Covid-19 and Business Law

De Gruyter Studies in Global Asia

Series Editors
Pervaiz K. Ahmed and Mahendhiran S. Nair

Volume 3

Covid-19 and Business Law

Legal Implications of a Global Pandemic

Edited by
Adnan Trakic

DE GRUYTER

ISBN 978-3-11-072358-8
E-ISBN (PDF) 978-3-11-072369-4
E-ISBN (EPUB) 978-3-11-072380-9
ISSN 2698-4776

Library of Congress Control Number: 2021942775

Bibliographic information published by the Deutsche Nationalbibliothek
The Deutsche Nationalbibliothek lists this publication in the Deutsche Nationalbibliografie; detailed bibliographic data are available on the internet at http://dnb.dnb.de.

Cover image: titoOnz/iStock/Getty Images Plus
Typesetting: Integra Software Services Pvt. Ltd.
Printing and binding: CPI books GmbH, Leck

www.degruyter.com

Preface

The idea behind this book came from a conversation I had with Professor Pervaiz K Ahmed, Head of School of Business, Monash University Malaysia, in the middle of 2020. At that time, we were all working from home due to the restrictions of movement introduced by the Malaysian Government to curb the spread of the COVID-19. A little while before this conversation, the Department of Business Law and Taxation (BLT), School of Business, Monash University Malaysia, which I have been privileged to lead, had organized a public seminar, "The Impact of COVID-19 on Contractual Obligations," to share ideas on how best to remedy contractual breaches caused by the COVID-19 pandemic. The seminar offered some unique perspectives on the topic, and I am very grateful to the team of distinguished speakers, Dr Abdul Majid, Justice Datuk Vazeer Alam bin Mydin Meera (the authors of Chapter 2), and Mr Jeremiah Gurusamy, for their insightful presentations. The impact of the pandemic, however, has not been limited to contracts alone. Other business law areas such as employment, tourism and hospitality, corporate governance, competition, human rights and the rule of law, trafficking of migrant workers, and legal services underwent similar challenges, if not worse. Therefore, the conversation with Professor Pervaiz served as a helpful reminder that the seminar was an excellent start to the discussion, and I needed to expand these to other business law areas. They, too, merited scholarly consideration to see how problems caused by the pandemic could be mitigated if not fully resolved. This is precisely what this book set out to accomplish. I hope we did justice to the discussed areas of law and that our findings and recommendations prove to be helpful to governments, industry, and community at large when dealing with legal challenges caused by the COVID-19 pandemic.

I want to use this opportunity to express my heartfelt appreciation to Professor Pervaiz for his guidance and mentorship and all the BLT colleagues (authors) for their painstaking efforts and participation in this project. The authorship, however, was not only limited to BLT. To ensure that every chapter is authored by subject experts, we also have contributions from scholars from other esteemed institutions. I am immensely grateful to you all. The book attests to your great collegiality and lucid scholarship, from which I have benefited greatly.

I should also like to record a debt of gratitude to the De Gruyter team, particularly Ms Lucy Jarman, for her timely assistance and helpful guidance throughout the publication process.

I want to thank my family for graciously allowing me to dedicate my time and effort to this book so that it may see the light of day.

Finally, thank you to you, dear reader! I hope you will find the book interesting and helpful. Happy reading!

Adnan Trakic
April 2021

https://doi.org/10.1515/9783110723694-202

Contents

Adnan Trakic

1 COVID-19 and Business Law: Challenges and Opportunities

Introduction

The Coronavirus Disease 2019 (COVID-19) pandemic has had extraordinary effects on human lives and economies around the world. As of 21 February 2021, there have been a staggering 110,749,023 confirmed cases of COVID-19, including 2,455,131 deaths.[1] Many countries have introduced various measures to stop the spread of the virus and preserve human lives and livelihoods. Some of these measures have been extreme, like the restrictions imposed on people's movement and lockdown of countries' borders. It has been reported that over half of the world's population, more than 3.9 billion people, have been confined to their homes due to the restrictions and lockdowns imposed by countries due to COVID-19.[2]

China was the first country to put Wuhan City, a place where the coronavirus originated from, on lockdown on 23 January 2020.[3] As the virus spread, many other countries followed suit. Malaysia, for example, promulgated a nation-wide movement control order (MCO) on 18 March 2020.[4] Around the same time, some states in the USA and Australia also began to impose strict social distancing measures,[5] while Singapore and most of the EU countries introduced nation-wide lockdowns

1 "WHO Coronavirus Disease (COVID-19) Dashboard," World Health Organization, February 21, 2021, https://covid19.who.int/.

2 Alasdair Sandford, "Coronavirus: Half of Humanity Now on Lockdown as 90 Countries Call for Confinement," *Euronews*, April 3, 2020, https://www.euronews.com/2020/04/02/coronavirus-in-europe-spain-s-death-toll-hits-10-000-after-record-950-new-deaths-in-24-hou.

3 Kaisha Langton, "China Lockdown: How Long Was China on Lockdown?," *Express*, May 30, 2020 https://www.express.co.uk/travel/articles/1257717/china-lockdown-how-long-was-china-lockdown-timeframe-wuhan.

4 The MCO was promulgated under the Prevention and Control of Infectious Diseases Act 1988 and the Police Act 1967. "Restriction of Movement Order," Prime Minister's Office of Malaysia, March 16, 2020, https://www.pmo.gov.my/2020/03/movement-control-order/.

5 James Glanz and Campbell Robertson, "Lockdown Delays Cost At Least 36,000 Lives, Data Show," *The New York Times*, May 20, 2020, https://www.nytimes.com/2020/05/20/us/coronavirus-distancing-deaths.html. See also "Australia Starts Lockdown Measures as Coronavirus Cases Jump," The Straits Times, March 23, 2020, https://www.straitstimes.com/asia/australianz/australia-starts-lockdown-measures-as-coronavirus-cases-jump.

https://doi.org/10.1515/9783110723694-001

in April and May 2020.[6] The medical professionals, who have been advising the governments, have claimed that such measures are critical in the time of a pandemic.[7]

While these measures have undoubtedly saved lives and curbed the spread of the deadly virus, they have also produced some unintended legal implications for individuals and businesses, particularly in the areas of contractual obligations, employment relationships, tourism and hospitality industry, company law, competition law, human rights and the rule of law, protection of vulnerable groups like migrant workers, and access to judicial and legal services.

Key Objectives and Research Approach

This book has five major objectives that underpin the analysis of the legal impacts of the COVID-19 pandemic on individuals and businesses. First, to identify and discuss specific legal challenges caused by the COVID-19 pandemic in earlier mentioned business law-related areas. Second, to increase the awareness about parties' rights and obligations in the time of the pandemic. Third, to enable the scholars and practitioners to present their views and solutions to the issues at hand in an appropriate manner. Fourth, to enable the public and interested parties to learn from the presented views. Fifth, to suggest to governments reforms of the existing laws and policies, where considered necessary.

These objectives lead to the following questions:

1. What are the specific legal implications of the COVID-19 pandemic for individuals and businesses?
2. How to address and remedy the legal implications of the pandemic in an effective manner?

6 "PM Lee: the COVID-19 Situation in Singapore (3 Apr)," A Singapore Government Agency Website, April 3, 2020, https://www.gov.sg/article/pm-lee-hsien-loong-on-the-covid-19-situation-in-singapore-3-apr. See also "Coronavirus: What Are the Lockdown Measures Across Europe?," DW, accessed February 22, 2021, https://www.dw.com/en/coronavirus-what-are-the-lockdown-measures-across-europe/a-52905137.

7 Esther Landau, "Doctors Call on Govt to Impose Nationwide Lockdown After Covid-19 Spike," *New Straits Times*, March 15, 2020, https://www.nst.com.my/news/nation/2020/03/574894/doctors-call-govt-impose-nationwide-lockdown-after-covid-19-spike; Doug Hendrie, "Thousands of doctors call for lockdown," *NewsGP*, March 18, 2020, https://www1.racgp.org.au/newsgp/clinical/thousands-of-doctors-call-for-lockdown.

Structure and Framework

This book consists of ten chapters. Chapters 1 and 10 are written by the editor. Chapter 1 introduces the topics and sets the expectation of all other chapters. It highlights the areas that are sought to be discussed. The legal implications of the COVID-19 pandemic are many, and they could be examined through the lens of different areas of law. This book, however, limits the scope of the discussion only to business law-related areas mentioned above. It is noted that some of these areas, like the reference to human rights and vulnerable groups, may not, in a traditional sense, be considered as business law areas. Nonetheless, the editor has taken the liberty of including them due to their significance and correlation with business and commerce. Fundamental human rights and liberties cannot be divorced from business and commerce, especially when it comes to employment matters, responsible business conduct, and social and environmental considerations in the global supply chain.

Chapter 2 begins with the most fundamental aspect of business law: the impact of COVID-19 on the performance of the contractual obligations. Many individuals and businesses became unable to perform their contractual obligations either due to COVID-19 (i.e. the disease) or the measures adopted by governments to contain the spread of the disease (i.e. the lockdown). This unintended non-performance of contractual obligations is a legal risk that burdens the non-performing parties. But why should they be burdened when they are not responsible for the non-performance? Chapter 2 examines the extent of the parties' liability in these circumstances with reference to two relevant legal concepts – frustration and force majeure. While, at first glance, the common law doctrine of frustration appears to be the solution to the problem, the doctrine could only be invoked to provide relief to individuals and not to the whole segments of the society affected by the pandemic. There is also a concern about whether the doctrine's remedy of avoidance of the contract is suitable for the breaches of contract caused by COVID-19 or related events.

For the aforesaid reasons, the contract law concept of force majeure has been viewed by many as a more appropriate instrument to absolve liability for the non-performance of the contract caused by the pandemic. That said, there are also some concerns around force majeure, like how the clause should be drafted and whether the commonly used "Act of God" term is wide enough to include the event such as a global pandemic. Chapter 2 addresses the frustration and force majeure–related concerns, mainly with reference to relevant Malaysian legislative provisions and judicial decisions.

Both frustration and force majeure remedies are normally sought by the affected contracting parties through litigation. But why should parties have to experience the discomfort of having to go to court and seek remedies that they may or may not get? In addition, the court processes are likely to be lengthy and costly. They would also take the court's time and resources, which could be put to better use in times of the pandemic. This is where the governments should be proactive in mitigating the

COVID-19's impact on individuals and businesses. This chapter specifically examines Malaysia's Temporary Measures for Reducing the Impact of Coronavirus Disease (COVID-19) Act 2020 and compares it with Singapore's COVID-19 (Temporary Measures) Act 2020. The detailed analysis of the COVID-19 Act will show whether the legislative measures are sufficient and broad enough in scope to provide the appropriate relief for the contractual breaches caused by both the COVID-19 (the disease) and the measure (the lockdown) adopted to contain the spread of the disease. While Chapter 2, for the most part, considers issues with reference to the relevant laws of Malaysia, occasional comparisons with other jurisdictions such as India, Singapore, and the UK are also made.

Some contract law principles that apply to general commercial contracts may not necessarily apply in the same manner to other more specific types of contracts, like employment contracts. This is why Chapter 3 specifically examines the impact of the COVID-19 pandemic on employment contracts and relationships, particularly with regard to employers' rights and duties in relation to downsizing, reducing salaries, temporary changing scope of work, and annual leaves. These measures have been generally considered legitimate options at the disposal of employers to navigate uncertain economic times. They are meant to prevent lay-offs and redundancies. In addition, many counties have introduced various job retention schemes (also known as furlough schemes) to support employers and workers through government grants to pay the workers' salaries.[8] While these schemes have been effective in preventing unemployment, they have also put significant constraints on countries' economies and their fiscal costs.[9]

The health of workers has been another primary concern. Employers are under obligation to provide a safe working environment to their workers, including the protection against the COVID-19. Many employers have allowed workers to work from home to ensure their safety. This has reignited the need for well-designed flexible work arrangement policies, which would ensure workers' productivity and, at the same time, provide adequate protection to workers against possible abuses.

8 See, for example, Malaysian Wage Subsidy Programme – Nuradzimmah Daim and Arfa Yunus "Wage Subsidy Programme: 2.6mil Workers, 322k Employers to Benefit," *New Straits Times*, November 10, 2020, https://www.nst.com.my/news/government-public-policy/2020/11/639865/wage-subsidy-programme-26mil-workers-322k-employers and the UK Furlough Scheme – "Coronavirus: Government to Pay up to 80% of Workers," *BBC*, March 20, 2020, https://www.bbc.com/news/business-51982005. See also Furlough Schemes in other European countries – Josh Sandiford "Furlough: How Other Countries Are Supporting Workers Through the Covid Crisis," *The Big Issue*, October 28, 2020, https://www.bigissue.com/latest/furlough-in-other-countries-supporting-workers-through-the-covid-crisis/.

9 "Furlough Schemes Delay Sharp Rise in European Unemployment to 2021," Fitch Ratings, November 5, 2020, https://www.fitchratings.com/research/sovereigns/furlough-schemes-delay-sharp-rise-in-european-unemployment-to-2021-05-11-2020.

In examining these challenges, this chapter offers solutions that are reflective of legal as well as social justice. What is required is a balanced approach that will not discriminate either against employers or workers. The tremendous economic challenges caused by the pandemic can only be overcome if both sides are prepared to offer their cooperation and understanding. This is even more so in sectors of the economy that have been affected the most by the pandemic, such as the tourism and hospitality industry.

Chapter 4 addresses the legal implications of COVID-19 for the tourism and hotel industry. Many hotels, tour companies, and transport operators had to close down as a result of the travel restrictions introduced by governments, which have been seen as a necessary means of preventing the spread of the virus. For countries like Malaysia, which heavily rely on the tourism industry's revenues, the COVID-19 pandemic presented major economic challenges and tremendous job losses. It is estimated that the Malaysian tourism industry lost RM100 billion in revenue in 2020 alone due to the pandemic.[10] Malaysian Association of Hotels has said that approximately 90 hotel establishments have closed permanently or temporarily since 2020, affecting around 7,000 employees, some of who have been retrenched and others have been on pay cuts or placed on unpaid leaves.[11] In addition, some 95 tourism agencies have been closed.[12] The Malaysian Government projected that average hotel occupancy for 2020 was 61.1%, while in 2021, it is projected to be 58.4%, the figure described as unrealistic by some critiques.[13]

While the governments have been working to save their ailing tourism industries, there has been little talk about the consumers whose bookings and package tours had been cancelled due to the pandemic. Are these consumers adequately protected under the existing laws? What is the extent of the compensation that they are entitled to if any? Are there any differences in treatment by law between outbound and inbound travellers? The Malaysian Tourism Industry Act (TIA) and Tourism Industry (Tour Operating Business and Travel Agency Business) Regulations 1992 seem to provide more protection to outbound travellers. Should this type of discrimination be acceptable? Also, what happens when a tour operator winds up?

---

10 Lim Guan Eng, "Can the Emergency and Suspension of Parliament Help to Save Our Hotels and Tourism Industry?," *Focus Malaysia*, January 28, 2021, https://focusmalaysia.my/politics/can-the-emergency-and-suspension-of-parliament-help-to-save-our-hotels-and-tourism-industry/.

11 G Vinod, "Covid-19: Hotel Equatorial Penang Bows Out, Hoteliers Call for Help," *Focus Malaysia*, January 26, 2020, https://focusmalaysia.my/featured/covid-19-hotel-equatorial-penang-bows-out-hoteliers-call-for-help/.

12 Lim Guan Eng, "Can the Emergency and Suspension of Parliament Help to Save Our Hotels and Tourism Industry?," *Focus Malaysia*, January 28, 2021, https://focusmalaysia.my/politics/can-the-emergency-and-suspension-of-parliament-help-to-save-our-hotels-and-tourism-industry/.

13 Lim Guan Eng, "Can the Emergency and Suspension of Parliament Help to Save Our Hotels and Tourism Industry?," *Focus Malaysia*, January 28, 2021, https://focusmalaysia.my/politics/can-the-emergency-and-suspension-of-parliament-help-to-save-our-hotels-and-tourism-industry/.

Are there any insolvency protection measures accorded to the affected consumers, or will they be treated as unsecured creditors with little hope of being adequately compensated? These and similar questions are addressed in Chapter 4.

The chapter explores the strengths and weaknesses of the existing regulatory framework under the TIA and the Regulations 1992 and offers suggestions by reference to the laws of the EU and the UK. More specifically, it considers insolvency protection measures under the EU Package Travel Directive 2015, and the UK's 2015 Directive and the Package Travel Regulations 2018, which implemented the EU Directive 2015. As a result of the comparison with the EU and UK laws, the chapter proposes several changes in the Malaysian regulatory framework intended to provide adequate protection to both the consumers and the tourism industry. It also discusses travel companies' response through their representative, the Malaysian Association of Tours and Travel Agents, to the unprecedented demand for refunds and compensations. In addition to these challenges, the travel companies, like all other companies incorporated under the Malaysian Companies Act (CA) 2016, have also been presented with a number of other company law-related challenges resulting from the pandemic.

Chapter 5 explores the implications of the COVID-19 pandemic for the CA 2016. Companies have been hit very hard financially in the pandemic. Many of them have been struggling to keep afloat and provide wages for their employees. They have been, especially small and medium-size enterprises, under enormous financial distress due to the fall in revenues caused by the pandemic and related lockdowns. Their creditors have been pressuring them to service their outstanding debts. If they default, the creditors would then initiate insolvency proceedings to recover the debt. As a result, many people will lose jobs, and ultimately, the whole country's economy will be adversely affected. This is why many countries have provided temporary relief to financially distressed companies through their COVID-19 legislation. However, it is interesting to note that the Malaysian COVID-19 Act 2020 does not contain any provisions on the application of the CA 2016. Why is that so? Does this mean that the CA's provisions, which require strict compliance from companies, will be enforced even though they have been passed, not with the pandemic in mind?

This chapter examines the measures undertaken by the Malaysian Government in terms of insolvency proceedings where companies have faced difficulties paying their debts due to the pandemic. What is the current minimum statutory threshold of debt before creditors can serve the statutory notice of demand? Is it high enough to make a difference for companies? Also, what is the time period given by the law for the company to respond to the statutory demand, and is it sufficient? Is the insolvency proceeding the only way the creditors can resolve their problem with the indebted company? Are there any other less informal ways of resolving this problem? These and similar questions are answered in this chapter with reference to the legislative and regulatory solutions in Singapore, the UK, and Australia.

This chapter also discusses various corporate governance challenges that businesses have had due to the COVID-19 pandemic. Companies' ability to display normal compliance of corporate governance and reporting became increasingly difficult during the pandemic. Some flexibility would need to be allowed by the company boards and regulators, but that should not be seen as an amnesty for poorly governed businesses. Therefore, company boards and regulators are encouraged to focus on the areas where businesses are particularly vulnerable during a global pandemic, such as monitoring and oversight responsibilities of directors, liquidity and capitalization, executive compensation, and takeover defences and preparedness. One area of concern that some companies might have underappreciated during the pandemic is collusive and anti-competitive behaviour.

The role of the competition law during the COVID-19 pandemic is specifically examined in Chapter 6. It may not be reasonable to expect that strict compliance with competition laws would be the first thing on the minds of businesses struggling to keep afloat during the pandemic. They are more likely to be thinking about how to generate enough revenue, reduce cost, and mitigate risk exposure to keep the business going. To do that, they may have to cooperate and share information and resources with each other. There is nothing wrong with cooperation as long it does not involve anti-competitive behaviour. Any anti-competitive conduct or agreements, horizontal or vertical, to prevent, restrict, or distort the competition are prohibited under completion law.

That said, strict compliance with competition law, particularly Competition Act 2010 in the Malaysian context, may not always be possible during the pandemic or even desirable. Should the competition regulators, like, for example, the Competition Commission of Malaysia, allow for some flexibility in the implementation of the law during the COVID-19 pandemic so that businesses can remain afloat and save jobs? Also, should businesses be allowed to work together, and if so, to what extent to ensure that there is a steady supply of essential items to the public, especially pharmaceutical products that are in high demand in the pandemic? Would not this be a win–win situation both for the businesses and the public? That said, how to make sure that businesses do not abuse the relief measures offered by the governments during the pandemic. There have been many reports where some businesses have been investigated because of the price hikes of some of the essential items.[14] Is the exploitative pricing related to competition law, and is it indicative of anti-competitive conduct or abuse of dominant position? These and similar questions will be answered with reference to examples in several jurisdictions.

14 Sachin Dave & Deepshikha Sikarwar, "Amid Covid-19 Outbreak Sudden Price Hikes Under the Scanner," *The Economic Times*, March 24, 2020, https://economictimes.indiatimes.com/news/politics-and-nation/amid-covid-19-outbreak-sudden-price-hikes-under-the-scanner/articleshow/74782650.cms?from=mdr. See also "Exploitative Pricing in the Time of COVID-19," OECD, May 26, 2020, https://www.oecd.org/competition/Exploitative-pricing-in-the-time-of-COVID-19.pdf.

Chapters 7 and 8 may not seem to be business law related at first sight as they consider the legal impacts of the COVID-19 pandemic on human rights law. However, without adequate protection of human rights and the rule of law, individuals and businesses would be unable to operate freely and effectively. Therefore, Chapter 7 is dedicated to examining the impact of the COVID-19 pandemic on human rights and the rule of law. There have been multiple reports about serious human rights violations as a result of extreme measures imposed by governments around the world due to COVID-19.[15] Some of these measures, including lockdowns, intense policing and checkpoints, and strict quarantines, are claimed to have been justified on the ground of a genuine emergency. There is no question that the COVID-19 pandemic presented a real challenge to the governments worldwide, which needed to be addressed with decisive and robust measures. However, whenever those measures result in a derogation or limitation of individuals' basic human rights guaranteed by the UN Universal Declaration of Human Rights, such as liberty (article 3), freedom of movement (article 13(1)), freedom of religion in community with others (article 18), freedom of peaceful assembly and association (article 20(1)), work and protection against unemployment (article 23(1)), education (article 26(1)), and free participation in community (article 27(1)), there must be the system of checks and balances in place to ensure that the derogation and limitation of the rights is proportionate, legal, necessary, and timely.[16]

Abusive policing in the enforcement of quarantine measures has been reported in many countries. In the UK, police have been accused of using drones to spy on people taking walks at nature spots, stopping dog-walkers from driving their pets to open spaces, and even urging some shops not to sell Easter eggs as they were not considered as essential items.[17] The government minister in the UK has reportedly said that the police may have gone "further than they should have."[18] In Malaysia, the senior government minister reported that there had been 20,011 arrests for violation of the government-imposed MCO between 18 March 2020 and 26 April 2020. Lawyers have questioned these arrests on the basis that the violation of the regulation is

15 See Kelly Shea Delvac, "Human Rights Abuses in the Enforcement of Coronavirus Security Measures," *The National Law Review*, May 25, 2020, https://www.natlawreview.com/article/human-rights-abuses-enforcement-coronavirus-security-measures.

16 "The Universal Declaration of Human Rights," United Nations, accessed February 5, 2021, https://www.un.org/en/universal-declaration-human-rights/.

17 "UK Police Accused of Abusing Power to Enforce COVID-19 Lockdown," *Aljazeera*, March 31, 2020, https://www.aljazeera.com/news/2020/03/uk-police-accused-abusing-power-enforce-covid-19-lockdown-200331084607759.html.

18 "UK Police Accused of Abusing Power to Enforce COVID-19 Lockdown," *Aljazeera*, March 31, 2020, https://www.aljazeera.com/news/2020/03/uk-police-accused-abusing-power-enforce-covid-19-lockdown-200331084607759.html.

not an arrestable offense.[19] Chapter 7 considers the legality of these measures with reference to international law, especially the principles of derogation and limitation of human rights.

This chapter also explains the appropriate way of providing the necessary emergency powers to the executive branch of government so that it can respond to the pandemic challenges effectively. Does this include a full fledge declaration of the state of emergency as done by a number of states, thereby removing parliament's scrutiny over the executives' actions? Or is there a way in which emergency powers could be legislated by parliaments for specific purposes and for a specific duration so as to avoid a complete lack of accountability and transparency? This chapter provides answers to these and similar questions.

The chapter also dedicates special attention to the alleged violations of privacy rights by governments worldwide through the centralized collection of private information of the citizens through the COVID-19 tracing apps, temperature-sensing drones, and phone apps to monitor location and distancing. Are governments allowed to collect that information? If the answer is no, how to do effective contact tracing then? Should not the health of the nation be prioritized over the individual's rights to privacy? These are also some of the questions that this chapter attempts to answer.

One of the most detested forms of human rights violations is human trafficking or trafficking in persons. Chapter 8 explores the trafficking of migrant workers for the exploitative purpose of forced labour. As a result of the COVID-19 pandemic, vulnerable individuals like migrant workers have become even more vulnerable. The police and other enforcement agencies have been preoccupied with the enforcement of the measures implemented by governments worldwide to contain the spread of the virus. The lack of police oversight has encouraged the elusive traffickers to become even more oppressive in their actions against the victims of human trafficking. The trafficked migrant workers, in particular, have been exploited for forced labour. They often live and work in deplorable conditions without any proper oversight by the regulators. The victims of the trafficking may even sometimes be treated as smuggled persons. As such, instead of being given the protection and help of the state, they end up being treated as suspected criminals and prosecuted under immigration laws. The Palermo Protocol[20] provides clear guidance as to how trafficking in persons should be regulated by national legislation.

19 V Anbalagan, "MCO Violations Do Not Warrant Arrest, Say Lawyers," *FMT*, April 16, 2020, https://www.freemalaysiatoday.com/category/nation/2020/04/16/mco-violations-do-not-warrant-arrest-say-lawyers/. See also Hafiz Yatim, "Bar Cautions of Consequence of Jailing More MCO Violators," *The Edge Markets*, April 17, 2020, https://www.theedgemarkets.com/article/bar-cautions-consequences-remanding-and-not-compounding-mco-violations.

20 A United Nations (UN) Protocol to Prevent, Suppress, and Punish Trafficking in Persons Especially Women and Children, supplementing the United Nations Convention against Transnational

This chapter examines specifically the extent of Malaysia's Anti-Trafficking in Persons and Anti-Smuggling of Migrants Act 2007 compliance with the protocol. In 2010, the act was amended to include smuggling of migrants' offences. Was this the right move? What are the possible repercussions of this? There has also been an issue pertaining to the definition and scope of the trafficking in persons' offices in the act. The courts, in several cases, considered the term "coercion" narrowly in the context of human trafficking, limiting it to the physical use of threat or force. However, should mental, emotional, and psychological coercion also be considered as a valid form of coercion for the purpose of the offence? How does Palermo Protocol define coercion in the context of trafficking in persons. The chapter also considers other legislation and to what extent they protect migrant workers, especially those that have been trafficked for forced labour. There is a lot of talk about the contract for labour and how it encourages workers' exploitation. The chapter proposes the necessary changes to the laws to tackle this issue.

To protect migrant workers and other vulnerable groups against exploitation and trafficking during the pandemic, judicial and legal services must be open and accessible. Chapter 9 considers the importance of legal services in a pandemic like COVID-19. Legal services are typically not included in the list of essential services that may continue to operate even during the total lockdown. As a result, the law firms in many countries have shut down for the duration of the lockdown. These shutdowns have caused significant cash flow problems for these firms as they continued to incur ordinary expenses, such as rentals and employees' salaries, while, at the same time, their ability to earn revenue significantly diminished.[21] Most of the law firms were not able to proceed with their clients' instructions. Also, conveyancing lawyers were unable to register land titles as land offices were closed. This also impacted ordinary business conduct by the individuals, businesses, and event governments as the necessary legal documentation could not be processed without the help and oversight from the legal representatives.

This chapter explores if legal services should be included in the list of essential services. What happens to the legal system when lawyers are unable to represent clients? How justice will be attained in cases where individuals are brought before the court without adequate legal representation. The criminals do not retire during the pandemic and the lockdowns. Therefore, the legal and judicial system must continue to operate to secure the public's interest and protect the offenders' rights when brought to face justice. Furthermore, what happens to ordinary businesses and

Organized Crime, accessed February 21, 2021, https://www.ohchr.org/EN/ProfessionalInterest/Pages/ProtocolTraffickingInPersons.aspx.

21 "RWC Impact Webinar: Impact of Covid 19 on Law Firms & Legal Services," *RWC*, April 13, 2020, https://www.richardweechambers.com/rwc-impact-webinar-impact-of-covid-19-on-law-firms-legal-services/.

countries' economies when legal services are suspended? How can the judicial system operate without support from legal services?

One way in which the continuance of the legal service was ensured in many countries was through the intensive digitalization of the legal and judicial practice.[22] Many countries have allowed court proceedings to be fully in a digitalized form where the parties could present their arguments and evidence online. However, the online court hearings have also presented many challenges, from equal access to essential IT infrastructure by the parties involved to the credibility of the evidence adduced through online means. This chapter examines the use of online technology by the courts and legal services and presents prospects for the future in this respect.

The last chapter of the book, Chapter 10, is written by the editor. It provides a brief recapitulation of each chapter's findings and pens concise recommendations based on what was discussed by the authors in their respective chapters. This chapter, however, is not a replacement for the actual discussion presented by the authors in their respective chapters. Rather, it is the editor's summary and review of what was discussed by the respective authors. Therefore, the readers are encouraged to read the actual chapters for a more detailed account of the respective topics.

Conclusion

One of the main questions that come to mind after detailing the legal impacts of the COVID-19 pandemic on the respective business law areas covered in this book is how to best remedy the problems? Should affected parties be left to negotiate the solution or, should governments step in to provide temporary relief measures to the affected parties? In other words, is there a need for COVID-19 legislation?

It has been suggested that, at an early stage of the pandemic, some of the administrative measures undertaken by the Malaysian Government provided the necessary protections for individuals and businesses but only for their transactions with the government link companies and agencies.[23] Apart from banking and financial institutions, which have also been mandated to provide certain protections, other private business transactions have remained largely unregulated. The question that comes to mind is: what relief is available for the contractual breaches caused by the

22 Edwin Lee and Daphne Sit, "The New Normal from Covid-19 Pandemic: Embrace Legal Technology and Innovation," *Asian Legal Business*, July 1, 2020, https://legalbusinessonline.com/house-news/new-normal-covid-19-pandemic-embrace-legal-technology-and-innovation-brought-you-glt.

23 Khairah N Karim, "Malaysian Bar: The Country Needs Covid-19 Law," *New Straits Times*, April 29, 2020, https://www.nst.com.my/news/nation/2020/04/588438/malaysian-bar-country-needs-covid-19-law.

COVID-19 pandemic in contracts that have not been covered by these administrative directives? Should the unintended non-performance of these contracts lead to their temporary suspension for the duration of the pandemic or complete termination? Furthermore, what remedies, if any, should the parties in the event of the suspension or termination of contracts due to the pandemic be entitled to?

It is submitted that the governments should enact laws that would protect the parties from legal actions arising from the non-performance of the contractual obligations in private business transactions. The Government of Singapore has done that with the introduction of the COVID-19 (Temporary Measures) Act 2020, which came into force on 20 April 2020.[24] The act provides temporary relief measures by suspending non-performing parties' liabilities in certain contracts for a period of 6 months. The act also allows for the extension of this period for up to a year. The contracts covered by the act are construction and supply contracts (e.g., contract for the supply of materials), event or tourism-related contracts (e.g., venue or catering for weddings; cruises, hotel accommodation bookings), hire purchase agreements, or conditional sales agreements for plant or machinery used for commercial purposes or commercial vehicles, and leases and licenses of non-residential property (e.g. lease for factory premises).[25] The act imposes a moratorium on legal action in order to encourage the affected parties to talk and negotiate their way out. Suppose the non-performing party is entitled to the relief under this act and has given a notice of his/her inability to perform his/her contractual obligation due to COVID-19 to other party or parties to the contract. In that case, the other party or parties are prohibited from taking certain legal actions against the non-performing party, including starting or continuing court proceedings or insolvency proceedings, enforcing security over commercial or industrial immovable property, enforcing security over the plant, machinery, or fixed assets that are used for manufacturing, production, or other business purposes, terminating lease or licence of commercial or industrial property on the basis of non-payment of rent, and repossession of any goods under a hire-purchase agreement.[26] Any action in contravention of the provisions of the act would amount to an offence.

Other countries have also taken lessons from Singapore and have introduced similar legislation. For example, Malaysia passed Malaysia's Temporary Measures for Reducing the Impact of Coronavirus Disease 2019 (COVID-19) Act 2020, which came into force on 23 October 2020. The act is seen as a step in a good direction.

---

24 See COVID-19 (Temporary Measures) Act 2020 at https://sso.agc.gov.sg/Act/COVID19TMA2020#pr1-. See also https://www.mlaw.gov.sg/news/press-releases/2020-04-20-covid-19-temporary-measures-act-provisions-relating-to-temporary-reliefs-to-commence-on-20-april-2020.

25 https://www.mlaw.gov.sg/files/news/press-releases/2020/4/Annex_Commencement_of_COVID-19_(Temporary_Measures)_Act.pdf

26 https://www.mlaw.gov.sg/files/news/press-releases/2020/4/Annex_Commencement_of_COVID-19_(Temporary_Measures)_Act.pdf

But, unlike Singapore's COVID-19 Act 2020, the Malaysian COVID-19 Act 2020 is said to be relatively narrow in scope. It, for example, provides temporary relief for the contractual breaches caused by the resulting measures introduced by the government to contain the spread of the virus (like the lockdowns) but not the COVID-19 (the disease itself). Also, it does not provide relief to the affected parties in employment contracts, nor does it contain any provision relating to the temporary relaxation of the Companies Act 2016 provisions. Malaysia's COVID-19 Act 2020 and its exact scope and limitations are extensively discussed in the chapters by the respective authors with reference to similar legislation in other countries. As a general rule, however, it is worth saying that governments' temporary relief measures in response to the COVID-19 pandemic should be substantial and comprehensive.

Vazeer Alam Mydin Meera, Abdul Majid and Mei Yee Lee

2 The Impact of COVID-19 on Contractual Obligations in Malaysia

Introduction

The coronavirus was first reported by China as a pneumonia-like disease in December 2019 in the city of Wuhan in Hubei province. Although the former US President Trump[1] and his Foreign Secretary, Mike Pompeo,[2] have claimed that the coronavirus is something that escaped from a Chinese lab in which it was created, they have advanced no evidence to substantiate this assertion. The coronavirus may well have emerged spontaneously in nature. In any case, after its first appearance in China, it seems to have spread to Thailand, Australia, Europe, and thence to the USA. It was first detected in Malaysian ports of entry in foreigners returning from Wuhan in January 2020.

With the foregoing as background, the rest of this chapter is organized as follows. In the beginning, the chapter identifies the legal or statutory basis of the measures instituted, taken, or introduced by the Malaysian Government to control or stop the spread of the coronavirus in the realm. The measures taken by the Government were inimical of the economic life of the nation and the citizenry. To reduce the impact of the coronavirus in the country, the Malaysian Government enacted a statute entitled, "Temporary Measures for Reducing the Impact of Coronavirus Disease (COVID-19) Act 2020" (the COVID-19 Act). The chapter then considers why, in common law jurisdictions such as Malaysia, the normal devices to allocate the damage flowing from the outbreak of an unexpected infectious disease – the doctrine of frustration and the force majeure clauses – were not available or were unsatisfactory. The penultimate section considers the legislative purpose of the COVID-19 Act. Where a statute purports to provide temporary relief to those whose economic well-being is adversely affected by legislation to achieve a social good – the control and prevention of infectious disease – the statute must be evaluated in terms of what it sets out to do. This is attempted by the final section, which is the conclusion.

1 "Coronavirus: Trump Stands by China Lab Origins Theory for Virus," *BBC*, May 1, 2020, https://www.bbc.com/news/world-us-canada-52496098.

2 Jordan Fabian, Jennifer Jacobs, and Iain Marlow, "Trump Promises Conclusive US Report on Virus's China Origins," *Bloomberg*, May 3, 2020, https://www.bloomberg.com/news/articles/2020-05-03/pompeo-says-enormous-evidence-links-virus-to-wuhan-laboratory.

https://doi.org/10.1515/9783110723694-002

The Statutory Basis of Measures Adopted by the Malaysian Government to Counter the COVID-19 in Malaysia

The word "epidemic" is defined in Section 2 of Malaysia's Prevention and Control of Infectious Diseases Act 1988 to mean "the extension of a disease by a multiplication of cases in an area". The website of the World Health Organization says that a "pandemic" is the worldwide spread of a new disease.[3] In Malaysia, Section 11 of the Prevention and Control of Infectious Diseases Act 1988 provides that if any area in Malaysia is threatened with an outbreak of an infectious disease or if any area in Malaysia is threatened with an epidemic of an infectious disease, the Minister may declare such an area to be "an infected local area". Section 11(2) of the same Act empowers the Minister to make regulations to prescribe the measures to be taken "to control or prevent the spread of any infectious disease within or from any infected area". In March 2020, when the cases of the coronavirus were proliferating, the Malaysian Government acted under Section 11 of Prevention and Control of Infectious Diseases Act 1988 by declaring the whole country an "infected" area and prescribing measures to control or prevent the spread of the disease in the form of the Prevention and Control of Infectious Disease (Measures within the Infected Local Area) Regulations 2020 (the 18 March 2020 Regulations).[4] The 18 March Regulations were expressed to be in effect from 18 March 2020 to 31 March 2020.

Since the virus was spread by droplets exhaled by an infected person, the measure adopted by the Malaysian Government to control or prevent the spread of the virus was a "lockdown" that isolated people from each other.[5] Save where essential, the regulations prohibited all travel from one part or district of the country to another. Only those holding jobs in or involved in essential services could travel to and from work.[6] In Malaysia, a person could travel from one area to another with the prior written permission of an officer authorized to issue such permission.[7] The Regulations prohibited any gatherings or events for sporting, recreational, social, or cultural purposes.[8] However, persons were permitted to gather at a funeral ceremony

3 "What Is a Pandemic?" World Health Organization, February 24, 2020, https://www.who.int/csr/disease/swineflu/frequently_asked_questions/pandemic/en/#:~:text=A%20pandemic%20is%20the%20worldwide,people%20do%20not%20have%20immunity.

4 Published in the Federal Gazette on 18 March 2020.

5 The Malaysian 18 March Regulations, r 3(1); the Singapore Regulations, rr 3 and 4.

6 The Schedule to the Malaysian 18 March Regulations listed 21 "essential services".

7 The Malaysian 18 March Regulations, r 3(2); the Singapore Regulations, r 7(3).

8 The Malaysian 18 March Regulations, r 3(2).

provided that the number of attendees at such a ceremony was kept to a minimum.[9] The list of prohibited travel in Malaysia included travel for a "religious" purpose.

The Doctrine of Frustration and the Force Majeure Clause in Contract Law

The doctrine of frustration, as we shall see, could not be invoked against the pandemic on account of its inherent limitations. The doctrine of frustration emerged to provide relief to individuals and not to whole sectors of society. The doctrine of frustration holds that if, without fault of either party, after the formation of the contract and before it is due to be performed, there occurs some unforeseeable event (the frustrating event) which so alters the circumstances in which the contract has to be performed as to make the contract impossible or illegal to perform or radically different from what the parties had contemplated when they made the contract, then the contract is at an end and the parties shall be relieved from further performance.

The doctrine of frustration emerged and was expanded in scope by common law decisions on the facts and circumstances of particular cases. Though the principles established in particular cases might have been generalized and applied in similar or analogous facts and circumstances, the doctrine was applied to individual cases. It was not meant to and did not provide relief to a whole swath of individuals affected by government action. The reference here is to the state enacting legislation to prevent economic activity – the regulations that prevented the individual from leaving his/her home to engage in economic activity. By reason of its genesis in the common law, the doctrine of frustration cannot deal with multiple cases simultaneously.

The relief provided by the doctrine of frustration is rather limited. The common law declared that upon being engaged, the doctrine of frustration dropped the guillotine to bring the contract to an end and let the loss "lie where it falls".[10] Section 57 of the Malaysian Contracts Act 1950 and Section 56 of the Indian Contract Act 1872 declare that a contract which, after it is made, becomes impossible or unlawful ipso facto becomes void. Each of Section 65 of the Malaysian Contracts Act 1950 and Section 64 of the Indian Contract Act has the effect of requiring a person who has "received a benefit under a contract declared to be frustrated to restore that benefit, so far as may be, to the person from whom it was received". Section 66 of the Malaysian Contracts Act 1950 and Section 65 of the Indian Contract Act 1872 impose upon a person who has "received any advantage under a void contract to restore it or

9 The Malaysian 18 March Regulations, r 3(3); funerals in the Singapore Regulation were governed by s 7(3).

10 *Fibrosa Spolka Akcyjna v Fairbairn Lawson Combe Barbour Ltd [1942]. 2* All ER 122, 126H; 127 para C and D per Viscount Simon LC.

make compensation for it, to the person from whom he received it". Illustration (d) to Section 66 reads:

> A contracts to sing for B at a concert for RM1,000, which are paid in advance. A is too ill to sing. A is not bound to make compensation to B for the loss of the profits which B would have made if A had been able to sing, but must refund to B the RM1,000 paid in advance.

Clearly, the contract between A and B is rendered void by frustration caused by A's supervening illness. And A has to make restitution of the RM1,000 paid in advance or any other benefit she/he has received.

In Malaysia, Section 15 of the Civil Law Act 1956 has provisions adjusting the rights and liabilities of parties to frustrated contracts. Section 15(2) of the Civil Law Act 1956 enacts that money payable before a contract is frustrated ceases to be payable, and money paid before a contract is frustrated is recoverable. However, the section recognizes that in some circumstances, it would be unjust to allow a payer to recover all the money he/she has paid. In such circumstances, the proviso to Section 15(2) empowers the court, if it considers it just, to permit a payee to retain the whole or part of any payment made before the frustrating event occurred. The court may exercise discretion if the payee has incurred expenditure in the performance of the contract or for the purpose of performing it. Section 15(3) of the same statute enables the court to order a party who had received a valuable benefit under the contract before the frustrating event occurred to pay to the other party whatever the court thinks just, not exceeding the values of that benefit.

The provisions of sections 15 and 16 of Malaysia's Civil Law act were based on the UK Law Reform (Frustrated Contracts) Act 1943. Both India and Malaysia were under British rule when the UK Law Reform (Frustrated Contracts) Act 1943 was enacted. The colonial administration in India does not seem to have been impressed by either the need to adjust the rights and obligations of parties to a frustrated contract or by the Law Reform (Frustrated Contracts) Act 1943 itself. This is indicated by India not following the English to enact a statute similar to the Law Reform (Frustrated Contracts) Act 1943. As India and the different states of the Commonwealth of Australia had not incorporated the doctrine of frustration in a statute, the doctrine in operation is defined by the common law. Consequently, the common law developments in the doctrine of frustration were, historically, more directly relevant in Hong Kong and Australia than they are in India and Malaysia.

However, Hong Kong and the Australian states have recognized the harshness of the common law doctrine, especially in apportioning losses flowing from the frustration of contract, and have enacted statutes that, by and large, mirror the provisions of the UK Law Reform (Frustrated Contracts) Act 1943. In Hong Kong, this was done, in 1986, by way of the Law Amendment and Reform (Consolidation) Ordinance (Cap 73) (LARCO). In Australia, to mitigate the harshness of the common law rule on frustration, three states enacted legislation *a la* the UK Reform (Frustrated Contracts) Act 1943. New South Wales had the Frustrated Contracts Act 1978, South

Australia had the Frustrated Contracts Act 1988, and Victoria had the Australian Consumer Law and Fair Trading Act 2012. The Victorian statute has since been replicated in all Australian states. Whatever may be the differences in the wording and syntax of Hong Kong's LARCO and the Victorian Australian Consumer Law and Fair Trading Act 2012, their effect is the same.

The doctrine of frustration works when the party invoking it is satisfied with just the contract being voided. However, where a party wishes to have the contract continue subject to him/her being relieved from the consequences of his/her breach, frustration does not work. Where the lockdown being imposed under statutory authority prevents a party from performing his/her contract, frustration is available but the remedy it provides – termination of the contract – is not acceptable for what is required is bold action which would address the unsatisfactory features of the doctrine of frustration.

We shall next consider the efficacy of force majeure clauses. A force majeure clause is a contractual term that seeks to deal with the parties' rights and obligations in the face of a superior force (a war, a typhoon, an epidemic, etc.) over which they have no control. Basically, a force majeure clause seeks to absolve the parties from non-performance of their contractual obligations, though it may also seek to govern the relationship of the parties following the force majeure event.

A force majeure clause is a creature of contract. It exists because of its incorporation into a contract. In this, it differs from the common law doctrine of frustration, the bounds of which are potentially expendable by the court recognizing a "new" frustrating event or one analogous to a recognized kind of frustration. Thus, if an event is not identified as a force majeure event in the contract, the court cannot declare such an unexpected event over which a party has no control, a force majeure event. Consequently, a force majeure is more difficult to resort to than is the doctrine of frustration; the existence of the force majeure clause in the contract is a condition precedent to its being invoked. The difficulty of invoking force majeure may be seen in the following cases.

In *Bank Pembangunan Malaysia Berhad v. Pesaka Technologies Sdn Bhd*,[11] the defendant pleaded force majeure and argued that the implementation of the project, that is, the contract, was impeded by various unforeseeable events that were beyond its control. However, the contract did not provide for force majeure. Thus, the High Court held that the defendant was not absolved from its contractual obligations. *In Getaran Unggul Sdn Bhd v Syed Ahamed bin Mohamed Ghani and others*,[12] the High Court held that the stop-work order issued by Majlis Perbandaran Pulau Pinang, the local authority, did not fall within the force majeure clause.

11 [2019] 1 LNS 412.
12 [2004] MLJU 485; [2004] 1 LNS 436.

In Araprop Development Sdn Bhd v Leong Chee Kong & Anor,[13] the Court of Appeal held that the delay in delivering vacant possession was not a delay as stipulated in the force majeure clause as it was caused by the appellant's subcontractors who were under the control of the appellant. *In Golden Bay Realty Pte Ltd v Orchard Twelve Investments Pte Ltd,*[14] where the Court of Appeal of Singapore held that the force majeure clause does not come into play where the delays caused were within the contemplation of the appellant and were within their control.

In *Progressive Ocean Sdn Bhd v Northern Corridor Implementation Authority ("NCIA"),*[15] the contract had a "force majeure" clause that defined force majeure to mean:

> . . . an act, omission or circumstance relied on by a Party to this Agreement as a force majeure event and over which that Party could not reasonably have exercised control, including, but not limited to, acts of God, acts of omissions of government, **epidemics**, quarantines, earthquakes or other natural disasters, or government regulations imposed after the commencement of this Agreement. An event or act shall not be excused or delayed by Force Majeure if it could reasonably be circumvented through use of alternative source, work around the plans or other means within the control of such party.

It should be noted that the force majeure clause may be defeated by the claimant's failure to take reasonable measures to circumvent it through the use of alternative sources, work around the plans, or other means within the control of such party.

In the foregoing passage from *Progressive Ocean Sdn Bhd v Northern Corridor Implementation Authority ("NCIA"),* COVID-19 will clearly fall within the formulation "epidemics, quarantines . . .". However, whether the COVID-19 pandemic is "an act of God" is very much an open question. This counter-intuitive tentativeness flows from "an act of God" having been defined as "an injury which results from natural causes which could not have been foreseen and could not have been avoided by any amount of foresight and care which could reasonably have been expected . . .".[16] In *Khoo Tham Sui v Chan Chiau Hee,*[17] there was no force majeure clause and no contractual reference to a storm, a typhoon, or a cyclone, and the court had to decide whether a cyclone, a typhoon, or other exceptionally inclement weather was an "act of God" or a frustrating event. The court held that the sudden storm at sea was not a frustrating event because the defendant could have foreseen the sudden storm. The logic would have seen a claim in force majeure being dismissed not only because it was not in the verbal contract between the parties but also because the defendant could have foreseen that a storm at sea was likely when it was towing logs.

---

13 [2008] 1 MLJ 783; [2008] 1 CLJ 135.

14 [1989] 2 MLJ 70; [1990] 3 CLJ (Rep) 499.

15 [2016] MLJU 304.

16 97 *Halsbury's Law of England (5th Ed) para 469, 404.*

17 [1976] 1 MLJ 25.

On 18 March 2020, the Malaysian Government enacted Regulations to control the spread of COVID-19. These would be government regulations imposed after the commencement of any agreement signed before 18 March 2020. Thus, the Malaysian Regulations may be incorporated into the force majeure clause quoted above.

The problems associated with invoking either the doctrine of frustration or the requirement that the force majeure clause be already incorporated into a contract disable anybody but the most experienced business party from using them. This is particularly true of individuals who were caught flat-footed by the Regulations in Malaysia. The basic case seems to be simple enough. The National Government enacted subsidiary legislation that imposed the lockdown, the ban on gatherings, and the requirement of social distances on pain of criminal sanctions. The Government may argue that in taking this action, it was merely performing its primary governmental function of protecting its citizenry from a dangerous disease. The Government may also argue that its demands via the subsidiary legislation were the lesser of two evils, the greater evil being COVID-19.

Frustration may have been applied where supervening illegality made a contract impossible to perform, but in Malaysia, from March 2020 onwards, the State deliberately used a statute to prevent the citizens from entering into or performing other than specified classes of contracts. It was not the parties to the contract that broke them but the law which made the contracts illegal through legislation, making them impossible to perform. Conceptually, all its good intentions to stop the spread of the disease notwithstanding, it was the State that either brought about a cessation of economic activities or the breach of contract. This raised the issue of who was to pay the victims of state-mandated cessation of economic activity and/or breach of contracts. The State, of course, saw itself as discharging a governmental function – that of protecting the citizenry – and did not see itself as liable for the economic woes it visited upon the community. The remedy of frustration was, as we saw earlier, definitely not equal to the task.

Where the lockdown being imposed under statutory authority prevents a party from performing his/her contract, frustration is available, but the remedy it provides – termination of the contract – is not acceptable. What is required is bold legislation that would address the unsatisfactory features of the doctrine of frustration. For instance, the state could transfer directly to the taxpayer's bank account the wages he/she has lost by reason of the lockdown. The amount could be determined from the income taxes paid in the preceding tax year.

The COVID-19 Act

The Malaysian Government enacted a statute to respond to the COVID-19 pandemic. The first step in the enactment of the statute was a Bill, the "Temporary Measures for Reducing the Impact of Coronavirus Disease (COVID-19) Bill" (the

Bill). The Bill was passed by the House of Representatives on 25 August 2020 and by the Senate on 22 September 2020. It received the Royal assent on 16 October 2020 and was gazetted on 23 October 2020 as the "Temporary Measures for Reducing the Impact of Coronavirus Disease (COVID-19) Act 2020".

Section 1(2) of the COVID-19 Act provides that except where the date of commencement and period of operation have been provided with respect to the respective Parts in the COVID-19 Act, the COVID-19 Act shall come into operation on the date of its publication and shall continue to remain in operation for a period of 2 years from such date of publication. Section 1(3) empowers the Prime Minister by order published in the Gazette, to extend the operation of the COVID-19 Act, and such an order for extension may be made more than once. Legislative control over such extensions is purported to be exercised by Section 1(4) requiring such an order to be laid before Parliament as soon as practicable after it is made. The purpose of the statute is sufficiently and succinctly indicated by its short title: to reduce, by way of temporary measures, the impact of COVID-19.

The COVID-19 Act raised hopes that it would provide relief to those who were unable to perform their contractual obligations. And Section 7 in Part II of the said Act headed "Inability to Perform Contractual Obligations" might have suggested that the Act would provide relief to the individual unable to perform his/her contractual obligations. Further, Section 7 does enumerate the categories of contract against the breach of which the innocent party will not be entitled to enforce their rights. The categories of contracts immunized are:

1. Construction work contract or construction consultancy contract and any other contract related to the supply of construction material, equipment, or workers in connection with a construction contract.
2. Performance bond or equivalent that is granted pursuant to a construction contract or supply contract.
3. Professional services contract.
4. Lease or tenancy of non-residential immovable property.
5. Event contract for the provision of any venue, accommodation, amenity, transport, entertainment, catering, or other goods or services, including for any business meeting, incentive travel, conference, exhibition, sales event, concert, show, wedding, party or other social gathering, or sporting event, for the participants, attendees, guests, patrons, or spectators of such gathering or event.
6. Contract by a tourism enterprise as defined under the Tourism Industry Act 1992 [Act 482] and a contract for the promotion of tourism in Malaysia.
7. Religious pilgrimage-related contract.

The list above is limited largely to businesses and organizations' contracts and does not include contracts of employment, particularly contracts of personal service. Thus, the first criticism of the COVID-19 Act is that it is not wide enough in scope to encompass employees and those individuals and small businesses that actually required protection for having breached their contracts. Where employees are concerned, the lockdown caused contractual obligations that had to be personally performed to be breached. Employment contracts were terminated. The Industrial Court has held that an employer may not reduce wages without the consent of the employee.[18] Anecdotal evidence exists that employers did reduce the wages of employees during the lockdown but that such reductions were "consensual". One wonders whether such employees had to make the difficult choice between a wage reduction and retrenchment. It has to be noted that retrenchment benefits are provided for in the Employment Act which covers just those employees whose pay does not exceed RM2,000 a month. Whether the absence of retrenchment benefits would have prompted those earning more than RM2,000 per month to accept a pay cut is very much an open question.

Just as the doctrine of frustration is not equal to the task of providing meaningful relief against the coronavirus disease, so is the COVID-19 Act powerless to solve the issue of termination benefits for those not covered by the Employment Act. This is not to deny that the COVID-19 Act extended the period in which employees dismissed without just cause or excuse could file a claim with the Industrial Court. But that extension would not economically support workers who were dismissed because they refused to accept a unilateral pay cut. The COVID-19 Act did not have provisions to remedy the plight of other employees too. To begin with, there were the daily paid workers. Their work was not an "essential service" and the Regulations did not authorize workers paid a daily wage to travel to work. As a result, such workers found that they had no source of income. Workers on monthly wages fared no better as they could not attend work which was non-essential.

Teachers in private educational institutions came under undue pressure. Following the 18 March Regulations, all face-to-face teaching ceased and was replaced by online instruction. This went on for months. Then, the rule requiring only online teaching was relaxed. An educational institution decided that some of the courses currently taught online had to revert to the traditional face-to-face teaching mode. One of the teachers objected to having to conduct such classes. Her reason: that she had an infant child and did not want to risk carrying the virus home and exposing her child to it. The representative of the institution responded: "Surely the institution is within its rights to ask any of its teachers to conduct regular classes. Especially since our competitors are doing it." In the words of the institution's representative, there is an implied threat that if the teacher declines to carry out the function she was hired to perform (to teach), she had better be prepared to quit.

If the teacher is then directed to conduct face-to-face teaching despite her concerns for her infant child, could the teacher claim "constructive dismissal" and file for relief for dismissal without "just cause or excuse" under Section 20 of the

18 Amirul Izzat Hasri, *"Can an Employer Reduce Your Salary?" Donovan & Ho, April 5, 2018,* https://dnh.com.my/can-your-employer-reduce-your-salary/.

Industrial Relations Act 1967? The teacher would argue that under her contract of service, her employer could not place her or her child in a situation in which either she or her child would risk danger to their health by the disease, which she did not by the said contract undertake to assume. One can imagine the employer's counsel declaim that the teacher's claim for constructive dismissal was "premature" in that neither she nor her child had succumbed to COVID-19. Counsel could also argue that the risk of the teacher or her child being infected was so minimal as to be speculative. Such a stance would be contradicted by the Regulations requiring citizens to stay at home to avoid all but essential contact with others to prevent contagion by the Coronavirus.

To succeed in a claim for constructive dismissal, the employee must exercise the right expeditiously; otherwise, the employee runs the risk of being deemed to have accepted the variation in terms of employment. One hopes that counsel will not submit that the employer can always compensate the employee the cost of having and raising it to the age at which earlier child died of COVID-19. It would be a rare employee who would refuse to comply with the directive herein or use "constructive dismissal" to seek relief in the Industrial Court. The point is that that would have been in the situation of the teacher herein, and the COVID-19 Act has no provision to aid her.

The control of movements and gatherings under Regulation 3 of 18 March 2020 and similar provisions in later Regulations were inimical to economic activity. People who could not, during the lockdown, travel to and from work were in breach of their contracts of employment. Retailers who rented stalls in shopping malls had, in the pre-lockdown days, been subject to very onerous tenancy terms. These stallholders were contractually required to obtain their landlord's consent before they could close their stalls, whether on account of family emergencies or religious duties, or otherwise. The lockdown literally placed them on the horns of a dilemma. The 18 March 2020 Regulations and similar provisions in later Regulations would not permit them to travel to their stalls, and the landlords would not approve their applications to keep their stalls closed. Such landlords still demanded, unfairly, the contractual rent in full. The doctrine of frustration, if invoked, might have operated to discharge the remainder of the tenancy. However, what the stallholders wanted was the tenancy itself continued but needed relief other than that, which would have flowed from the tenancy being voided by frustration.

Another class of contracts breached was those for the rental of employee parking lots in parking facilities owned or operated by employers. Such contracts were standard form contracts that pre-dated the Regulation. In these standard form contracts, the employers, as landlords/owners, reserved to themselves the right to raise the rent from time to time and required that the rental be paid quarterly in advance. The standard form contracts also entitled the landlord to terminate the contract upon the tenant not paying the rent upon expiry of each quarter and not to renew the rental at any time without assigning any reason for the same. When the Regulations went into effect, employers instructed their employees to comply with the Regulations, which prohibited travel within the whole of the Federation, not to come to work. Some employers even notified employees that their attempting to enter the workplace during the lockdown would be a severe disciplinary offence. Thus, employees were prevented, by both the law and the employer, from using the parking lot for which they had pre-paid.

When the lockdown expired, the landlord notified the renters that their rental for the next quarter was due and payable. Frustration would operate to discharge the contract, but the employees would still require parking facilities after that. And landlords informed their renters that if they opted to terminate their rental contracts, the renewal of the rental of their parking lots would be decided upon their payment history. A renter would have to be very optimistic if he/she avoided the contract on the grounds of frustration and yet expected to renew the lease of his/her parking lot. Thus, the car park lot renters required relief from having to pay for parking facilities that they were unable to use during the lockdown without having their contracts to rent the parking space terminated by the landlords.

Also, landlords of parking facilities used their contractual power to raise the rent for the parking bays at this time. The Consumer Protection Act 1999 (CPA) makes procedurally and substantively unfair contract terms void. However, sections 2(4) and 24B denude the CPA of any meaningful impact by making the application of the CPA "supplemental" and "without prejudice" to "any other law regulating contractual relations". As a matter of statutory interpretation, the other Acts regulating contractual relations, therefore, prevail over the CPA. Since Malaysia has adopted the common law on exemption clauses, the provisions of the CPA may be nugatory and of no assistance to parking bay renters.

The relief enacted is only available if the inability of the party to perform any contractual obligations arising from any category of contract specified in Part II of the Act is caused by measures undertaken pursuant to the Prevention and Control of Infectious Disease Act 1988 to curb the spread of COVID-19. In short, the inability to perform his/her contractual obligation must be caused by a measure undertaken pursuant to the Act (i.e. the lockdown), not otherwise. Thus, if a sole trader breached his/her contractual obligation because he/she was infected by the COVID-19 and was hospitalized for a long period, and this rendered him/her unable to perform his/her contractual obligation, he/she would not be covered by the Act because his/her breach of contract is not attributable to any of the measures undertaken pursuant to the 1988 Act.

Regulation 3(1)(e) in the Prevention and Control of Infectious Disease (Measures within the Infected Local Area) Regulations 2020 (the Regulations) provides that a person could travel for "any special purposes as may be permitted by the Director General". But no mechanism was provided for obtaining the permission of the Director General. However, the onus is likely to be on the individual to discover how to make the necessary application and to make it in such form and such detail as may be demanded by the Director General.

Support for the proposition that the retailer has to apply to the Director General for permission to travel to and from his retail business may appear to be provided by *Dato Yap Peng & Ors v Public Bank Bhd & Ors.*[19] In this case, Bank Negara "froze" the first appellant's assets (publicly quoted shares and land) under the Essential (Protection of Depositors) Regulations 1980 (the 1980 Regulations). The freezing of his/her assets prevented the first appellant from servicing his/her loans from the respondent banks. The first appellant claimed frustration by supervening legislation. The banks referred to the fact that the 1980 Regulations had a provision that permitted the sale or disposal of the "frozen" assets with Bank Negara's consent. The respondent banks continued that a supervening prohibition of some contractually undertaken obligation which could be overcome by obtaining the consent from Bank Negara would be frustrated only when the person affected by the prohibition could show that his/her application had been rejected by Bank Negara. The Court of Appeal accepted the banks' stance and dismissed Dato Yap Peng's appeal.

Applying *Dato Yap Peng* to our retailer, only if permission is declined can the retailer take the next step. One may be sure that counsel for the victim of a breach of contract seeking to enforce his/her rights will argue that the contract breaker who claims that it was the prohibition on travel imposed by the Regulations that caused him/her to breach the contract had to establish that he/she had applied for permission to the Director General for a special purpose and that the Director General had rejected his application. Only then, counsel would argue, is the contract breaker entitled to the protection of Section 7. Not many people under the lockdown are likely to have been familiar with the Regulation. It may be noted that it would not make any sense for the retailer to seek the Director General's permission to open his/her stall when his/her potential customers would be house-bound under the Regulations.

Does the COVID-19 Act 2020 contain any provisions that could come to the aid of a person unable to perform his/her contractual obligation? It would seem that a contract breaker may be able to resort to s 3(1), which provides:

> In the event of any conflict or inconsistency between the provisions of this Act and any other written law, the provisions of this Act shall prevail and the conflicting or inconsistent provisions of such other written law shall be deemed to be superseded to the extent of the conflict or inconsistency.

Another commentator has observed that Section 9 provides that disputes "may" be settled through mediation.[20] The use of the word "may" makes mediation optional.

19 [1997] 1 MLJ 484 (CA).

20 "Temporary Measures for Reducing the Impact of Coronavirus Disease 2019 (COVID-19) Bill 2020," Christopher & Lee Ong, Last Modified August 2020, https://www.christopherleeong.com/media/4063/clo_covid9_bill.pdf.

Section 9(2) enacts that the procedure for mediation shall be decided by the Minister of Law. If mediation is not available, the only other avenue for redress is the court. Thus, if the announcement of the procedure is delayed, the courts may well be flooded with applications for relief.

One admires the elegance and simplicity of Section 26(2) of the COVID-19 Act, which relieves the purchaser on credit whose payments are in arrears of the need to pay the credit service provider interest on overdue payments. This definite provision provides certainty for both parties to the transaction and the credit purchaser relief from overdue interest payments. Section 26(2) of the COVID-19 Act provides that this relief is available only if the credit sale agreement was entered into before 18 March 2020; and if the purchaser had no overdue instalments before 18 March 2020.

Comparison with Singapore's COVID-19 Act 2020

In Singapore, the statute comparable to Malaysia's COVID-19 Act is the COVID-19 (Temporary Measures) Act 2020 (the Singapore COVID-19 Act). Under Section 34(1) of the Singapore COVID-19 Act, the Minister may make regulations (called "control orders") for the purpose of preventing, protecting against, delaying, or otherwise controlling the incidence or transmission of COVID-19 in Singapore. In exercise of this power, the Minister issued COVID-19 (Temporary Measures) (Performance and Other Activities – Control Order) Regulations 2020.

The Singapore COVID-19 Act does not limit relief to contractual breaches caused by the measures adopted to prevent the spread of the disease. All that is required is that the breach be caused by the disease. Further, the Singapore Act requires a party seeking the protection of the Singapore COVID-19 Act to serve a notice of that on the other party. The party whose rights have been breached may then apply to an assessor to ascertain the cause of the breach. The Malaysian legislation has no such provision, and litigation may be necessary to establish that a breach of contract was caused by measures instituted under the Act or Regulations. Singapore thus has a more efficacious way of settling the issue.

A party to a contract who breached a contractual obligation may have had a performance bond forfeited, paid damages, had legal proceedings, arbitration or mediation commenced, or a judgement or award, or been the subject of execution proceedings (collectively "sanctions"). The Malaysian Regulations declares any of the sanctions effected from 18 March 2020 until the date of publication of the COVID-19 Act valid. By contrast, the Singapore Regulations does not provide for transactions entered into before the enactment of the COVID-19 Act.

Limitation

Section 12 of the COVID-19 Act provides that the limitation period for contracts during the period 18 March 2020 to 31 August 2020 is extended to 31 December 2020. The Sabah Limitation Ordinance and the Sarawak Limitation Ordinance similarly have the period of limitation extended to 31 December 2020.

Bankruptcy

Under the Insolvency Act, bankruptcy proceedings could be launched against an individual for the indebtedness of RM50,000. The COVID-19 Act raised the minimum for this purpose to RM 100,000 until 31 August 2021. This should provide a breathing space for financially distressed individuals.

The Hire Purchase Act 1967

The Hire Purchase Act 1967 has been amended. During the period 1 April 2020 to 30 September 2030, any owner may not repossess goods comprised in the hire purchase agreement for non-payment of instalments.

Defect Liability Period for Housing Accommodation

The period from 18 March 2020 to 31 August 2020 shall be excluded from the calculation of the defects liability period after the purchaser has taken vacant possession of a housing accommodation. The period from 18 March 2020 to 31 August 2020 shall also be excluded from the calculation of the time for the developer to carry out works to repair and make good the defect, shrinkages, and other faults in a housing accommodation.

The Housing Development (Control and Licensing) Act 1966

The Housing Development (Control and Licensing) Act 1966 has been amended. The purchasers cannot be charged late payment charges for failing to pay their instalments on time during the period from 18 March 2020 to 31 August 2020. Balanced against this, developers do not have to pay damages for later delivery of vacant possession and for failing to effect repairs to defects during the period 18 March to 31 August 2020. Both developers and purchasers may apply to the Minister to exercise power vested in him/her to extend the period until 31 December 2020. These provisions do not extend to legal proceedings already commenced, any judgement or award relating to late payment charges by purchasers, or liquidated damages payable by developers after 18 March 2020.

The Consumer Protection Act and Credit Sales

Part IIIB of the Consumer Protection Act 1999 (as amended in 2019) is entitled "Credit Sales Transactions". It provides for the sale of goods and services by credit. It also enacts the details that must be included in the credit sales agreement. In the event of default in payment of two consecutive instalments by a purchaser under a credit sale agreement, Section 24U(2)(a) provided that "the purchaser may elect to pay the overdue instalments and the late payment charges to the credit facility provider". The COVID-19 Act amends Section 24U(2)(a) to read: "to pay the overdue payments to the credit facility provider". The COVID-19 Act thus relieves the purchaser from having to pay the credit facility provider any of the late payment charges. Section 26(2) of the COVID-19 Act provides that this relief is available only if the credit sale agreement was entered into before 18 March 2020; and if the purchaser has no overdue instalments before 18 March 2020.

Conclusion

The purpose of the "Temporary Measures for Reducing the Impact of Coronavirus Disease (COVID-19) Act 2020" is clearly indicated by its title. It is meant to provide temporary or limited relief and not to extinguish the liability of the contract breakers. The COVID-19 Act has identified a limited number or classes of contracts which it deems worthy of receiving the temporary relief it provides. The classes of contracts concerned are listed in Section 7, and they concern construction works, the supply of construction materials, and performance bonds related to construction contracts. The next two are professional service contracts and tenancies of non-residential buildings. The second last class is of contracts by a tourism enterprise, and the last is a religious pilgrim-related contract. These are, in the main, business contracts. The COVID-19 Act is thus very narrow in scope in limiting itself to business contracts and not providing for employment contracts, residential tenancies and vehicle parking facilities, and small businessmen and sole traders. Further, such relief as is provided is contingent on a condition precedent: that the breach of contract must have been caused by one of the measures embodied in Regulations issued under the Prevention and Control of Infectious Diseases Act 1988.

The Covid-19 Act seems to have been enacted to provide relief only to the contract breakers who fell into the classes of contracts listed above. It is clear that the COVID-19 Act is not bold enough to attempt to provide complete relief to all contract breakers. If so, it would be unfair to criticize the COVID-19 Act for not doing what it never set out to do. Perhaps, the COVID-19 Act has actually achieved the rather limited goals it set itself.

Ashgar Ali Ali Mohamed and Chithra Latha Ramalingam

3 COVID-19 and Its Influence on Selected Employment Relationship Issues

Introduction

The unprecedented worldwide COVID-19 pandemic has forced all countries around the globe to contain the deadly virus through the stringent measure of either emergency orders or movement control orders. These measures have resulted in anxiety and suffering for many corporations and negatively impacting the well-being of workers, with many being asked to take a salary cut or even retrenchments as a measure for the company to remain afloat. It is worth noting that while the law recognizes workers' security of tenure in employment, the employer's prerogative to make commercial decisions to reorganize or restructure the company as a cost-saving measure is equally recognized. This prerogative, however, is subject to the rule that the company must act bona fide in the interest of the company as a whole and not capriciously or with motives of victimization or unfair labour practice.

Having said the above, this chapter discusses the selected issues of employment law arising from the current COVID-19 pandemic, which a prudent employer would take to withstand its harsh business impact, namely, the pay-cut, flex-work arrangement, and retrenchment of surplus labour, among others. In relation to retrenchment, it is worthwhile mentioning that in Malaysia, the terms "retrenchment", "termination", and "lay-off" are used interchangeably.[1] These terms, however, have different meanings. At the outset, it must be noted that all retrenchments are terminations, but all terminations are not retrenchments. When an employee is retrenched, this amounts to a termination of his services. But when it is said that an employee has been terminated, it cannot only mean that he is retrenched because retrenchment is one method in which an employee's services can be terminated.

Flexible Working Arrangements and Conflict of Interest

With modern technology, where communication via telephone, handphone, and emails among others, is easily accessible, it would completely be viable for employers to direct their employees to arrange for the remote workplace. In fact, the work

1 See the Employment (Termination and Lay-Off Benefits) Regulation, 1980, where the "lay-off" has been used.

https://doi.org/10.1515/9783110723694-003

patterns have evolved rapidly in the last few decades, with flexible working arrangements seen much favoured and widely accepted in many countries. This includes the flexibility of working hours, arrangements regarding work schedules such as part-time work and job sharing, and flexibility in the place of work, such as working from home or at a certain location, among others. Such working arrangements are seen as beneficial to both the organization and the employees. It brings inter alia, empowerment, and improved employability and staff retention. Since the beginning of last year, the working from home arrangement has become the preferred work arrangement worldwide, including Malaysia, thanks to the COVID-19 pandemic, which has brought along the "new normal" that includes, inter alia, the social distancing rule.

It may be added that Malaysia is highly dependent on migrant workers, skilled and unskilled, who undeniably have contributed significantly to Malaysia's economic growth, especially in sectors with an acute shortage of workers such as construction and plantation. What is evident is that the country is swarmed with unskilled or low-skill migrant workers who cannot contribute meaningfully to Malaysia's aspiration of becoming a high-income economy.[2] Such high dependency on unskilled migrant workers impedes the country's progress towards a high-productivity nation and, if not addressed, could give rise to issues that could affect the people's support for the government. Efforts are underway to reduce the country's dependence on low-skilled migrant workers. However, such efforts cannot be done away with overnight, as sudden repatriation of migrant workers can have serious repercussions on the economy, especially in sectors like manufacturing, construction, and plantation.[3] Alternative measures should be considered, and this includes providing attractive incentives to the national workforce, including implementing flexible working arrangements. Such arrangements, however, can be challenging since the existing employment law lacks a legal framework for flexible working. Hence, a review of the existing labour legislation to suit the COVID-19's "new normal" is urgently required.

Aside from the above, in relation to working from home with limited supervision, the worker's duty of fidelity and fiduciary towards the employer must not be underrated. An essential component of the duty of fidelity is his obligation to serve the best interest of the employer.[4] He must avoid any conflict of interest or even potential conflict of interest where his personal interests could inappropriately influence or appear to influence the business judgement. In the performance of his official duties, workers should avoid giving preferential treatment to an individual,

2 Billy Toh, "Malaysia Lacks Skilled Jobs for the Able, While the Unskilled Gets Displaced," *The Edge Financial Daily*, March 10, 2017, https://www.theedgemarkets.com/article/%E2%80%98malaysia-lacks-skilled-jobs-able-while-unskilled-gets-displaced%E2%80%99.

3 "It's a Long Journey Towards Solving Labour Shortage in Plantation Sector," *The Sun Daily*, September 27, 2020, https://www.thesundaily.my/local/it-s-a-long-journey-towards-solving-labour-shortage-in-plantation-sector-DH4283162.

4 *Worldwide Rota Dies Sdn Bhd v. Ronald Ong Chew Joon* [2010] 8 MLJ 297.

corporation, or organization in which he or a relative or friend has an interest, financial or otherwise. For example, hiring a family member as a vendor or buying goods or services from a family business on their employer's behalf. It is common that by transacting business with a family member or friend, the employee may feel the urge to favour the interests of the family member over the interests of his employer. Further, no employee should use a company's property, facilities, equipment, or other resources to pursue his personal interests or the interests of another organization. Likewise, he should not conduct his private business dealings during working hours' even if the activities did not directly compete with the employer's business as such acts are plainly unacceptable and wrong and in breach of the fiduciary relationship.

An employee who finds himself in a conflict-of-interest situation must disclose the matter to his superior or the designated officer of the organization. The disclosure must be made as soon as the employee knows of the conflict and thereafter for as long as the conflict continues to exist. The disclosure is primarily to safeguard the interests of the employer. Any non-disclosure of a conflict of interest or even a potential conflict of interest is viewed seriously and may warrant disciplinary action. Further, knowingly making a false declaration that he was not having any outside business interests or serving or being on the board of directors of any other company is gross misconduct. An employee who acts against the best interests of the employer would clearly be perceived as being dishonest, which inevitably reflects both on the fitness of the employee to continue in office and the discipline and morale of the service.

Annual Leave and Absenteeism

It is an established rule that a person who has undertaken responsibilities ought to discharge it faithfully.[5] While working from home, the employee ought to faithfully discharge his duties and obligations, and this includes the duty to be present for work at the working hours and to render the services expected of him. An unauthorized absence on a scheduled workday would disrupt employers' work schedules and affect their customers' commitments. To minimize work disruption due to the slack caused by an absent employee, a regular worker would, in normal circumstances, assume added workload. Whilst an employee is entitled to annual leave, medical leave, maternity leave, paternity leave, compassionate leave, emergency leave, calamity leave, and unpaid leave, such leave, however, cannot be claimed as of

5 *Pan Global Textiles Bhd, Pulau Pinang v Ang Beng Teik* [2002] 2 MLJ 27, FC.

right but is subject to the discretion of the employer.[6] It is normal in any organization for the employer to maintain the procedure in applying for leave, which may take several forms such as completing a leave application form, notifying the company ahead of time as to when the employee intends to take leave, and applying for annual leave in accordance with a leave roster. The leave is not granted automatically or indiscriminately because many factors and circumstances have to be taken into consideration before the leave is approved. In approving or otherwise the leave application, the employer is required to exercise its discretion in a manner that is tenable with their business needs at that particular time. It is worth mentioning that an employer cannot force their workers to utilize the annual leave or unpaid leave throughout the movement control order period. Be that as it may, it is equally important for the employee to be cooperative with the employer to minimize the COVID-19 impact on their business by agreeing inter alia, to utilize the annual leave or go on unpaid leave, which is primarily intended to evade reduction of the workforce due to business losses.

An employee should not absent himself from work unless and until the leave request has been formally and properly approved by the employer. An unauthorized absence from the workplace without any prior approval or permission of the employer is a gross violation of discipline. Absenteeism is considered a fundamental breach of the employment contract. It justifies the employee's dismissal after adequate opportunity is given to the employee to refute the allegations framed against him. The Employment Act 1955 (Malaysia) provides that an employee who absents himself from work for a continuous period of 2 days or more without prior permission or approval of the employer or without notifying the employer of such absence constitutes a gross violation of discipline. An employee with a valid excuse for being absent from work, for example, due to ill-health or emergency has a statutory duty to inform his employer of such sick or emergency leave within 48 h of the commencement of the said leave, and his failure to so inform the employer at the earliest opportunity during such absence shall be deemed an absent from work without reasonable excuse.

With the easily accessible modern communication tools, it would be inexcusable for an employee not been able to inform his employer of his absence from work on account of illness or other emergencies as soon as possible and in any case within 48 h from the commencement of his leave. The communication can even be done through his family members, friends, or colleagues. It is, however, unconscionable for an employee to assume that he could stay away from work either without prior approval of the employer or notifying the employer. No employer would or should tolerate the behaviour of an employee who deliberately stayed away from work for days and returning to work at his whim and fancy as this would set a bad

6 *Metromix Sdn Bhd v Ismail Bin Sulaiman* [1998] 1 ILR 336.

example to the other employees. In establishing absenteeism, the employer is merely required to show that the employee was absent from work for more than 2 consecutive days or had been frequent in taking unauthorized leave. Once the employer has established the above, the burden of proof will then shift on the employee to justify his absence. The employee must be able to produce proof that he/she had a reasonable excuse for such absence and had made reasonable attempts to inform the company of his absence. Hence, with the imposition of movement control order as a measure to combat the spread of the COVID-19 in this country, workers selected to work from office must follow the order and instructions of the employer without excuses, and any leave application is subject to prior approval of the employer as discussed above.

Deduction of Worker's Wages

A person normally seeks employment for various personal reasons. However, the majority of them work for a monetary consideration. Undoubtedly, the wages earned would be used to provide the employed and his family with the basic necessities of life such as food, clothing, education, housing, leisure activities, and eventually, saving for retirement. Wages payable must be adequate to meet the basic needs of the worker and his or her family. In practice, however, the level of wages is generally set by the market force (supply and demand) or by a collective agreement. In fact, many workers are paid substandard wages. Realizing this, many countries have introduced a minimum wage law that prohibits the employer from engaging workers for less than a given hourly, daily, or monthly minimum wage. The Minimum Wages Order 2012 (Malaysia) makes it mandatory for employers to pay their employees basic wages that meet the minimum wages requirement stipulated in the Order. The above Order aims to increase the standard of living of workers and reduce poverty, among others. Workers are, however, entitled to contractually agree to higher wages than the minimum set in the Order.

Undeniably, the wages of an employee are a fundamental factor in a contract of employment. It must be paid within the period specified by the law or as agreed to by the parties. An employer cannot delay the payment of wages to the employees. The Employment Act provides that wages must be paid not later than the seventh day after the last day of any wage period the wages.[7] Failure of the employer to pay the wages to its workers when it falls due may result in criminal prosecution, and on conviction, the employer can be subject to a fine of up to RM10,000.[8] The non-payment

7 Employment Act 1955, Section 19.

8 Employment Act 1955, Section 99A provides: "Any person who commits any offence under, or contravenes any provision of, this Act, or any regulations, order, or other subsidiary legislation

of wages would also constitute a fundamental breach of the employment contract where the affected worker may, besides making a formal complaint to the Labour Department, resign from employment and have his resignation treated as a constructive dismissal pursuant to Section 20(1) of the Industrial Relations Act 1967 (Malaysia) as the employer had repudiated an essential term of the contract.

Further, no employer may deduct any portion of a worker's wages except when it is authorized by law or where the employer has written authorization from the employee for the deduction. Any unilateral deduction of an employee's wages would amount to a significant breach going to the root of the contract. The employee in the aforesaid circumstances was placed in a position that he had no choice but to leave the company and thereafter allege constructive dismissal. However, the COVID-19 pandemic has severely impacted many businesses, with many having to close. Despite the government's wage subsidies and employment retention programmes, many employers have resorted to pay cuts – and hence the issue of legality arises.[9] It is argued that employees should understand their employers' predicament and be cooperative by agreeing to a temporary pay cut, a measure primarily intended to avert retrenchment. An employee who resists pay cut measures, thereafter alleging constructive dismissal, may not find their claim favourable because the pay cut is made for legitimate business reasons.

It must be noted that the Malaysian labour legislation promotes social justice and not legal justice, where a balance is drawn between competing claims. The court is required to balance, for instance, a worker's right to contractually agreed wages with the employer's legitimate reasons for pay cut measures during the current harsh economic conditions. The notion of social justice was aptly noted by the Industrial Court in *Vincent Pillai Leelakanda Pillai v Subang Jaya Hotel Development*:[10]

> A workman's right and status under his employment contract are not to be decided solely on the basis of the law of contract, and neither is a workman's security of tenure to be dependent on the absolute discretion of his employer or on the terms and conditions of his contract of employment. His rights are to be determined on the basis of fair labour practice, equity and good conscience to ensure that the principle of security of tenure is not undermined and social justice is dispensed.

---

whatsoever made thereunder, in respect of which no penalty is provided, shall be liable, on conviction, to a fine not exceeding ten thousand ringgit."

9 "Small Businesses Start to Cut Salaries to Survive Covid-19," Federation of Malaysian Manufacturers, accessed February 9, 2021, https://www.fmm.org.my/FMM_In_The_News-@-Small_businesses_start_to_cut_salaries_to_survive_Covid-19.aspx.

10 [2018] 2 ILR 158.

Force Majeure Clause in Employment Contract

The force majeure clause and the doctrine of frustration scientifically can be considered to be dizygotic twins.[11] The justification to this stems from the question that ties these two important pieces of law in that both identify with the question "when should a contracting party which, through no fault of its own, can no longer perform its obligations be relieved of the obligations or liability for not performing them".[12] The Malaysian industrial jurisprudence dictates that a workman's right and status under his employment contract are not to be decided solely based on the law of contract,[13] and neither is his security of tenure to be dependent on the absolute discretion of his employer or the terms and conditions of his contract of employment. His rights are to be determined based on fair labour practice, equity, and good conscience to ensure that the principle of security of tenure is not undermined and social justice is dispensed with.

Employees enter into a contract with the employers generally in good faith. Their focus would be to perform the terms of the contract to their best possible ability. Therefore, the intention of breaching the contract is never at the forefront of the employees' minds when it is signed. The employment contract is about and should be about the performance of the contract rather than focussing on the breach.[14] The unprecedented COVID-19 pandemic has brought about a major impact on the economy, and many industries have considered triggering the force majeure clause in their employment contracts in retrenching the workers. Hence, the question arises as to whether the employer is allowed to invoke the force majeure clause in the employment contract to excuse their inability to perform the contractual obligations due to the COVID-19 pandemic outbreak?[15]

---

11 "There are two types of twins – identical (monozygotic) and fraternal (dizygotic). To form identical twins, one fertilised egg (ovum) splits and develops two babies with exactly the same genetic information." Cited from "Twins – Identical and Fraternal," *Better Health Channel*, accessed February 8, 2021, https://www.betterhealth.vic.gov.au/health/ConditionsAndTreatments/twins-identical-and-fraternal.

12 "COVID-19 – Issues Affecting Performance of Contractual Obligations in Construction Contracts Governed by English Law," Quinn Emanuel Trial Lawyers, accessed February 8, 2021, https://www.quinnemanuel.com/media/je2pl3td/client-alert-covid-19-issues-affecting-performance-of-con_.pdf.

13 *Hong Guan & Co. Ltd. v. R. Jumabhoy & Sons Ltd.* [1960] AC 684.

14 Judge Oliver Wendell Holmes said that parties entering into a contract primarily focus on performing the contract rather than on breaching it, and that contractual provisions therefore generally concern the results of performance rather than the results of a breach. See Oliver Wendell Holmes, *The Common Law* (Cambridge: Harvard University Press, 2009), https://doi.org/10.4159/9780674054011.

15 "A pandemic is defined as 'an epidemic occurring worldwide, or over a very wide area, crossing international boundaries and usually affecting a large number of people'. The classical definition includes nothing about population immunity, virology or disease severity." Cited from Heath Kelly, "The Classical Definition of a Pandemic is Not Elusive," Wold Health Organization, accessed February 8, 2021, https://www.who.int/bulletin/volumes/89/7/11-088815/en/.

This worldwide epidemic has been much of the debate in the legal field concerning the force majeure clause. The earliest known case that recognized that epidemic may institute a force majeure event was in the case of *Lebeaupin* in 1920. Justice Macardie, in this case, stated that:

> This term [i.e. force majeure] is used with reference to all circumstances independent of the will of man, and which it is not in his power to control, and such force majeure is sufficient to justify the non-execution of a contract. Thus, war, inundations, and epidemics, are cases of force majeure; it has even been decided that a strike of workmen constitutes a case of force majeure. . . [But] a force majeure clause should be construed in each case with a close attention to the words which precede or follow it and with due regard to the contract. The effect of the clause may vary with each document.[16]

This is subject to the issue of whether the force majeure clause is recognized in the industrial jurisprudence of the country and, further, whether it warrants the satisfaction of an event or effect that can be neither anticipated nor controlled.

In Malaysia, the force majeure clauses have been dealt with in non-employment cases. In the case of *Intan Payong*,[17] it was decided that the party relying on the force majeure clause to be discharged from the obligation of the contract bears the burden of proof. Further, the case of *Saujana Triangle*,[18] the court decided that the force majeure clause cannot be implied into a contract where it is silent on the same clause. The recent cases further applied the Singapore High Court's decision in *Magenta*[19] where the court decided that there is no clear rule on what amounts to force majeure, and it is much dependent on the intention of the parties in the drafted contract.

The courts in Malaysia have been seen to be reluctant in applying this clause as opposed to the doctrine of frustration. In the case of *Ramanazan*,[20] the court was asked to decide whether the claimant's employment contract had been frustrated. The court held that a supervening event, through the operation of law, can terminate a contract of employment due to his medical condition as the same was not the fault of either parties. If the decision of *Magenta's* case as approved in *Saujana Triangle's* case is accepted, then parties in the employment contract must clearly "define" what should constitute "force majeure" event in the said contract, and this is decided through precise and accurate questioning on the facts of the case.[21] The party relying on the clause has to ensure that all reasonable steps ought to have been taken to manoeuvre away from the application of the clause, and the party took every step to mitigate the unintended or unplanned outcome.[22] This is the very essence of the freedom of contract.

16 *Lebeaupin v R Crispin & Co* [1920] 2 KB 714.
17 *Intan Payong Sdn Bhd v Goh Saw Chan Sdn Bhd* [2004] 1 LNS 537.
18 *Muhammad Radhieddeen bin Abdul Khalid v Saujana Triangle Sdn Bhd* [2017] MLJU 950.
19 *Magenta Resources (S) Pte Ltd v China Resources (S) Pte Ltd* [1996] 2 SLR(R) 316.
20 *Ramanazan a/l Kathmuthu v Southern Latex Products Sdn Bhd* [2016] ILJU 54.
21 *RDC Concrete Pte Ltd v Sato Kogyo* [2007] 4 SLR(R) 413 at [54].
22 *RDC Concrete Pte Ltd v Sato Kogyo* [2007] 4 SLR(R) 413 at [54].

Therefore, it is argued that while the parties to the employment contract may define clearly the unforeseen circumstances that will be covered under the force majeure clauses, thereby avoiding future disputes, the Malaysian industrial jurisprudence, however, leans in favour of protecting workers with the Industrial Court being able to free parties from any unfair terms of their contracts entered into because of the inequality. The most significant aspect of industrial adjudication is following social justice and not legal justice. Unlike an ordinary court of law, which is bound by contractual rights, duties, or obligations with no authority to transform, alter, or even create rights when the justice of the matter demands, the Industrial Court is not purely judicial – it is not confined to the administration of justice following the law. In the interest of industrial peace, the prevention of unfair labour practice or victimization, the Industrial Court may confer rights and privileges on either party, which it considers reasonable or proper, irrespective of whether it is within the express contract between the parties. Hence, there is no guarantee that the employer could absolve liability by merely relying on the force majeure clause. Where there is a challenge of dismissal, the employer will still have to show on a balance of probability that the dismissal was with just cause or excuse. Aristotle's statement that "unpredictable events happen, random 'acts of God' for which no one is responsible. But how we respond to them is not random, and responsibility for that lies squarely on our shoulders"[23] is a timely lesson to prepare Malaysia for employment contracts in the future catastrophe.

"Redundancy", "Retrenchment", and "Lay-Off"

While the law recognizes the security of tenure in employment, the employer's overriding interest of business efficiency is equally emphasized. It is trite law that the employer is entitled to organize his business in the manner he considers best, and in this regard, he is empowered to retrench workers based on the operational requirements of the organization.[24] An employee's services may become surplus if there is a reduction, diminution, or cessation of the type of work the employee was performing. For example, an employer may reduce its workforce due to automation, or the employer may choose to restructure his business by combining two or more departments or units, among others. Again, when the business is less profitable, the surplus labour may be discharged so as to save costs. In the aforesaid circumstances,

---

23 Julian Baggini, Christine Korsgaard, Ursula Coope, Peter Singer, Susan Haack, Kenneth Taylor and Slavoj Žižek, "I Watch Therefore I Am: Seven Movies That Teach Us Key Philosophy Lessons," *The Guardian*, April 15, 2015, https://www.theguardian.com/film/2015/apr/14/force-majeure-films-philosophy-memento-ida-its-a-wonderful-life.
24 *TWI Training and Certification (SE Asia) Sdn Bhd v Jose A Sebastian* [1998] 2 ILR 879.

unless the employer can absorb them into performing other jobs in the organization, the affected workers would have to be retrenched.

As a result of the COVID-19 pandemic, businesses are facing disruptions or even closures to some extent, thereby causing major changes in most of the industries across the world. This unprecedented event brings about an economic downturn or recession. The fact is that no companies are immune to the recession. Hence, when this occurs, markets become volatile and force the employers to reduce their workforce. If the employer does not resort to discharging the redundant worker but carries on the business and loses money, this may lead to insolvency, bankruptcy, or winding up of the organization.

It is appropriate to note that the terms "redundancy", "retrenchment", and "lay-off" whilst used interchangeably, have, nevertheless, distinct legal connotation. "Lay-off" means the suspension of an employee's employment contract arising from the company's temporary or long-term business strategy or economic conditions. It is a mere suspension of the employee from employment for a certain specified period of time. During the current COVID-19 pandemic, there is temporary inactivity. Thus, it is a common industrial practice to lay off part of the labour force because of not much work to warrant that many workers. If the employee is laid off due to temporary diminution in the particular kind of work done by him, and subsequently re-engaged without claiming the lay-off benefits payment under the Employment (Termination and Lay-Off Benefits) Regulations 1980 (Malaysia), it will be considered that there is no break in the continuity of his services with the organization. However, if the employee considers himself to have been terminated, he will have a right to termination benefits and at the rate mentioned in the 1980 Regulations. Once he has been paid the benefits, there will be a break in the continuity of his service, even if he is re-employed in the same organization later in time.

"Retrenchment", on the other hand, means termination of employee's services because the employee has become a surplus to the requirement of the organization, which may be due to several factors such as the closure of business, restructuring, reduction in production, mergers, technological changes, take-over, and economic downturn. The discharge of surplus labour was for reasons otherwise than as a punishment inflicted by way of disciplinary. Whilst retrenchment could be justified when it is carried out for profitability, economy, or convenience of the employer's business, it should be carried out bona fide and not for the purpose of victimization.

Meanwhile, "redundancy" means a surplus of labour, and due to this superfluity, workers need to be removed or retrenched. Redundancy occurs when the employer has ceased or intends to cease in continuing the business. It can also arise where work has ceased or diminished. All these are brought about because of changes in business strategy as times are not always booming in the business world. Redundancy may be established by showing that the business requires fewer employees of whatever kind resulting from a reorganization exercise or due to other legitimate reasons of business operations.

In light of the above, there must first be redundancy or surplus of labour before there can be retrenchment or termination of the surplus. To determine whether a retrenchment exercise in a particular case was bona fide or otherwise would depend upon each case's peculiar facts and circumstances. While lay-off stands on its own, it is merely a suspension of the employee from employment for a specified period. The worker will return to work when his services are required and that there is no break in the continuity of his service.

Retrenchment Procedure and Compensation

Redundancy in an organization that necessitates the retrenchment of workers would expect the employer to take a range of steps that go beyond payment of retrenchment benefits. The employer is expected to explore all possible alternatives to retrenchment by taking the necessary interim measures as follows: cutting down working hours, overtime, and the number of shifts; extending time off without pay; freezing bonuses and increase in salaries; reducing wages (by agreement); ceasing all new recruitment except for critical areas; decreasing the number of contractors or casual labourers; rationalizing costs and expenditure; temporary lay-off; early retirement offers; gradual reduction of workforce by way of natural turnover; and conducting retraining programmes for skill development to enable employees to move into different positions.[25] The decision to retrench should only be made when the job is redundant and that the employer had exhausted all available options to avert retrenchment. These options are primarily asking the employees to sacrifice for the good of the company, thereby minimizing retrenchment.

Hence, when retrenchment is inevitable, the employer is required to adhere to the proper procedure before retrenching its workers.[26] The guidelines that are discussed below are important to be observed as they tend to establish that the termination on the grounds of redundancy is bona fide and in accordance with established principles and procedures of industrial jurisprudence. The guidelines include adequate notice to the affected workers, which is primarily to prepare them for the impending retrenchment and find suitable alternative employment. The notice must contain relevant information such as reasons for retrenchment, the number of workers likely to be affected and their various job categories, selection criteria, when the retrenchment is likely to take place, the assistance the employer will offer such as time off to attend interviews for other jobs, an early release should a new job be found, issuing letters of reference, and psychological counselling. The issuance of

25 *Woo Chee Khoon v Citibank Berhad* [2011] 2 LNS 0495 (Award No. 495 of 2011).

26 See *William Jacks & Co (M) Sdn Bhd v S Balasingam* [1997] 3 AMR 2585; [1997] 3 CLJ 235 at 241, CA.

prior notice is a good industrial practice as this could minimize the traumatic impact of the retrenchment on the workers and their families.

Further, the employer should engage or consult with the workers likely to be affected by the proposed retrenchment or the representatives from the trade union. The discussion could focus on finding ways, for example, to avoid retrenchment, to reduce the number of people retrenched, to limit the harsh effects of retrenchment, and the method and criteria for selecting workers to be retrenched, among others. The consultation would reflect on the genuineness of the retrenchment and that the employer cares about their workers, and that they are doing their best to cope with the difficult time.

A generous gesture of an employer in an impending retrenchment exercise would also include exploring suitable alternative employment in the organization for the affected workers. The employer should take constructive action to place the affected workers in alternative positions within the organization, including their subsidiaries. Workers should not be retrenched until all options to place them elsewhere in the organization have been exhausted. Although there is no legal duty on the company to offer alternative employment to the affected employees, nevertheless, effort must be made to avert retrenchment by exploring alternative employment within the organization.

Aside from the above, a significant part of any retrenchment plan is a strategy to help these workers find new employment. The employer could assist the retrenched workers in securing alternative employment by submitting their names to labour exchange organizations or programmes and to local companies known to be recruiting new employees. The company could also make arrangements with the outsourcing company to re-employ the affected workers.

Another commonly used alternative to retrenchment is requesting the selected workers to take early retirement under the "Voluntary Separation Scheme" (VSS) by offering an attractive retirement package, which normally is better than the statutory minimum for retrenchment under the Employment (Termination and Lay-Off) Benefits Regulations 1980. The VSS is a voluntary arrangement reached between the employer and employee, and it has the effect of putting an end to the employee's employment by providing him a tangible inducement or reward for his early retirement.[27] The VSS scheme introduced by the company will invite the selected workers of the organization to submit their application and this means that the workers are making the offer to retire from the company. The offer would then be open to acceptance or rejection by the employer on the basis of its operational needs. When it is accepted by the company, a legally binding contract is thereby concluded, and there is said to be a mutual agreement to bring the contract of employment to an end, which in effect is not a dismissal.

27 *Jamil Arshad & Ors v CNA Manufacturing Sdn Bhd* [2010] 2 LNS 1305.

An enforceable contract would only come into existence upon acceptance of the offer by the employer and not when the employee volunteers. It is important for the company to inform the employees selected for VSS of the need to reduce the current workforce in accordance with the requirements of the organization's operational needs. Upon completing the VSS exercise, if the company still finds a surplus in its workforce, the company may embark on retrenching the excess labour, including potential workers selected for the VSS but who had declined the offer.

It is worth mentioning that by the very nature of the scheme, it has to be on a voluntary basis without forcing the employee into retirement. This means that the company cannot harass, force, coerce or induce the workers to accept the VSS. Further, the VSS offer should not be used for any ulterior purpose, for example, removing the underperforming staff or replacing the existing staff with migrant workers. In order to ensure that the VSS is genuine, the scheme must be offered to employees who have been advised that their position has been declared redundant and only after all redeployment, retraining, relocation, or transfer options available in the organization have been explored and eliminated.

Aside from the VSS scheme, workers to be retrenched or laid off from employment on genuine commercial reasons should be paid appropriate compensation for the loss of employment. The employer should recognize that a workman who loses his job arising from a genuine redundancy situation in the company has done nothing wrong, and therefore, the retrenchment benefit is to be paid to him in order to reflect the above. The payment of retrenchment benefits would ensure that the retrenched workers and their families have some form of financial compensation to cushion the often-harsh effects of losing their livelihood.

In Malaysia, where an employee's contract of service is terminated by his employer, the employee, who is within the purview of the Employment Act 1955, would be entitled to termination benefits pursuant to the Employment (Termination and Lay-Off Benefits) Regulations 1980. The amount of compensation they are entitled would depend on their last drawn monthly salary and the length of time they have been with the organization. The Act, however, is only applicable to the category of employees specified in the First Schedule, and workers falling within the purview of the First Schedule will be paid the retrenchment benefits as per the Regulation. As for workers who do not come within the purview of the Act, their entitlement for such benefits would depend on whether there is any contractual arrangement between the parties for such payment or whether the collective agreement to which the workers are members stipulates for such payment. Suppose the worker does not fall within the ambit of the Employment Act, and there are no retrenchment benefits prescribed in his contract of employment or collective agreement. In that case, there is no obligation on the company to pay any retrenchment benefits and if any such payment was made, it would have been made purely at the discretion of the company.

It would be inequitable to compel a company struggling to keep itself financially afloat and could hardly sustain itself financially to incur additional losses by making it pay retrenchment benefits to the retrenched workers. Hence, the recently enacted Employment Insurance System Act 2017 (Malaysia) is aimed at addressing the above by providing inter alia, financial assistance to affected workers for a limited period.[28] The Act establishes a social security scheme known as the Employment Insurance System, administered by Social Security Organization. It is applicable to all private-sector employers with more than one employee between 18 and 60 years old irrespective of the wages. The Organization shall determine the relevant benefits to be provided to the insured person. These are as follows: job search allowance, early re-employment allowance, reduced income allowance, and training allowance and training fee. Undeniably, this Act would be able to minimize the financial hardship of the retrenched workers arising from a genuine redundancy in the organization, and the benefits provided therein are not an unemployment benefit system, as practiced in some developed countries. It may be further added that the claims for benefits under the Act would not bar a worker from making a claim for unfair dismissal under Section 20 of the Industrial Relations Act 1967, termination or lay-off benefits under the Employment (Termination and Lay-Off Benefits) Regulations 1980 or any complaint relating to premature retirement under the Minimum Retirement Age Act 2012.

It is worth mentioning that an employee who alleged that his retrenchment from the organization was carried out with ulterior motives or accepted the compensation under protest will not be stopped from questioning the validity of his termination in the Industrial Court pursuant to Section 20(1) of the Industrial Relations Act 1967. The Act provides that a worker cannot be dismissed save and except with just cause or excuse. Where the matter is adjudicated in the Industrial Court, the employer would be required to justify his actions by offering reasons showing that the termination was with just cause and excuse. The employer must establish that there was a redundancy situation in the organization justifying the retrenchment exercise, and further, the consequential retrenchment was in compliance with the accepted standards of procedure as discussed above. The above is also in line with the International Labour Conference's Convention No. 158 that requires termination of employment on a justifiable basis.[29] It provides, inter alia, that an employee cannot be terminated unless there are valid reasons for the termination, such as the operational requirement of the employer's undertaking, establishment, or service.[30] It further provides that when the employer contemplates major changes in production, programme, organization, structure, or technology that are likely to entail

28 See "Job Losses Surged in March, But All Is Not Lost," *The Star*, April 3, 2020, available at https://www.thestar.com.my/news/nation/2020/04/03/job-losses-surged-in-march-but-all-is-not-lost (accessed May 25, 2020).

29 "C158 – Termination of Employment Convention, 1982 (No. 158)," International Labour Organization, accessed February 10, 2021, https://www.ilo.org/dyn/normlex/en/f?p=NORMLEXPUB:12100:0::NO::P12100_ILO_CODE:C158.

30 Termination of Employment Convention, 1982 (No. 158), art 4.

termination, they should hold prior consultation with the affected workers' or their representatives.[31]

Occupational Stress

Finally, in the present globalized world, occupational stress has fraught a tremendous concern to the employees and the stakeholders of the organization. There are many working conditions that a person encounters daily that affect his physical and emotional well-being. This includes the excessive work demand, workload and stressful deadlines, long working hours, insufficient number of staff, lack of support from co-workers and supervisors, annoying co-workers, angry customers, and hazardous working conditions. Job uncertainty such as impending lay-offs, restructuring, and management changes are also likely to affect workers psychologically. It also arises due to employer's wrongful conduct such as harassing or humiliating worker in the presence of other workers, victimizing or targeting a particular member of staff, falsely accusing worker of criminal misconduct, inappropriately demoting worker with a substantial reduction in salary, bonus, benefits, status, responsibilities, and authority, making a significant change in his job location at short notice and forced resignation.

There is a significant relationship between stress and job performance.[32] Stress is the common denominator for depleting work performance and productivity. Workers affected by occupational stress often show high dissatisfaction in terms of job mobility, burnout, taking excessive sick leave, and repeated absences. Long-term stress or traumatic events at work can affect the physical health of the worker. Studies have shown that an employee who is preoccupied with job responsibilities will counter irregular eating habits and would be lacking in regular exercise, with the resulting consequences such as weight problems, high blood pressure, and elevated cholesterol levels, the onset of heart disease.[33]

In this regard, occupational stress should be viewed seriously by the employer who has a common law obligation to take reasonable care of its workers' health and safety at the workplace.[34] An employer who neglects or disregards the safety and health of the workers is not only deemed to have committed an offence under the Occupational Safety and Health Act 1994 (Malaysia) but also a violation of their

---

31 Termination of Employment Convention, 1982 (No. 158), art 13.

32 Manshor, A. T., Rodrigue, F. and Chong, S. C. (2003), Occupational Stress Among Managers: Malaysian Survey, *Journal of Managerial Psychology*, 18(6): pp. 622–628.

33 Ornelas, S. and Kleiner, B. H. (2003), New Development in Managing Job Related Stress, *Journal of Equal Opportunities International*, 2(5): pp. 64–70.

34 *Malik v Bank of Credit and Commerce International S.A. (in Liquidation) and Mahmud v Bank of Credit and Commerce International S.A. (in Liquidation)* [1997] 3 All ER 1, HL.

common law obligation and thus, is exposed to civil liability. For example, incidents of sexual assault contribute immensely to low self-confidence, self-esteem and more detrimentally, it affects the psychological well-being of the victims. In *Mohd Ridzwan Abdul Razak v Asmah Hj Mohd Nor*,[35] Zaharah Ibrahim JCA, delivering the judgement of the court held, inter alia, that "where the acts of sexual harassment were serious enough to cause adverse psychological effect on the victim, those acts would fall within the tort of intentionally causing nervous shock similar to that in *Wilkinson v Downton*".[36]

In *Mohd Ridzwan Abdul Razak*, the appellant, general manager of the Pilgrims Fund Board, was alleged to have sexually harassed the respondent, a staff who was under his supervision, with vulgar remarks, dirty jokes that were sexually oriented, and had repeatedly offered to take the respondent as his second wife. However, disciplinary action could not be taken against the appellant as there was insufficient evidence. Nevertheless, the company issued a strong administrative reprimand to the appellant and transferred the respondent to the legal division in the company. In the meantime, the appellant lodged a complaint with the employer seeking disciplinary action to be taken against the respondent for defaming him without basis. However, the request was declined by the employer. Hence, this defamation action by the appellant against the respondent seeking damages. Meanwhile, the respondent counterclaimed damages for mental distress arising from the appellant's alleged sexual harassment.

The High Court dismissed his application as the appellant had failed to prove the claim. However, the respondent's counterclaim was allowed as she had followed the proper procedure in lodging the complaint with the employer and that there was ample evidence to show that the appellant had uttered vulgar and/or sexually explicit statements directed at the respondent or within the presence of the respondent. Dissatisfied with the decision, the appellant appealed to the Court of Appeal. The appellant alleged that the trial judge had erred in dismissing his claim for defamation and allowing the respondent's counterclaim. In dismissing the appeal with costs, Zaharah Ibrahim JCA, delivering the judgement of the court, stated:

> The evidence led before the High Court indicated that the defendant was an emotionally vulnerable person, in the sense that she appeared to be under some emotional pressure and had migraine and pains in her leg. She clearly would be more susceptible to being adversely affected by the kind of objectionable remarks made by the plaintiff, and the fact that the plaintiff continually made such remarks indicated that he knew that such remarks would make the

---

35 [2015] 4 CLJ 295.

36 [2015] 4 CLJ 295, [42]. See also *Wilkinson v Downton* [1897] 2 QB 57. In *Wilkinson's* case, the defendant deliberately and falsely told the plaintiff that her husband had been injured in a road accident and this had caused the plaintiff to suffer severe shock and become seriously ill. The court held that the plaintiff was entitled to recover in tort for the psychiatric illness which she suffered as a result of the defendant's wilful act.

> defendant extremely uncomfortable. After her complaint was investigated, the defendant was placed in another department, assigned to do duties which had nothing to do with the job she was hired to do. This transfer had a direct nexus to the acts of the plaintiff that she lodged a complaint about. A psychiatrist had diagnosed her as having major depression which was caused by being harassed by the plaintiff that continued to haunt her even after she left LTH. The defendant was under so much emotional stress that she could no longer bear being in LTH and left to take up a post in Sabah. The acts of the plaintiff uttering the remarks which amounted to sexual harassment and with the knowledge of her vulnerability fell within the ambit of the tort of intentionally causing nervous shock.[37]

On a further appeal to the Federal Court, the court, in affirming the decision of the Court of Appeal, stated inter alia that:

> sexual harassment is a very serious misconduct and in whatever form it takes, cannot be tolerated by anyone. In whatever form it comes, it lowers the dignity and respect of the person who is harassed, let alone affecting his or her mental and emotional well-being. Perpetrators who go unpunished, will continue intimidating, humiliating and traumatising the victims thus resulting, at least, in an unhealthy working environment.[38]

Hence, it is important for the employer to ensure workers' well-being and this necessarily includes not overburdening workers beyond their capacity to carry out the task or assignment. Further, workers should also be treated with courtesy, politeness, and kindness regardless of their position in the organization. Likewise, the employer must ensure that incidents of bullying or harassment do not occur. It goes without saying that the treatment of workers with dignity and respect will make a great difference in the level of worker productivity and creativity, besides fostering greater employee engagement within a business organization.

Having said the above, with the current COVID-19 pandemic accompanied with restricted movements imposed by the authority, it is important for the employer to understand workers constraints of working from home. They should assist workers with the necessary facilities and equipment so that they can work effectively. Falsely accusing an employee of being incapable of carrying out his or her job, victimizing or targeting particular members of staff, demotion involving reduced responsibilities and/or positioning within the corporate hierarchy with reduction in salary, bonus, benefits, status, responsibilities, authority or a combination of any of them and forced resignation, among others, should be avoided as this would only add on to their already stressful life arising from the current situation.

---

37 [2015] 4 CLJ 295, 297, [50]–[54].

38 *Mohd Ridzwan Abdul Razak v Asmah Hj Mohd Nor*, Federal Court of Malaysia (Appellate Jurisdiction) Civil Appeal No: 01(F)-13-06/2013 (W), [81].

Conclusion

It is trite law that the employer is entitled to organize his business in the manner he considers best. They are empowered during the current COVID-19 pandemic to take various measures to keep the business afloat and the harshest of which is to retrench workers. The services of an employee may become surplus if there is a reduction, diminution, or cessation of the type of work the employee was performing. The above undeniably is undermining job security recognized by the Industrial Relations Act 1967. Hence, compensation is payable to workers retrenched pursuant to the Employment (Termination and Lay-Off) Benefits Regulations 1980 at the rate specified therein. If a worker does not fall within the purview of the Employment Act 1955, and there being no provision for payment of retrenchment compensation prescribed in his contract of employment or collective agreement, the company is not obliged to make such payment, and if any such payment was made, it would have been purely at the discretion of the company. If the company is struggling to keep itself financially afloat and could hardly sustain itself financially, it would be undoubtedly inequitable to compel the company to incur additional losses by making it pay retrenchment benefits to the retrenched employees. The harsh reality of this had led to the enactment of the Employment Insurance System Act, which provides, inter alia, financial assistance to affected workers for a limited period.

Be that as it may, the decision to retrench worker should only be made when the job is redundant and that the employer had exhausted all available options to avert retrenchment, such as cutting down working hours, overtime, and the number of shifts; extending time off without pay; freezing bonuses and increase in salaries; reducing wages (by agreement); ceasing all new recruitment except for critical areas; decreasing the number of contractors or casual labourers; rationalizing costs and expenditure; temporary lay-off; early retirement offers; gradual reduction of workforce by way of natural turnover; and conducting retraining programmes for skill development so as to enable employees to move into different positions. It is also worth noting that job uncertainty such as impending lay-offs, restructuring, and management changes are likely to affect the employee psychologically. Occupational stress should be viewed seriously by the employer who has an obligation to take reasonable care of its workers' safety and health at the workplace, breach of this duty may place the employer in a legal predicament. Apart from an alleged constructive dismissal claim, the affected worker may file a civil claim against the employer for negligence or for failure to provide a safe place of work. It is therefore important for the employer to ensure the workers' health and safety at the workplace. Apart from treating workers with courtesy, politeness, and kindness regardless of their position in the organization, they are not to be burdened beyond their capacity to carry out the task or assignment. It goes without saying that the treatment of workers with dignity and respect will make a great difference in the level of worker productivity and creativity, besides fostering greater employee engagement within a business organization.

Joo-Ee Gan

4 Look What COVID-19 Unveiled: The Lack of Insolvency Protection by Malaysian Travel Companies

Introduction

The travel ban was one of the strategies adopted by governments in the fight against the novel coronavirus (COVID-19) pandemic. With the imposition of Movement Control Order (MCO) or, more colloquially, "lockdown", the tourism industry was among the worst hit. As more and more countries closed their borders to non-citizens, outbound travels were virtually impossible. The airline industry was devastated, with an estimated reduction of 1,302 to 1,432 million passengers or approximately USD 237 to 260 billion potential loss of gross operating revenues in 2020 from international travels alone.[1] Until recently, domestic travels were strictly regulated and discouraged.[2]

The detection of COVID-19 in Wuhan, China, in December 2019, the virus's speculative origin, its failed containment, and rapid spread to reach a pandemic scale have been much documented.[3] Suffice to note that 18 months later, infections exceeded 36 million cases, with more than 3.8 million deaths worldwide.[4] The severe economic fallout led to the contraction in global trade, including the collapse of cross-border tourism.[5] Tour cancellations were rift, and revenue losses quickly plunged travel companies into a downward spiral of cash-flow depletion, which affected the financing of loans, the payment of salaries, tax instalments, and other fixed costs.

The plight of Malaysia travel companies was not dissimilar. Since the imposition of the MCO on 18 March 2020 pursuant to the Prevention and Control of Infectious Diseases Act 1988, the Ministry of Tourism, Arts and Culture (MOTAC) had cancelled

1 "Effects of Novel Coronavirus (COVID-19) on Civil Aviation: Economic Impact Analysis," The International Civil Aviation Organization (ICAO), accessed September 2, 2020, https://www.icao.int/sustainability/Documents/COVID-19/ICAO_Coronavirus_Econ_Impact.pdf.

2 Shannon Teoh, "Coronavirus: Malaysia to Ease Curbs from June 10 to Allow Domestic Travel, Social Activities," *The Straits Times*, June 7, 2020, https://www.straitstimes.com/asia/se-asia/coronavirus-malaysia-to-ease-curbs-from-june-10-to-allow-domestic-travel-social.

3 Caroline Kantis, Samantha Kiernan and Jason Socrates Bardi, "Updated: Timeline of the Coronavirus," *Think Global Health*, January 15, 2021, https://www.thinkglobalhealth.org/article/updated-timeline-coronavirus.

4 "Covid-19 Coronavirus Pandemic," Worldometer, accessed 28 December, 2020, https://www.worldometers.info/coronavirus/?utm_campaign=homeAdUOA?Si.

5 "World Economic Outlook Update: A Crisis Like No Other, An Uncertain Recovery," The International Monetary Fund (IMF), accessed September 2, 2020 https://www.imf.org/en/Publications/WEO/Issues/2020/06/24/WEOUpdateJune2020.

https://doi.org/10.1515/9783110723694-004

the Visit Malaysia 2020 campaign.[6] The country's tourism industry suffered losses amounting to RM45 billion in the first half of 2020.[7] As of April 2020, 68% of Malaysian travel companies had applied for various government aid, while 51% relied on wage subsidies to sustain their employees. Worse, 29.5% of these travel companies were contemplating business closure.[8] Cash-strapped travel companies faced with demands for a refund of tour fares have issued holiday vouchers or "refund credit notes" instead of cash. But the problem becomes more complicated where the travel companies have become insolvent as a result of the COVID-19 pandemic.[9]

This chapter examines the impact of the COVID-19 pandemic on the consumers who purchased package tours from Malaysian travel companies. Foremost is the issue of tour cancellation – does the tourism regulatory framework accord adequate remedies to the consumers? In the next section, the regulatory framework laid down by the Tourism Industry Act 1992 (TIA) will be examined. This is followed by a discussion on the Malaysian Association of Tour & Travel Agents (MATTA), which serves as the travel companies' mouthpiece, on account of its membership of over 3,400 industry players.[10] More specifically, MATTA's response to the unprecedented demand for refunds and compensations and its call for legislative reform will be highlighted. It is argued that the COVID-19 pandemic has brought to the fore weaknesses in the Malaysian tourism regulatory framework. A comparative approach that reveals the consumer-centric philosophy in other jurisdictions shows that the TIA is in need of an overhaul.

Regulatory Safeguards Under the Tourism Industry Act 1992

A Malaysian entity that wishes to provide tourism services must be licensed by MOTAC pursuant to the TIA. Under Section 5(2), the Commissioner of Tourism (the Commissioner) is responsible for the licensing and regulation of "tourism enterprises", which

6 "Visit Malaysia 2020 Cancelled Over Virus Impact," *The Star*, March 19, 2020, https://www.thestar.com.my/news/nation/2020/03/19/visit-malaysia-2020-cancelled-over-virus-impact.
7 "Covid-19: Malaysia's Tourism Industry Hit with RM45 billion in Losses," *The New Straits Times*, June 27, 2020, https://www.nst.com.my/news/nation/2020/06/604012/covid-19-malaysias-tourism-industry-hit-rm45-billion-losses.
8 "Travel Agencies' Response to the Prihatin Plus Packages," The Malaysian Association of Tour & Travel Agents (MATTA), accessed September 3, 2020, http://matta.org.my/downloads/93281-travel-agencies-response-to-the-prihatin-plus-packages.
9 Ben Clatworthy, "Holiday Vouchers Will Be Valid Even if the Company Goes Bust," *The Times*, July 18, 2020, https://www.thetimes.co.uk/article/holiday-vouchers-will-be-valid-even-if-the-company-goes-bust-lbjgmbpcc.
10 "About MATTA: History," MATTA, accessed September 3, 2020, https://matta.org.my/about-us.

include tour operators, travel agents, and tourism training institutions.[11] The Commissioner's licensing jurisdiction is far-reaching – without his/her consent, no entity can call itself a "tourist agency" or "travel agent" or "tour operator" or use the words "tourism", "tour", or "travel", or any derivative of these words in any language, or any other words in any language capable of being construed as indicating the involvement in the tourism industry.[12] The hotel sector also comes under the Commissioner's purview in that premises that offer accommodation to tourists must be registered as "tourist accommodation premises".[13]

The licensing of travel companies safeguards the interests of the consumers in several manners. First, the licensing process minimizes the risk of fraudulent practices by bogus travel companies. Section 14 of the TIA requires a tourism enterprise to display its licence in a conspicuous place at its principal place of business and at every branch where it carries on its business. In a brick-and-mortar business model, customers are presumably alert to the possibility of fraud where a travel company is unable to show that it is licensed by the government. But given the prevalence of Internet intermediaries today, the potency of Section 14 is greatly diminished. Arguably, Section 14 can be interpreted to require the equivalent practice online. But until a government directive is made to this effect, compliance, to date, on the online platform is not observed. This weakness in implementation means that complaints of bogus travel companies by swindled consumers do surface from time to time.[14] But at the very least, the licensing process empowers the Commissioner to investigate and take action against unlicensed entities that offer travel services. MOTAC recently published on its official portal a list of travel companies that violated the registration requirement in Section 5 of the TIA. As of 3 September 2020, there were 161 violators.[15]

Secondly, under Section 15(1) of the TIA, the Commissioner may, from time to time, require a travel company to submit information pertaining to its business operations, including financial statements, audited balance sheets, and profit and loss account. This enables the Commissioner to assess the financial standing of a travel company, especially prior to the renewal of a licence. Moreover, Section 8(1)(g) provides that the Commissioner may revoke a licence where "a winding up order has been made against the licensed tourism enterprise or a resolution for its voluntary

---

11 The Secretary General of MOTAC serves as the Commissioner of Tourism. The term "tourism enterprise" is defined in s 2 of the TIA.

12 TIA, s 13.

13 TIA, ss 31A–31D.

14 Mohd Farhaan Shah, "Fake Agents on MATTA Radar," *The Star*, August 13, 2017 https://www.thestar.com.my/news/nation/2017/08/13/fake-agents-on-matta-radar-travel-group-wants-to-send-illegal-tour-operators-on-a-oneway-trip.

15 "List of Companies NOT Registered with MOTAC," MOTAC, accessed September 3, 2020, http://www.motac.gov.my/en/check/list-of-companies-not-registered.

winding up has been passed". In short, the TIA prescribes a monitoring mechanism whereby MOTAC can weed out financially precarious entities from the tourism industry. This indirectly protects the consumers against the expense and/or mental distress that the insolvency of a travel company may cause. Section 16(3) requires a licensed tour operator operating outbound tour packages to purchase an insurance policy or deposit either cash or bank guarantee with the Commissioner. Section 16(3) is silent on the risks that the insurance should cover or the quantum of cash deposit/bank guarantee. However, regulation 6(1)(m)(i) of the Tourism Industry (Tour Operating Business and Travel Agency Business) Regulations 1992 (the 1992 Regulations) makes clear that "for purposes of compensation or refund for the protection of outbound tourists", an insurance policy for the value of RM100,000 or cash in the sum of RM20,000 or bank guarantee in the sum of RM100,000 should be deposited with the Commissioner. Read together, Section 16(3) and regulation 6(1)(m)(i) impose on travel companies operating outbound tours the duty to provide insolvency protection for outbound travellers.

Lastly, travel companies are not at liberty to impose one-sided contractual terms to the consumers' detriment. Their contractual freedom is curtailed by the 1992 Regulations. Regulation 6(1)(m)(ii) provides that a travel company that intends to obtain an operating licence for outbound tours must adopt the standard terms and conditions laid out in The Fourth Schedule of the 1992 Regulations (the Fourth Schedule).[16] Notably, clause 4 of the Fourth Schedule states that a travel company that cancels a tour due to force majeure must provide alternative tours or refund the tour fare. In short, there are attempts to safeguard the consumers' interests through the imposition of legislative-sanctioned standard contract terms.

MATTA's Role in Consumer Protection

With the largest membership of travel companies in Malaysia, MATTA is well placed to influence the development of the sector through constructive engagement with MOTAC and the regulation of its members' activities. Although MATTA is not a professional body and the functions it assumes vis-à-vis its members cannot strictly be deemed self-regulation, the tourism regulatory framework expressly recognizes MATTA's role in the licensing of tourism enterprises and the handling of consumer complaints.

16 Although the Fourth Schedule does not apply to booking contracts for domestic (inbound) tour packages, most tour operators/agents use identical booking contract for outbound tour and domestic tour. This means that the standard terms and conditions prescribed by the Fourth Schedule invariably apply to domestic tours.

Under regulation 9A(1) of the 1992 Regulations, every licensed tourism enterprise must become a member of MATTA. Where this condition precedent is not satisfied, the Commissioner may refuse to approve any application for a renewal of licence.[17] Indirectly, regulation 9A puts all tourism enterprises under MATTA's regulatory radar. In particular, every member must abide by MATTA's Code of Ethics for Members (the Code of Ethics).[18] Among other things, the Code of Ethics lays down the codes of business practice for travel agents and tour operators, respectively. Additionally, specific clauses in the Code of Ethics require a member to comply with the 1992 Regulations, which of course, include the Fourth Schedule.[19]

Investigations into alleged infringements of the Code of Ethics are conducted by two bodies – the Members' Affairs Board (MAB) and the Consumers' Affair Board (CAB). As the names indicate, the former deals with members' affairs while the latter handles consumer affairs and complaints. Where the MAB/CAB forms the view that an allegation is not groundless, a hearing will be convened by the Ethics Disciplinary Board (EDB). Where a member is found to have infringed the Code of Ethics, the EDB may issue a written warning; administer a reprimand; impose a fine; demand from the member an undertaking that he/she will comply with the Code of Ethics; suspend his/her membership for a period not less than 90 days and not exceeding 12 months; or terminate his/her membership. The EDB's findings will be communicated to MOTAC within 14 days from the date the Board sat. An aggrieved member may appeal to the Appeal Board. The decision of the Appeal Board is final and binding, subject to an application for judicial review. Similarly, the Appeal Board's decision will be communicated to MOTAC within 14 days from the date of the decision (where the penalty is suspension or termination of membership).[20]

Since regulation 9A(1) of the 1992 Regulations requires a licensed tourism enterprise to be a member of MATTA, the suspension or revocation of membership has severe repercussions. A travel company that ceased to be a member of MATTA might not have its licence renewed by the Commissioner – this would sound a death knell to its business. Thus, MATTA's members are under pressure to conform to the Code of Ethics, even though it has no legal force. The upside for the consumers is that those compliant travel companies are more likely to provide satisfactory services.

17 The 1992 Regulations, reg 9A(2).

18 "Code of Ethics for Members," MATTA, accessed September 11, 2020, https://www.matta.org.my/downloads/matta-code-of-ethics.pdf.

19 For instance, cl 5.2.8 of the Code of Ethics states that "[m]embers shall fulfil any programme in which their name and/or logo are used with their permission for advertising and for promoting travel and tourism. All such advertisement and promotion by members shall comply with all the relevant Code(s) and regulations including that provided in Regulation 6 Standard Terms and Conditions for Outbound Tour Package of the Tourism Industry (Tour Operating Business and Travel Agency Business)".

20 The Code of Ethics, cl 5.3 and cl 5.4.

Disruptions in the COVID-19 Environment

There were already grouses with the TIA and the 1992 Regulations pre-COVID-19, specifically the Fourth Schedule's standard terms and conditions for outbound tours that must be adopted by travel companies. MATTA had repeatedly urged MOTAC to amend or remove the Fourth Schedule on the ground that its compensation regime was outmoded.[21] In particular, clause 4 of the Fourth Schedule is deemed onerous since it requires a full refund of tour fare in the event of cancellation due to force majeure regardless of the sunk cost from a travel company's own commitments to third-party service providers. Moreover, paragraph 4.2.3 states (in the context of group packages) that where a travel company cancels due to insufficient passengers or inability to secure seats or accommodation, the company will, in addition to a refund, pay compensation in the range of RM50 to RM100 per person, depending on the duration of notice given.

In the wake of mass cancellations, Malaysian travel companies have suffered huge losses, with the potential liability of approximately RM500 million from demands for refund and compensation.[22] Bearing in mind that a travel company would have made payments to third-party service providers (e.g., airlines, hotels, and ground handlers) in respect of tour bookings, the duty to refund and compensate consumers has plunged many travel companies into a financial abyss. A survey conducted by MATTA showed that as of 6 April 2020, 62.54% of travel companies were undergoing or planning retrenchment exercises. Despite the government's wage subsidy programme, the taking of unpaid leave on the employers' request and salary reduction were the norm during the MCO.[23] Financial woes exacerbated by the duty to refund tour fares might drive almost one-third of Malaysian travel companies out of business.[24]

MATTA had called for the 1992 Regulations to be amended, with de-regulation as an objective. According to MATTA, "it was best to let travel agents operate freely as consumers were adequately protected by existing laws".[25] In the meantime, MATTA expressed the view that, even though cancellations are governed by the 1992 Regulations, where a travel company has made payments to hotels and airlines, and there is no refund from these parties, the consumer must be bound by the hotels' and airlines'

---

21 Farah Solhi "MATTA: Tourism Industry Act 1992 Should Be Amended," *The New Straits Times*, March 12, 2020, https://www.nst.com.my/news/nation/2020/03/574054/matta-tourism-industry-act-1992-should-be-amended.

22 n 21.

23 "Travel Agency Workforce Status," MATTA, accessed September 21, 2020, http://matta.org.my/downloads/75965-travel-agency-workforce-status-infographic.

24 n 8.

25 n 21.

policies in respect of cancellation and cannot insist on a full refund.[26] This position is inconsistent with clause 4, which provides for a *full refund* of the booking price. It would seem that, cognizant of the threat of business closure that its members face, MATTA has lobbied for the lesser evil of *partial* refund of the booking fees.

The stance adopted by MATTA raises several issues. First, is clause 4 of the Fourth Schedule unduly harsh to the travel companies? Secondly, should the compliance with clause 4 be waived in light of the mass cancellations caused by COVID-19? Lastly, are travel consumers adequately protected by existing laws, and should the travel industry be allowed to "operate freely"? It is worth noting that MATTA was reported to have commented that "it is counter-productive for MOTAC to micro-manage holiday contracts between travel agents and customers by imposing the same terms and conditions on services delivered by diverse tourism sectors and different countries, each having their own rules and policies for cancellations, postponements, re-routings and refunds".[27]

The European Package Travel Directive as a Benchmark

Travel companies in the European Union (EU) operate within a stringent regulatory framework that prioritizes consumer protection. Under the EC Directive on Package Travel 1990 (the 1990 Directive), travel companies were required to provide extensive information to consumers concerning their package travel contracts, and they must have in place insolvency protection to meet the consumers' demand for refund, the cost of repatriation from abroad, or accommodation expenses pending repatriation.[28] Insolvency protection could be in the form of a travel guarantee fund, a bank guarantee, a liability insurance, a trust, or a combination of these measures. The 1990 Directive did not herald the inception of insolvency protection in Europe. Some member states had implemented laws to this effect before the Directive came into force. For instance, the Danish Travel Guarantee Fund Act 1979 introduced a private, self-governing travel guarantee fund to protect leisure travellers from the insolvency of travel companies. This statute was later amended to implement the

26 "MATTA Covid-19 Frequently Asked Questions (FAQ) – Employment, Financial Support, Cancellations & Refunds," MATTA, accessed September 21, 2020, http://matta.org.my/downloads/01300-covid-19-frequently-asked-situation-employment-financial-cancellations-refund.
27 "MATTA Urges Amendment of the Fourth Schedule of the Tourism Industry Act 1992 to Prevent Further Financial Repercussion," *Business Today*, March 12, 2020, https://www.businesstoday.com.my/2020/03/12/matta-urges-amendment-of-the-fourth-schedule-of-the-tourism-industry-act-1992-to-prevent-further-financial-repercussion/.
28 EEC/314/1990.

1990 Directive.[29] In the UK, the structure of the travel industry was such that most travel companies that sold outbound package holidays were members of the Association of British Travel Agents (ABTA). Members of ABTA were required to provide a bond for the protection of their consumers, which could be called on in the event of insolvency. This meant that prior to the implementation of the 1990 Directive (through the EC Package Travel Regulations 1992), a consumer financial protection scheme already existed in the UK.[30]

The 1990 Directive has been superseded by the Package Travel Directive 2015 (the 2015 Directive) that came into force in 2018.[31] The latter was necessary because online booking has blurred the distinction between service providers and intermediaries. Where travel services are sold online, it is often difficult to differentiate between the retailer and the organizer responsible for the proper performance of a holiday package. This is especially so where multiple travel services are purchased at a single point of sale (e.g. a travel website) before the consumer agrees to pay for them. Consequently, it is difficult to pinpoint the party responsible for the poor or non-performance of a package travel contract. In the past, 98% of holidays contracted by European travellers were under the purview of the 1990 Directive. The rise in online booking had reduced the applicability of the 1990 Directive to less than 50%.[32] It was, therefore, important "to adapt the legislative framework to market developments".[33] It would be impossible to examine the 2015 Directive in detail here. However, specific features of this new European package travel regulation will be highlighted to facilitate a comparison with the Malaysian tourism regulatory framework.

Expansion in the Regulation of the Tourism Industry

The 2015 Directive shows the trend towards more regulation, as opposed to deregulation. This is evident from its expanded scope. Like the 1990 Directive it replaces, the 2015 Directive applies only to "package travel". Whereas the former defined package travel as a combination of two or more travel services within one contract by one organizer;[34] the 2015 Directive has broadened the definition of "package

29 Susanne Storm and Hanne Hvelplund, "Tourism and Travel Organizer Bankruptcy – The Danish Travel Guarantee Fund Act Part One," *International Travel Law Journal* (1998): 137–151.

30 David Grant, "The Package Travel Regulations 1992 – Damp Squib or Triumph of Self-Regulation?," *Tourism Management* 17, no. 5 (1996): 319–321.

31 EU/2015/2302.

32 "The European Package Travel Directive," Centre for the Promotion of Imports (CBI), Netherlands Enterprise Agency, accessed September 21, 2020, https://www.cbi.eu/market-information/tourism/how-work-new-2018-european-package-travel-directive.

33 The Package Travel Directive (EU/2015/2302), para 1 of the Preamble.

34 EC Directive on Package Travel 1990 (EEC/314/1990), art 2.

travel" to cover a wider range of transactions. Article 3(2) of the 2015 Directive anticipates online purchases through intermediaries that facilitate booking from various service providers but do not "combine" the travel services, as previously done by high street travel agents. Hence, in addition to those services combined by one trader pursuant to a single contract, package travel is presumed (irrespective of whether separate contracts are concluded with individual service providers) where those services are:[35]

(i) purchased from a single point of sale and those services have been selected before the traveller agrees to pay;
(ii) offered, sold, or charged at an inclusive or total price;
(iii) advertised or sold under the term "package" or under similar term;
(iv) combined after the conclusion of a contract by which a trader entitles the traveller to choose among a selection of different types of travel services; or
(v) purchased from separate traders through linked online booking processes where the traveller's name, payment details, and e-mail address are transmitted from the trader with whom the first contract is concluded to another trader or traders and a contract with the latter trader or traders is concluded at the latest 24 hours after the confirmation of the booking of the first travel service.

Scenario (i) anticipates a booking through a travel website that offers multiple travel services that a consumer can add to "cart" or "shopping basket" before payment. By contrast, scenario (v) occurs where after selling a travel service, the first service provider (e.g. airline) links the consumer to another service provider (e.g. hotel booking website), and the consumer makes a second booking within 24 hours.

This example shows that, in order to protect consumers in the e-commerce era, the law must capture a myriad of online transactions that were previously unregulated. As the online platforms and the role of online travel agencies continue to evolve, more regulation is necessary to promote healthy competition, prevent the exploitation of small service providers, and enhance consumer protection.[36] In sum, an expanded regulatory framework for the tourism industry is inevitable. Against this backdrop, MATTA's call for less scrutiny by MOTAC seems wishful. While MATTA is right to point out that the TIA is anachronistic, an overhaul should expand the purview of its regulation, not the reverse.

35 The Package Travel Directive (EU/2015/2302), art 3(2)(b).

36 Margherita Colangelo and Vincenzo Zeno-Zencovich, "Online Platforms, Competition Rules and Consumer Protection in Travel Industry," *Journal of European Consumer & Marketing Law* 5, (2016): 75.

Modes of Providing Insolvency Protection

In this section, the UK's implementation of the 2015 Directive through the Package Travel and Linked Travel Arrangements Regulations 2018 (Package Travel Regulations 2018) is briefly discussed to illustrate the different avenues through which travel companies can provide insolvency protection.[37] It is argued that had the TIA imposed on Malaysian travel companies similar obligations, they might be more prepared to weather the impact of mass cancellations. A comparison with the duty to refund or repatriate pursuant to the Package Travel Regulations 2018 will also show that the obligations imposed by clause 4 of the Fourth Schedule are not unreasonable.

Under regulation 19(1) of the Package Travel Regulations 2018,

> [t]he organizer of a package who is established in the United Kingdom must provide effective security to cover, in the event of the organizer's insolvency, the reasonably foreseeable costs of (a) refunding all payments made by or on behalf of travellers for any travel service not performed as a consequence of the insolvency, taking into account the length of the period between down payments and final payments and the completion of the packages; and (b) if the carriage of passengers is included in the packages, and the performance of any package is affected by the insolvency, repatriating the traveller and, if necessary, financing the traveller's accommodation prior to the repatriation.

In short, regulation 19(1) imposes on an insolvent organizer the duty to refund payments or repatriate the traveller, where applicable. This duty is present regardless of a consumer's place of residence, the place of departure, or where the package is sold. Further, it is immaterial where the entity in charge of the insolvency protection is located.[38] In order to meet this duty to refund or repatriate, an organizer must at least ensure that the arrangements described in regulation 20 (bonding), regulation 21 (bonding where the approved body has reserve fund or insurance), regulation 22 (insurance) or regulation 23 (monies in trust), and regulation 24 (insurance where monies are held in trust) are in force.[39]

Regulations 20 and 21 envisage the existence of authorized institutions (e.g. ABTA) that administer the bonding system. Under regulation 20, where a body acts as the bonding institution for its members, it binds itself to pay, in the event of its member's insolvency, a sum calculated in accordance with the regulation in respect of package travel contracts that have not been fully performed. Where an authorized institution has a reserve fund or insurance to meet the potential pay-outs, the position is governed by regulation 21, which sets out the method of calculating the size of the bond. Interestingly, the sum derived in accordance with regulation 21 is likely to be lower than the sum calculated in accordance with regulation 20. This is clear

---

37 SI 2018/634.

38 Package Travel Regulations 2018 (SI 2018/634), reg 19(2).

39 Package Travel Regulations 2018 (SI 2018/634), reg 19(5).

when regulation 20(4) is compared with regulation 21(4) – the former provides that in any event, the sum payable shall not be less than 25% of all the payments that the organizer estimates he/she will receive under or in contemplation of contracts for packages in 12 months from the start date of the bond; in the latter, the percentage is stated to be 10%.

Regulation 22 allows organizers to procure insurance policies whereby the insurers undertake to indemnify the consumers against the loss of the sum paid under or in contemplation of package travel contracts should the organizers become insolvent. Regulation 23 permits an organizer to arrange for a trust where the monies can be applied to meet the claims of travellers whose package travel contracts have not been fully performed. Additionally, regulation 24 states that where a trust is set up, the organizer must procure an insurance policy to cover the cost of repatriation, and where applicable, the cost of the traveller's accommodation prior to the repatriation.

By contrast, the TIA's framework on insolvency protection is somewhat skeletal. Clearly, Sections 8 and 15 of the TIA do not fit the bill. They merely enable the Commissioner to identify financially precarious travel companies and, where necessary, revoke their licences. Although Section 16(3) of the TIA imposes on travel companies that operate outbound tour packages a rudimentary duty to provide insolvency protection, the provision is not applicable to domestic travellers. Distinguishing between outbound travellers and domestic travellers seems untenable when, in the European context, the 2015 Directive applies even to business travellers. It is acknowledged that while there are companies that make travel arrangements for their employees on the basis of a general agreement, there exist "representatives of small businesses or professionals who book trips related to their business or profession through the same booking channels as consumers".[40] Therefore, the 2015 Directive broadened its purview to include business travellers who do not make travel arrangements on the basis of a general agreement. In light of this development, the exclusionary approach of Section 16(3) seems anomalous.

Moreover, the threshold of insurance coverage or cash deposit/bank guarantee is arguably too low. Under regulation 6(1)(m)(i) of the 1992 Regulations, a licensed tour operator for outbound tours is required to purchase an insurance policy for a value of RM100,000 or deposit with the Commissioner cash in the sum of RM20,000 or furnish to the Commissioner a bank guarantee in the sum of RM100,000 for purposes of compensation or refund for the protection of outbound tourists. Needless to say, these sums are inadequate to meet the demands for a refund and/or compensation from COVID-19 mass cancellations.

The modes of insolvency protection prescribed by Section 16(3) are comparatively limited. The TIA does not list the bonding system and trusts as options. Perhaps one could ask whether the Malaysian tourism industry is prepared for the

40 The Package Travel Directive (EU/2015/2302), para 7 of the Preamble.

adoption of bonding. More specifically, is MATTA willing and/or able to assume the role of the bonding institution for its members? It is argued that had the TIA mandated a more sophisticated regime of insolvency protection, Malaysian travel companies would have been forced to buffer themselves against insolvency risk in more concrete ways. This would have enhanced their preparedness to face the COVID-19 travel cancellations. Unfortunately, the hazy regulatory road map for insolvency protection under the TIA does not encourage such contingency planning.

Turning to clause 4 of the Fourth Schedule – in essence, the provision is criticized as burdensome to the Malaysian travel companies. But benchmarked against the Package Travel Regulations 2018, is the duty to refund imposed by clause 4 too onerous? It is submitted that clause 4 is not unreasonable when compared to the obligations of an organizer under regulation 19(1) of the Package Travel Regulations 2018. To be effective, however, clause 4 should be revised in terms of clarity and scope. To facilitate a discussion, clause 4 is reproduced below.

4 Cancellation by Company
- 4.1 FIT Tour Packages[41]
  - 4.1.1 The company reserves the right to cancel the tour due to any act of God, war, strike, riot or order from the Government of Malaysia which is beyond its control.
  - 4.1.2 The company shall recommend alternative tours preferably to the same destination or other tours. Should any passenger decide not to accept the alternative tours, all moneys paid less the administrative fee chargeable will be refunded to the passenger.
- 4.2 Group Packages
  - 4.2.1 The company reserves the right to cancel the tour due to any act of God, war, strike, riot or order from the Government of Malaysia which is beyond its control.
  - 4.2.2 The company shall recommend alternative tours preferably to the same destination or other tours. Should any passenger decide not to accept the alternative tours, all moneys paid less the administrative fee chargeable will be refunded to the passenger.
- 4.3 In the event of a cancellation by the company due to insufficient passengers or inability to secure seats or accommodation, the company will refund the amount of money paid and also pay compensation as follows:

41 The term "FIT" refers to free independent traveller, who travels alone as opposed to travelling in a group.

Cancellation Received	*Cancellation Charges Per Person*
8-14 working days before the date of departure	Full refund of tour fare and a compensation of RM50.00 per person
1-7 working days before the date of departure	Full refund of tour fare and a compensation of RM75.00 per person
On date of departure	Full refund of tour fare and a compensation of RM100.00 per person

It is immediately apparent that clauses 4.1 and 4.2 provide for force majeure, the occurrence of which entitles a travel company to cancel a package travel contract and recommend alternative tours; and should the traveller declines the alternative tours, a refund is in order. The travel restrictions imposed in response to COVID-19 can be deemed "order from the Government of Malaysia" – an event of force majeure. In the circumstances, the issuance of travel vouchers for future alternative tours is justified, though many consumers have demanded a refund of tour fare instead.[42] Where a travel company is still trading, a claim for refund in respect of force majeure cancellation is within the ambit of clause 4. But it should be noted that a consumer could be the party that cancels a package tour in circumstances where tour refunds (in varying percentages) must still be made.[43] In other words, the duty to refund is broader since cancellations are not necessarily by a travel company or consequent upon force majeure. Negative cash flow from excessive demands for refund may well lead to the winding up of travel companies. When this occurs, where do the consumers stand under the current regulatory framework? While the requirement of insurance or cash deposit/bank guarantee in Section 16(3) of the TIA is intended to serve as insolvency protection for outbound travellers, clause 4 has failed to put this into effect. Indeed, there is no provision in the Fourth Schedule that deals with a package traveller's rights where a travel company becomes insolvent. Consequently, in the event that a travel company is wound up, the consumers rank as unsecured creditors with a slim chance of recovering their tour fares. This is why statutory priority through safeguards like bonding, guarantee fund, insurance, or trust is important. By providing a special channel for tour fare refunds, they remove the travel consumers from the vagaries of insolvency law.

42 n 21.

43 Clause 3 of the Fourth Schedule provides for cancellation by tour members and prescribes the cancellation charges that a travel company may impose. Other than a situation where notice of cancellation is given two days or less before the date of departure, partial refund of tour fare (in varying percentages) must still be made.

Further, clause 4 is confined to situations where a travel company cancels a tour package before its performance. This leaves unprotected the consumers whose package travel contracts are partly performed. By contrast, the Package Travel Regulations 2018 anticipates situations where insolvency prevents an organizer from discharging its outstanding contractual obligations. Hence regulation 19(1) requires an organizer to put in place arrangement for defraying the cost of repatriation or the cost of accommodation pending repatriation or both. So long as the ambit of clause 4 revolves around force majeure and pre-performance cancellations, there is no impetus for a Malaysian travel company to provide comprehensive insolvency protection.

Lastly, it is unclear what clause 4.2.3 seeks to achieve. The provision imposes on a travel company the obligation to refund the full tour fare and to pay compensation "[i]n the event of a cancellation by the company due to insufficient passengers or inability to secure seats or accommodation". Compensation (as opposed to a refund) is obviously not payable where the cancellation is due to force majeure. If clause 4.2.3 is intended to deter cancellations purely on the grounds of business efficiency or profitability, the paltry sum prescribed is hardly punitive of the travel company; and as compensation for the consumer, the sum is purely tokenistic. In short, the utility of clause 4.2.3 is limited.

The Role of the State

In the UK, a leisure traveller enjoys additional financial protection through the Air Travel Organizer's Licence (ATOL), operated by the UK Civil Aviation Authority (CAA). This scheme was introduced in 1973, and it protects most air package holidays sold by UK based travel companies.[44] Essentially, a consumer with an ATOL-protected package holiday is entitled to assistance should the travel company cease trading while the consumer is on holiday. If the travel company becomes insolvent, ATOL will provide a refund or replacement holiday. Of course, ATOL only applies to air package holidays. But given that ABTA's scheme provides protection to non-flight based holidays, it is fair to say that a British leisure traveller is adequately protected. The two systems complement one another, and many ABTA members also hold ATOL licences.

There is no similar scheme in Malaysia, and it is not suggested here that the lack of a comparable regime equates to poor regulation of the tourism industry. Rather, the existence of ATOL is highlighted to illustrate the proactive role that the state can play in the protection of travel consumers. Essentially, the UK government assumes the role of the guarantor where air package holidays are concerned. The viability of the Malaysian government taking on a similar role depends on many

44 "About ATOL," UK Civil Aviation Authority (CAA), accessed September 30, 2020, https://www.caa.co.uk/ATOL-protection/Consumers/About-ATOL/.

factors – the maturity of the sector, the buy-in among the industry players, cost-sharing, and the implementation platform, to name a few. Importantly, a private, self-funding insolvency protection regime must be in place if the state is reluctant to play a more substantial role. To this end, the TIA is sorely in need of a revamp.

Conclusion

The 2015 Directive and the Package Travel Regulations 2018 (which implement the former in the UK) demonstrate the norm of (full or partial) tour fare refund in the event of non-performance or failure to fully perform a package travel contract. Put in perspective, the duty to refund imposed by clause 4 of the Fourth Schedule is not unreasonable. This obligation can also be expressed in terms of Section 66 of the Contracts Act 1950, which states that where a contract is discovered to be void or when a contract has become void, the party that has received advantage under the transaction must restore it or make compensation for it. This means that consumers who find themselves with contracts discharged due to force majeure would have recourse to the civil courts or the Consumer Claims Tribunal where the claims do not exceed RM50,000.[45] What clause 4 of the Fourth Schedule does is to provide travel consumers with a more expeditious contractual right to a refund of tour fare where cancellation occurs due to force majeure. In short, clause 4 merely requires that outbound travel package contracts reflect a basic principle of contract law.

The issue is whether the COVID-19 pandemic justifies a travel company's breach of clause 4 where it forms part of a package travel contract. Pursuant to Section 16(3) of the TIA, every travel company that operates outbound tours would have obtained an insurance policy or caused a deposit in the form of cash or bank guarantee to be made to the Commissioner. This means that Malaysian travel companies with outbound operations are not completely without resources to meet the claims of their consumers. However, the scale of cancellations is unprecedented, and travel companies are already hard-pressed to keep their employees and remain in business. As many Malaysian travel companies are financially unprepared to honour their obligations pursuant to clause 4, it is unsurprising that they have sought government intervention.[46]

Since March 2020, the Malaysian government has introduced various economic stimulus measures that provide direct or indirect relief to the tourism industry.

---

45 Following the amendment of s 98 of the Consumer Protection Act 1999 by the Consumer Protection (Amendment) Act 2019, the Consumer Claims Tribunal now has jurisdiction to hear consumer claims within the ambit of this Act where the total amount of the award sought from the Tribunal does not exceed RM50,000. The threshold sum was RM25,000 prior to the amendment.
46 n 21.

Among other things, travel companies have benefitted from the deferment of monthly income tax instalment payments; 15% discount in monthly electricity bills for hotels, travel agencies and airline premises, shopping malls, conventions, and exhibition centres; and the exemption from Human Resource Development Fund levies for hotels and travel companies. To revive domestic tourism, the government has announced that personal tax relief of up to RM1,000 granted in respect of domestic tourism-related expenditure. In addition, Malaysians are eligible for digital vouchers for domestic tourism of up to RM100 per person for domestic flights, rails, and hotel accommodations.[47] Eligible travel companies have also benefitted from the government's wage subsidy programme, the deferral and rescheduling of employer's contribution to the Employees Provident Fund, and the RM50 billion guarantee scheme whereby the government guarantees up to 80% of the loan sum obtained for the purpose of financing working capital.[48] In the short run, these stimulus measures should ease the financial burden of travel companies, and hopefully, enable them to meet their obligations pursuant to clause 4.

Additionally, under regulation 6(1)(m)(iii) of the 1992 Regulations, the Commissioner can, in the event of a dispute, determine the quantum of compensation payable or the extent of the refund to a traveller. This means that MOTAC has the power to prescribe a lower percentage of tour fare refund or dispense with the compensation payable under clause 4.2.3 in this COVID-19 environment. In the long run, however, the TIA and the 1992 Regulations should be amended to introduce mandatory insolvency protection in respect of all package tours (not merely outbound travel).

It is plain from the comparison with the 2015 Directive that Malaysian laws do not adequately protect travel consumers. The lack of insolvency protection is the Achilles heel of the TIA and the 1992 Regulations because clause 4 fails where it matters the most. Presumably, under "normal" circumstances, a financially sound travel company is unshaken by the occasional cancellations due to force majeure before the performance of the package travel contract. What consumers really need is protection against insolvent travel companies, especially where they are stranded abroad after a partially performed contract. Should a travel company become insolvent from excessive demands for refund of tour fares, clause 4 is of no help.

The Temporary Measures for Reducing the Impact of Coronavirus Disease 2019 (COVID-19) Act 2020 (the COVID-19 Act) was enacted to mitigate the impact of COVID-19 on the Malaysian economy. The statute came into force on 23 October 2020. With retrospective effect (deemed to come into operation on 18 March 2020) and potential

47 "Economic Stimulus Package No. 1," MATTA, last modified March 3, 2020, https://www.matta.org.my/article/31296-economic-stimulus-package-no1.

48 "Economic Stimulus Package No. 2," MATTA, last modified April 2, 2020, https://www.matta.org.my/article/31756-economic-stimulus-package-no-2.

extensions to its period of operation,[49] the COVID-19 Act throws a lifeline to Malaysian businesses, including travel companies. Contract by a tourism enterprise as defined under the TIA and the contract for the promotion of tourism in Malaysia come under the ambit of Part II of the COVID-19 Act.[50] Section 7 of the Act states that

> [t]he inability of any party or parties to perform any contractual obligation arising from any of the categories of contracts specified in the Schedule to this Part due to the measures prescribed, made or taken under the Prevention and Control of Infectious Diseases Act 1988 to control or prevent the spread of COVID-19 shall not give rise to the other party or parties exercising his or their rights under the contract.

In the context of a package travel contract, this means that a consumer could not exercise his/her rights under the contract where the travel company failed to perform its contractual obligations due to the MCO. Moreover, by virtue of Section 10, any termination of package travel contract or forfeiture of deposit made from 18 March 2020 to the publication of the COVID-19 Act shall be deemed to have been validly made. In sum, the balance is tipped against the travel consumer. Section 7 of the COVID-19 Act arguably absolves a travel company's contractual duty to provide alternatives tours where the contract could not be performed due to the MCO. Section 10, applied ruthlessly, might allow travel companies to treat a package travel contract (where performance was due during the MCO period) as terminated and the booking deposit forfeited. But surely Section 10 of the COVID-19 Act does not sanction the forfeiture of the tour fare?[51] It would be a travesty to read "*any deposit or performance bond forfeited*" in Section 10 to mean the forfeiture of the entire contract price! Unfortunately, it is hardly reassuring to tell a consumer that his/her right to the refund of tour fare is intact despite the COVID-19 Act, where the travel company is financially incapable of meeting its contractual obligation. It is submitted that the Malaysian tourism industry needs a more sophisticated regulatory framework with a road map for a more comprehensive implementation of insolvency protection. This will enhance the preparedness of Malaysian travel companies in weathering the challenges of future black swan events. It should also be pointed out that the provisions pertaining to insolvency protection contained in the 2015 Directive apply to travel companies

---

49 Extension to the period of operation vary between different Parts of the Temporary Measures for Reducing the Impact of Coronavirus Disease 2019 (COVID-19) Act 2020 (the COVID-19 Act). Section 5 provides that where Part II Inability to Perform Contractual Obligations is concerned, extension shall not exceed the period of operation of the COVID-19 Act, that is, 2 years (s 1(2)) or any order of extension made by the Prime Minister (s 1(3)).

50 The COVID-19 Act, Schedule to Part II (Section 7), para 6.

51 The COVID-19 Act, s 10 states: "Notwithstanding Section 7, any contract terminated, *any deposit or performance bond forfeited*, any damages received, any legal proceedings, arbitration or mediation commenced, any judgment or award granted and any execution carried out for the period from 18 March 2020 until the date of publication of this Act shall be deemed to have been validly terminated, forfeited, received, commenced, granted or carried out." [Emphasis added.]

not established in the EU, where such travel companies sell or offer for sale packages in a member state or by any means direct such activities to a member state.[52] This means that a Malaysian travel company that sells package travels to European travellers is required to provide insolvency protection as per the 2015 Directive. Similarly, where a Malaysian travel company partners with an EU travel company in the provision of travel services to European travellers, the latter may require the former to obtain liability insurance. Since the 2015 Directive came into force in 2018, major Malaysian travel companies that provide travel services to European travellers would have been forced to provide insolvency protection in respect of these consumers. Two practices might have emerged among Malaysian travel companies, with the cynical outcome that insolvency protection is accorded to European travellers but not to local or other non-European travellers. To avoid such double standard, it is imperative that amendments are introduced so that the TIA mandates insolvency protection in respect of all travel services offered by Malaysian travel companies.

52 The Package Travel Directive (EU/2015/2302), art 17(1) states in the context of the scope of insolvency protection that ". . .Organizers not established in a Member State which sell or offer for sale packages in a Member State, or which by any means direct such activities to a Member State, shall be obliged to provide the security in accordance with the law of that Member State."

Loganathan Krishnan

5 Implications of the COVID-19 Pandemic for the Malaysian Companies Act 2016

Introduction

The Companies Act 2016[1] and the Companies Regulation 2016 replaced the Companies Act 1965.[2] The CA 2016 was passed by both the houses of Parliament[3] and was gazetted on 15 September 2016.[4] The Companies Commission of Malaysia[5] announced that the CA 2016 would come into force on 31 January 2017 except for section 241 (requirement of secretary to register with Registrar) and Division 8 of Part III (corporate rescue mechanism).[6] The CA 2016 comprises 5 parts, 620 sections, and 13 Schedules.[7] According to the Domestic Trade, Cooperatives and Consumerism Minister Datuk Seri Hamzah Zainuddin, during the launch of the CA 2016 Awareness Programme, the implementation of the CA 2016 is timely due to the number of companies that are registered in Malaysia.[8] He further stressed that the CA 2016 will have a major impact on companies due to the significant changes made.[9] Since the objective of the CA 2016 is to simplify the registration of limited companies, sole traders and partnership firms may be attracted to

1 Hereinafter referred to as CA 2016.

2 Hereinafter referred to as CA 1965. The legislature decided that the CA 1965 is in need of a major reform following the developments in the United Kingdom, Australia, Hong Kong and Singapore. The reforms made to the CA 2016, have been tested and are tried in those countries. For more details, see Adeline Paul Raj, "Companies Bill 2015 to Bring Major Reform," *The Edge Markets*, May 2, 2016, https://www.theedgemarkets.com/article/companies-bill-2015-bring-major-reform and Kenneth Foo Poh Khean and Lee Shih, *Companies Act 2016: The New Dynamics of Company Law in Malaysia* (Ampang: CLJ, 2017), 16.

3 On 4 April 2016 and 28 April 2016, respectively, and received the Royal Assent on 31 August 2016. See, "Phase One of Companies Act 2016 Comes into Effect," *The Star*, February 1, 2017, ttps://www.thestar.com.my/business/business-news/2017/02/01/phase-one-of-companies-act-2016-comes-into-effect

4 Choong Kwai Fatt, *Hallmark Legal Principles on Companies Act 2016* (Kuala Lumpur: Choong Consultants PLT, 2019), 7.

5 Hereinafter referred to as CCM.

6 Philip Koh Tong Ngee, "Reforming Malaysian Company Law," *The Star*, January 21, 2017, https://www.thestar.com.my/business/business-news/2017/01/21/reforming-malaysian-company-law.

7 "Companies Act 2016 – Shaping the Malaysian Corporate Regulatory Landscape," Ernst & Young, Vol. 5(1), March 2017.

8 Farezza Hanum Rashid, "Hamzah: Implementation of Act Timely," *New Straits Times*, May 12, 2017. 14.

9 SSM National Conference 2017, Implementing the Companies Act 2016: Moving Together, Greater Together, Companies Commission of Malaysia, Sunway Resort Hotel & Spa, Bandar Sunway, 22–23 August 2017.

https://doi.org/10.1515/9783110723694-005

register their businesses as a limited company.[10] During the preview for an Associated Chinese Chambers of Commerce seminar, Michael Chai, Legal Affairs Committee Chairman, remarked that many business-friendly policies have come into effect as a result of the CA 2016.[11]

Be that as it may, the pandemic caused a huge impact on businesses and the CA 2016. The research problem this chapter attempts to address is to understand the implications of the pandemic for the CA 2016 and the challenges faced by companies. The author is motivated to explore the implications and the challenges. The chapter then proceeds to discuss the temporary measures adopted by the Malaysian Government in addressing the implications. Whilst doing so, the temporary measures particularly on the minimum debt threshold for insolvency, conduct of board and general meetings and the moratoriums of extension of time for complying with the CA 2016 will be scrutinized to determine whether the measures do bring about any assistance to companies. Finally, the chapter draws the approaches taken in other countries and the way forward to improve the measures taken in Malaysia.

Prevention and Control of Infectious Diseases (Measures Within the Infected Local Areas) Regulations 2020

In an effort to contain the outbreak of COVID-19, the Malaysian Government issued the Prevention and Control of Infectious Diseases (Measures Within the Infected Local Areas) Regulations 2020.[12] The Regulations were issued under the Prevention and Control of Infectious Diseases Act 1988 and the Police Act 1967. Thus, under the Regulations, the Government implemented a Movement Control Order (MCO).[13] This was pursuant to Section 11 of the Prevention and Control of Infectious Diseases Act 1988, which imposed the MCO for 56 days, that is, phase 1 of the MCO was

10 Salleh Buang, "New Arena for Companies, Dramatic Changes: New Companies Act 2016 Offers Coherency," *New Straits Times*, December 15, 2016, 15.

11 Ooi Tee Ching, "New Laws Boon for Firms," *New Straits Times*, June 14, 2017, B6.

12 Hereinafter referred to as the Regulations.

13 Hereinafter referred to as MCO 1.0.

from 18 March 2020 till 1 April 2020,[14] phase 2 was from 1 April 2020 till 14 April 2020,[15] phase 3 was from 14 April 2020 till 28 April 2020,[16] and phase 4 was from 29 April 2020 till 12 May 2020.[17] Paragraph 3 of the Regulations prohibits the movement of individuals within an infected area unless they fall within the exceptions provided, such as providing for essential services.

The Conditional MCO (CMCO),[18] which was announced on 1 May 2020, ended on 9 June 2020.[19] The Recovery MCO (RMCO)[20] was announced by the Government of Malaysia on 5 June 2020 and was effective from 10 June until 31 August 2020.[21] On 28 August, Prime Minister Muhyiddin Yassin announced the extension of the RMCO by a further 4 months until 31 December 2020.[22] The second MCO was implemented across a number of federal territories and states until 4 February 2020.[23]

During the time of MCO, CMCO, and RMCO, companies carried on their business by implementing alternative arrangements to continue managing the affairs of their businesses in order to minimize the economic impact of the COVID-19.[24] Meanwhile, businesses wanted some form of legal solutions to address their challenges in managing their businesses during the pandemic.

---

14 Tang Ashley, "Malaysia Announces Movement Control Order After Spike in Covid-19 Cases," *The Star*, March 18, 2020, https://www.thestar.com.my/news/nation/2020/03/16/malaysia-announces-restricted-movement-measure-after-spike-in-covid-19-cases.

15 "MCO Period Extended to April 14 – PM," *Bernama*, March 25, 2020, https://www.bernama.com/en/general/news_covid-19.php?id=1824718.

16 "MCO Extended Until April 28 – PM Muhyiddin," *Bernama*, April 10, 2020, https://www.bernama.com/en/general/news_covid-19.php?id=1830577.

17 "MCO Extended Another Two Weeks to May 12 – Muhyiddin," *Bernama*, April 23, 2020, https://www.bernama.com/en/general/news.php?id=1835248.

18 Hereinafter referred to as CMCO.

19 "Essence of Conditional Movement Control Order," *Bernama*. May 1, 2020, https://www.bernama.com/en/general/news.php?id=1837487.

20 Hereinafter referred to as RMCO.

21 Loo Cindi, "CMCO Ends June 9, Recovery MCO from June 10 to Aug 31," *The Sun Daily*, June 7, 2020, https://www.thesundaily.my/home/cmco-ends-june-9-recovery-mco-from-june-10-to-aug-31-updated-EM2538754.

22 "Malaysia Extends Movement Control Order Measures till Year-end," *Xinhua*, August 28, 2020, http://www.xinhuanet.com/english/2020-08/28/c_139325562.htm.

23 Hereinafter referred to as MCO 2.0.

24 Tan Weng Hwee and Muhammad Azim bin Che Mokhtar, "COVID-19: Board of Directors Meetings and Shareholders' Meetings During the Movement Control Order," Lee Hishammuddin Allen & Gledhill, April 7, 2020, https://www.lh-ag.com/wp-content/uploads/2020/04/COVID-19-Board-of-Directors-Meetings-and-Shareholders%E2%80%99-Meetings-During-the-Movement-Control-Order-LHAG-update-20200407.pdf.

Temporary Measures for Reducing the Impact of Coronavirus Disease 2019 (COVID-19) Act 2020

Various calls were made to enact a COVID-19 Act, similar to that which was passed in Singapore.[25] To do this, legislators would have to go to the Parliament, and because of MCO, CMCO, and RMCO, this may prove to be rather difficult. Nonetheless, many countries that faced similar restrictions managed to enact a law on COVID-19.

Finally, on 23 October 2020, the Temporary Measures for Reducing the Impact of Coronavırus Disease 2019 Act 2020 (COVID-19 Act) was gazetted.[26] The legislation is aimed to provide for temporary measures to reduce the impact of COVID-19, including modifying the relevant provisions in other legislation.[27] Section 1(2) of the COVID-19 Act provides that where the date of commencement and period of operation have been provided in respect of the respective Parts in this Act, this Act shall come into operation on the date of publication of this Act and shall continue to remain in operation for a period of 2 years from such date of publication. This would mean that the Act came into force on 23 October 2020 and will remain in force till 22 October 2022. Notwithstanding subsection (2), the Prime Minister may, by order published in the Gazette, extend this Act's operation, and the order for extension may be made more than once.[28]

When the COVID-19 Act was in the drafting stage, it was predicted that it would impact CA 2016.[29] Nevertheless, it did not make any reference to CA 2016. Thus, the COVID-19 Act does not offer any form of assistance to businesses. The COVID-19 Act was not comprehensive enough.[30] Nevertheless, the impact of COVID-19 on businesses cannot be denied nor doubted. This is to be contrasted with COVID-19 (Temporary Measures) Act 2020 enacted in Singapore whereby Division 2, section 22 provides for modification to its Companies Act.

---

25 P. Aruna, "Companies Need More Relief," *The Star*, May 11, 2020, https://www.thestar.com.my/business/business-news/2020/05/11/companies-need-more-relief.

26 Hereinafter referred to as COVID-19 Act.

27 These include: The Limitation Act 1953, the Sabah Limitation Ordinance, the Sarawak Limitation Ordinance, the Public Authorities Protection Act 1948, the Insolvency Act 1967, the Hire-Purchase Act 1967, the Consumer Protection Act 1999, the Distress Act 1951, the Housing Development (Control and Licensing) Act 1966, the Industrial Relations Act 1967, the Private Employment Agencies Act 1981, the Land Public Transport Act 2010, the Commercial Vehicles Licensing Board Act 1987, the Courts of Judicature Act 1964, the Subordinate Courts Act 1948, and the Subordinate Courts Rules Act 1955.

28 COVID Act, s 1(3).

29 Adib Povera, "Expert: Take A Leaf from Singapore in Drafting Bill," *New Straits Times*, June 10, 2020, https://www.nst.com.my/news/nation/2020/06/599354/expert-take-leaf-singapore-drafting-bill.

30 Sothi Rachagan, "Covid-19 Act: Very Little, Very Late," *The Vibes*, October 7, 2020, https://www.thevibes.com/articles/opinion/2188/covid-19-act-very-little-very-late.

Implications of the Pandemic for the Companies Act 2016

The ensuing discussion will demonstrate the impact of COVID-19 on various aspects of a company and the CA 2016.

Virtual General Meetings

It was a norm to hold general meetings in the physical presence of the company's members and the management. However, due to COVID-19, which restricted public gathering and required social distancing, companies had no choice but to either cancel/defer their meetings or conduct virtual meetings. Fortunately, the CA 2016 facilitates the use of technology, which allows members reasonable opportunity to participate in virtual meetings. This can be observed in section 327(1) of the CA 2016, which provides that a company may convene a meeting of members at more than one venue using any technology or method that enables the members of the company to participate and to exercise the members' rights to speak and vote at the meeting. Thus, meeting at multiple venues is allowed, but the main meeting venue shall be in Malaysia, where the chairperson is present, as provided in section 327(2) of the CA 2016. The platform for virtual meetings could be Zoom, Google Meet, FaceTime, or Microsoft Teams. For instance, Bursa Malaysia's 42nd annual general meeting (AGM)[31] was held in Kuala Lumpur on Thursday, 28 March 2019, at 10:00 h. The shareholders who attended the 42nd AGM remotely through live streaming voted via an online platform, which was made accessible from 10:30 h.[32]

Moreover, section 340(2) of the CA 2016 provides that public companies must hold AGMs within 6 months of the company's financial year-end and not more than 15 months after the last preceding AGM. If an AGM was not held, the company and every officer commit an offence and shall, on conviction, be liable to a fine not exceeding RM20,000.[33] It is important to hold an AGM since approvals are required to declare final dividends, election and re-election of retiring directors, approval of directors' remuneration, appointment of auditors, remuneration for auditors, annual reports, and financial statements.[34]

31 Hereinafter referred to as AGM.

32 Serina Abdul Samad, Moo Eng Thing, and Lee Jee Yun, "COVID-19: The Effects on the Malaysian Capital Market," Azmi & Associates, April 3, 2020, https://amcham.com.my/wp-content/uploads/Article-20200403-COVID-19-The-Effects-on-the-Malaysian-Capital-Market.pdf.

33 CA 2016, s 340(6).

34 CA 2016, s 340(1).

Nevertheless, the provision only enables meetings at more than one venue using technological means, as the main meeting venue must still be held in the physical presence of the chairperson. The concern is whether this is possible if it was held during MCO 1.0. The second concern is whether, during MCO 2.0, CMCO, or RMCO, members will be able to attend the virtual meeting if it was held at a venue where inter-state/district travel was prohibited. The third concern is whether members are permitted to attend a general meeting using technological means from their own respective residences. The fourth concern is whether members have the necessary tools and skills to participate in virtual meetings. The final concern is whether the online platforms will be able to host a huge number of attendees since public companies usually have large numbers of members.

Written Resolutions

Written resolutions are only available for private companies as provided by section 290(1)(a) of the CA 2016. In doing so, the procedures in sections 300 and 301 of the CA 2016 must be complied with. It can be proposed by the board of directors[35] or any member.[36] It should be noted that a unanimous approval to pass a resolution is no longer required under the CA 2016, unlike the CA 1965. The percentage required will depend on the type of resolution required by the CA 2016.[37] Nevertheless, written resolutions cannot be used to remove the director or auditor before their term expires.[38] An additional safeguard is that any shareholder holding 5% or more of the company's total voting rights may require the company to circulate a resolution accompanied by a statement on the subject matter of the resolution prior to the passing of the written resolution.[39] Thus, private companies need not hold general meetings, including AGM, as they can resort to written resolutions. Fortunately, Digital Signature Act 1997 was enacted and will prove to be very useful since section 62 allows for digital signatures.

However, if a company's constitution requires the convening of a physical general meeting, then decisions cannot be passed via written resolutions. In that sense, a meeting must be held, but it could not be done during MCO 1.0 period except if it was MCO 2.0, CMCO, or RMCO periods unless inter-state/district travel was prohibited. Alternatively, the company should alter its constitution[40] to allow for virtual meetings. However, this is a catch-22 situation since the company still needs to

35 Hereinafter referred to as the board.
36 CA 2016, s 297(1).
37 CA 2016, s 305(4).
38 CA 2016, s 279(2).
39 CA 2016, s 302.
40 CA 2016, under s 36.

have a physical meeting in order to alter its constitution to allow for virtual meetings. If there are no such restrictions, a company may have virtual meetings. Hence, it is recommended that these meetings be held by way of teleconference or online meetings to avoid gatherings of people in confined spaces.[41] Nevertheless, if a company wishes to remove its director(s) or auditor, it must have a meeting. Since written resolutions are inapplicable to public companies, such companies are required to conduct meetings.

E-Notice for Company Meetings

The notice of a meeting of members may also be given by electronic form as provided by section 319(1)(b) of the CA 2016. The notice given in an electronic form shall be transmitted to the electronic address provided by the member to the company for such purpose or by publishing on a website.[42] Thus, the CA 2016 allows an alternative to sending a notice instead of sending it via hard copy. The latter form of sending the notice is certainly not possible during MCO 1.0. Be that as it may, sending an electronic notice has undoubtedly made it easier for companies to communicate with their members in light of the pandemic.

Nevertheless, if companies were in the practice of sending notice via electronic means, this is not an issue. Those companies sending out notices via electronic means would have to first acquire the electronic addresses of members. This may consume a considerable amount of time if it is a public company with a huge number of members.

Virtual Board Meetings

Section 211 of the CA 2016 provides that the business and affairs of a company shall be managed by or under the direction of the board. It further provides that the board has all the powers necessary for managing and for directing and supervising the management of the business and affairs of the company. Thus, they would be required to pass resolutions when making decisions at the board meetings. This can be seen in section 251 of the CA 2016, which provides that the financial statements of the company must be approved at the board meeting. Nonetheless, this could not be done during MCO 1.0.

---

41 Lee Shuk Yee, Chan Su San, and Arlene Lee, "Movement Control Order Updates from the Authorities in Malaysia, TaXavvy, PriceWaterHouseCoopers," April 1, 2020, https://www.pwc.com/my/en/assets/publications/Taxavvy/2020/pwc-taxavvy-17-2020-mco-updates-from-authorities.pdf.
42 CA 2016, s 319(2)(b).

Section 212 of the CA 2016 provides that, subject to the constitution, the provisions set out in the Third Schedule shall govern the proceedings of the board. Paragraph 6(b) reads that a meeting of the board may be held through audio, audio and visual communication, by which all directors participating and constituting a quorum can simultaneously hear each other throughout the meeting. Moreover, they may use their respective technological tools. It can be done by private and public companies. Regardless of whether it is MCO 1.0/2.0, CMCO, or RMCO periods, the board can meet in a virtual sense.

Paragraph 4 reads that a notice of a meeting of the board shall be sent to every director who is in Malaysia, and the notice shall include the date, time, and place of the meeting and the matters to be discussed. It does not provide whether the notice can be sent electronically. The legislature has expressly provided that notice can be sent via electronic means with regard to company meetings.[43] The legislature has omitted to do so with regard to board meetings. Nonetheless, in view of paragraph 6(b), it can be implied that notice via electronic means is allowed. Even if board meeting could not be held, paragraph 15 provides that a resolution in writing, signed or assented to by all directors then entitled to receive a notice of a meeting of the board, is as valid and effective as if it had been passed at a meeting of the board duly convened. Ultimately, paragraph 18 provides that except as provided in this Schedule, the board may regulate its own proceedings. Hence, the board may determine that notice can be sent via electronic means. The allowance of a digital signature under section 62 of the Digital Signature Act 1997 will prove useful in making decisions via virtual board meetings.

Lodgement of Statutory Documents

A company's annual return must be lodged with the CCM within 30 days from each anniversary of the company's incorporation date as provided by section 68(1) of the CA 2016. As for financial statements, section 259(1) of the CA 2016 provides that a company must submit its financial statements and reports in the case of a private company within 30 days from the date the financial statements and reports are circulated to the shareholders; in the case of a public company, within 30 days from the date of the company's AGM. Section 259(2) of the CA 2016, however, allows the Registrar to extend the period of filing of the financial statements and reports upon an application made by the company before the expiry of the periods specified in section 259(1) of the CA 2016.

Nonetheless, in view of MCO 1.0, MCO 2.0, CMCO, or RMCO, this could prove to be a challenge. In the event lodgement was not made in due course of time, the legal

43 CA 2016, s 319(1)(b).

consequence would ensue. In fact, every officer who contravenes this section commits an offence and shall, on conviction, be liable to a fine not exceeding RM50,000 and, in the case of a continuing offence, to a further fine not exceeding RM1,000 for each day during which the offence continues after conviction.[44]

Directors of a Company

The board hires a management team to run the organization on a day-to-day basis on their behalf. Nonetheless, at a time of existential crisis, the board should not forget that it is ultimately responsible.[45] Reliance is placed on the board to take actions in response to an evolving situation in light of the pandemic. As circumstances change, so too will the directors' focus, but the actions must always be based on the director's duties and obligations. Upon reaching the point where liquidation or administration cannot be reasonably avoided, the directors must consider when to cease trading.[46] The CA 2016 does not make any distinction between executive and non-executive directors or shadow and de facto directors. Essentially, certain aspects of directors' duties must be examined in light of the pandemic.

Duty to Act in Good Faith

A director owes a fiduciary duty both under common law[47] and the CA 2016 to act in good faith for the best interest of the company.[48] Hence, he/she must exercise his/her powers for a proper purpose,[49] avoid conflict of interest,[50] should not make any secret profit,[51] avoid bribe,[52] should not divulge confidential information,[53] should

44 CA 2016, s 259(3).

45 Roger Barker, "The Corporate Governance of Coronavirus – What Boards Should Consider," *IOD*, March 20, 2020, https://www.iod.com/news/news/articles/The-corporate-governance-of-coronavirus—what-boards-should-consider.

46 Nick Garland, Giles Hindle, and Richard Highley, "COVID-19 and Financial Distress: Duties and Key Considerations Applicable to All Directors," *DAC Beachcroft*, April 1, 2020, https://www.dacbeachcroft.com/en/gb/articles/2020/march/covid-19-and-financial-distress-duties-and-key-considerations-applicable-to-all-directors/.

47 *Re Smith and Fawcett Ltd.* [1942] Ch 304.

48 CA 2016, s 213(1). Other duties are listed out in CA 2016, ss 218, 219, 221, 222, 223, 224, 225, and 228.

49 *Howard Smith Ltd v Ampol Petroleum Ltd* [1974] AC 821.

50 *Aberdeen Railway Co v Blaikie Bros* (1854) 1 Macq 461 per Lord Cramworth LC.

51 *Regal (Hastings) Ltd v Gulliver* [1942] 1 All ER 378.

52 *Boston Deep Sea Fishing & Ice Co v Ansell* (1888) 39 Ch, D 339.

53 *Thomas Marshall (Exporters) Ltd v Guinle* [1978] 2 WLR 116.

not compete with the company,[54] should not misuse company's funds,[55] and should not take up the corporate opportunity for personal reasons.[56]

Nonetheless, the question is whether a director is able to make decisions to treat all company members fairly, having regard to the impact that the decision will have on employees, the community, the environment, the company's business relationships, and reputation. This changes when a company faces financial distress and more so in view of the pandemic. However, there may come the point at which a director knows or ought to know that liquidation or insolvency is unavoidable. At this point, the director's primary duty shifts to protecting the interests of the company's creditors, taking all reasonable steps to prevent increased losses to creditors. The burden of proof is on the director to prove to the courts that this was done. Otherwise, the director is in breach. He may rely on information, professional or expert advice, opinions, reports, or statements including financial statements and other financial data, prepared, presented, or made by others in making his/her decisions.[57] In some cases, the directors may delegate any power of the board to any committee of the board, director, officer, employee, expert, or any other person.[58]

Duty to Exercise Care, Skill, and Diligence

Directors are also required to act with reasonable care, skill, and diligence as required by common law[59] and section 213(2) of the CA 2016. The yardstick is based on what would be expected from a careful and diligent director in the same circumstances. Business decisions must always be taken in the interests of the company while taking into account the interests of other stakeholders such as employees and creditors. Failure to comply with these statutory duties could result in personal liability for a director. Additionally, a director must prudently have regard to the interests of customers and suppliers, as those relationships are integral to the success of the business. In light of the pandemic, this could be very challenging for directors.

Duty to Prevent Wrongful Trading

Directors may also be faced with the possibility of being personally liable for wrongful trading under section 539(3) of the CA 2016 as the offence was not suspended during the pandemic. Without such a measure, directors who are otherwise performing well

54 *Bell v Lever Bros Ltd* [1932] AC 161.
55 *Totex-Adon Pty Ltd v Marco* [1982] 1 ACLC 228.
56 *Cook v Deeks* [1916] 1 AC 554.
57 CA 2016, s 215(1).
58 CA 2016, s 216(1).
59 *Re City Equitable Fire Insurance Co Ltd* [1925] Ch 407.

may be pressured to enter into an insolvency process to avoid incurring any personal liability. The provision reads:

> If in the course of winding up of a company or in any proceedings against a company, an officer of the company who knowingly was a party to the contracting of a debt had, at the time the debt was contracted, no reasonable or probable ground of expectation, after taking into consideration the other liabilities, if any, of the company at the time, of the company being able to pay the debt, commits an offence and shall, on conviction, be liable to imprisonment for a term not exceeding five years or to a fine not exceeding five hundred thousand ringgit or to both.

The term officer in relation to a corporation includes any director.[60]

4 Duty to Avoid Improper Declaration of Dividends

A company may only make a distribution to the shareholders out of profits of the company available if the company is solvent.[61] If there has been an improper declaration of dividends, the company, every officer, and any other person or individual who contravene this section commits an offence and shall, on conviction, be liable to imprisonment for a term not exceeding 5 years or to a fine not exceeding RM3 million or to both. As stated earlier, the term officer in relation to a corporation includes any director. Thus, a director who authorizes the payment of a dividend that contravenes the provisions of the CA 2016 will be in breach of his duties and be personally liable to repay the company for any loss suffered.

Corporate Rescue Mechanisms

At the time when the CA 2016 came into force, that is, on 31 January 2017, Division 8 of Part III on corporate rescue mechanisms did not come into force yet. It came into force on 1 March 2018, together with the Companies (Corporate Rescue Mechanism) Rules 2018. The objective of corporate rescue mechanisms is to strike a balance between the interests of creditors, on the one hand, and protect companies from the dire consequences of being wound up, which would have a far-reaching effect on its employees, creditors, and the community at large.[62] This mechanism enables a sustainable company or a company at the growth stage to resolve its short-term distress by implementing a rehabilitation plan that results in a win-win situation between

---

60 CA 2016, s 2.

61 CA 2016, s 131(1).

62 "COVID-19 & Corporate Rescue Mechanisms," Jeeva Partnership, May 1, 2020, https://jeevaretnam.com.my/covid-19-corporate-rescue-mechanisms/.

the company and its creditors.[63] It offers legal assistance to suffering businesses in light of the pandemic.[64] There are three corporate rescue mechanisms, namely, judicial management, corporate voluntary arrangement, and scheme of arrangement. In view of the pandemic, the corporate rescue mechanisms are a blessing in disguise instead of the company being wound up.

Judicial Management

A financially distressed company may apply to the court for the appointment of an independent judicial manager.[65] He would be responsible for managing the company's affairs, business, and property to prepare a restructuring scheme that would be presented to creditors, whereby a 75% majority sanction is required.[66] The judicial manager then finds ways to restructure the company's debts and manage the company's business for a period of time.[67]

However, this judicial management is not applicable to a company that is subject to the Capital Markets and Services Act 2007, that is, public listed companies, as provided in section 403 of the CA 2016.[68] Furthermore, secured creditors have the veto power to reject an application for judicial management. Additionally, the court retains the power to issue a judicial management order if it considers the public interest. This shows that the powers of the court are wide since it may also allow for rejection of the order if the order was obtained without full and honest disclosure, or the company was acting in bad faith, or the application was defective.[69] Furthermore,

---

63 "Dealing with Creditors after Lockdown (Covid19)," Cheng & Co, March 29, 2020, https://chengco.com.my/wp/2020/03/29/dealing-with-creditors-after-lockdown/.

64 "COVID-19 Corporate Rescue Mechanism: Legal Steps to Financial Recovery," EST Advisory Management, September 30, 2020, https://estadvisorymanagement.com.my/covid-19-corporate-rescue-mechanism-legal-steps-to-financial-recovery/.

65 CA 2016, ss 403–430.

66 CA 2016, ss 404 and 405.

67 Alen Gomez, Sitpah Selvaratnam, Ganesan Nethi, and Michael Yap Chih Hong, "Debt Restructuring and Corporate Rescues in the Wake of Covid-19: Pointers and Options," Tommy Thomas, April 22, 2020, https://www.tommythomas.net/main/news/63-debt-restructuring-and-corporate-rescues-in-the-wake-of-covid-19-pointers-and-options.

68 Idza Hajar Ahmad Idzam, and Bailey Leong, "Corporate Rescue Mechanism for Companies in Distress: A Compromise Between Debtors and Creditors," Zul Rafique & Partners, June 5, 2020, https://www.zulrafique.com.my/ckfinder/userfiles/files/Article_%20Corporate%20Rescue%20Mechanisms%20for%20Companies%20in%20Distress_%20A%20Compromise%20between%20Debtors%20and%20Creditors.PDF.

69 Norziana Lokman, Julizaerma Mohamed Khudzairi, and Sarina Othman, (2020), "Rehabilitating Ailing Malaysia Companies Using the New Corporate Rescue Mechanism," *Journal of Administrative Science* 17, no. 1 (2020): 96.

a recent High Court decision in *Re Biaxis (M) Sdn Bhd*[70] has set a seemingly high benchmark to meet in obtaining the judicial management order.[71] Thus, it will be very difficult to obtain a judicial management order from the courts.

Corporate Voluntary Arrangement

In corporate voluntary arrangement,[72] a binding arrangement is made between the company and its creditors without involving the approval from court whilst the directors have management control over the company.[73] To initiate this, the directors must prepare a proposal for the creditors and nominate an insolvency practitioner to act as a supervisor.[74] The licensed insolvency practitioner will provide an opinion, amongst others, whether the proposed scheme is viable and whether it is likely to be accepted by the creditors.[75] If the nominee is of the view that the scheme should be tabled for consideration by the creditors, a written opinion would be provided by the nominee and the nominee will file the documents setting out the terms of the proposed voluntary arrangement, a statement of assets and liabilities, and a statement that the company is eligible for a moratorium.[76] While the papers relating to the voluntary arrangement are led in court, the court only acts as a depository of documents, and there is no court hearing before the voluntary arrangement can take effect.

However, section 395 of the CA 2016 provides that this mechanism is only limited to private companies with no secured debt.[77] This would mean that the mechanism is not an option for companies who have loans that carry a charge over their property. It is unclear why such a restriction is necessary when voluntary arrangements do not in

---

70 [2020] MLJU 1188.

71 Lum Man Chan, "The Case of Re Biaxis: Further Distress for Judicial Management Applications?," *Empower* 3, no. 11 (November 2020), https://hhq.com.my/wp-content/uploads/2020/11/HHQEmpowerNov_ReBiaxis.pdf.

72 CA 2016, ss 395–402.

73 CA 2016, s 396.

74 Mark Lim, Mohd Arief Emran Arifin, and Eddie Lim, "Survival of Companies Impacted by the COVID-19 Outbreak," Baker McKenzie, March 24, 2020, https://www.bakermckenzie.com/en/insight/publications/2020/03/survival-of-companies-impacted-by-covid19.

75 Siti Nurfatin Shikh Ab Wahab, "Corporate Rescue Mechanism: Application of the Law," *LaWorld*, July 6, 2020, https://www.laworld.com/malaysia-corporate-rescue-mechanism-application-of-the-law/.

76 Abdul Malek Mohamed Said, "The Financial Impact of COVID-19," Deloitte, May 4, 2020, https://www2.deloitte.com/my/en/pages/financial-advisory/articles/financial-impact-of-covid-19.html.

77 Melinda Marie D'Angelus, Hanani Hayati Mohd Adhan, and Demetria Rinesha Samuel, "COVID-19: The Threat to Insolvency – Options to SMEs," Azmi & Associates, April 11, 2020, https://amcham.com.my/wp-content/uploads/Article-20200412-COVID-19-The-Threat-to-Insolvency-Options-to-SMEs.pdf.

any event bind secured creditors unless with their consent.[78] Moreover, in most cases, companies have loans with a charge over their property. Hence, it is unlikely that this mechanism will be of any rescue to ailing companies.

Scheme of Arrangement

Scheme of arrangement is a court-supervised exercise whereby a scheme advisor will be tasked to evaluate a company's financial position to formulate a proposal to restructure any outstanding debts.[79] The applicant is required to seek the court's order to convene meetings of the members and various classes of creditors of the companies. When applying to the court to convene such a meeting, companies often resort to applying for an order restraining further proceedings in any action or proceeding for a period of 3 months, provided there is no winding-up order or resolution to wind up the company. Such a period may be extended for up to 9 months.

However, the companies must meet the stringent criteria stipulated under section 368 of the CA 2016, failing which the restraining order will not be granted by the court. Furthermore, the moratorium against legal actions by creditors is not automatic and is subject to the court's discretion.[80]

Nevertheless, if none of the corporate rescue mechanisms could be utilized by a company, the last resort would be to wind up the company.

Presumption of Insolvency

Section 465(1)(e) of the CA 2016 provides that one of the circumstances in which a company may be wound up by a court is where a company is being unable to pay its debts. A company shall be deemed to be unable to pay its debts if the company is indebted in a sum exceeding the amount as may be prescribed by the Minister, which is RM10,000,[81] and a creditor has served a notice of demand, requiring the company to pay the sum due, and the company has for 21 days after the service of the demand neglected to pay the sum. In practice, this is the most common reason for winding up a company.

---

78 Andrew Chiew Ean Vooi, "COVID-19: Time for Businesses to Rethink and Restructure," Lee Hishammuddin Allen & Gledhill, April 2, 2020, https://www.lh-ag.com/wp-content/uploads/2020/04/COVID-19_Time-for-Businesses-to-Rethink-and-Restructure-LHAG-update-20200402.pdf.

79 CA 2016, ss 365–371.

80 Alen Gomez, Sitpah Selvaratnam, Ganesan Nethi, and Michael Yap Chih Hong, "Debt Restructuring and Corporate Rescues in the Wake of Covid-19: Pointers and Options," Tommy Thomas, April 22, 2020, https://www.tommythomas.net/main/news/63-debt-restructuring-and-corporate-rescues-in-the-wake-of-covid-19-pointers-and-options.

81 Pursuant to the Federal Government Gazette dated 27.01.2017.

The concern is whether companies are able to pay their debts within 21 days in view of the pandemic, and also of concern is the amount that practically makes most companies fall within the category of being unable to pay their debts.

Measures Taken by the Regulators

The preceding discussions have shown the challenges faced by the CA 2016 and companies in light of COVID-19. Governments around the world are scrambling for formulas, strategies, stimulus packages, and bailout plans to keep their economy afloat. Malaysia is not spared by the pandemic, and thus its economy was severely impacted since there were reduced socio-economic activities, and consequently, many companies are struggling to survive. With the announcement of MCO 2.0, things are looking bleak for businesses. In view of this, interim measures were initiated by the regulators, namely CCM, Securities Commission (SC),[82] and Bursa Malaysia, to assist financially distressed companies from being wound up by the court and provide some form of flexibility in complying with the CA 2016.

Virtual General Meetings

The SC issued a Guidance Note on the Conduct of General Meetings for public companies.[83] It provided that such companies shall only conduct fully virtual general meetings during the MCO 1.0. However, there should not be more than 8 individuals physically present at the main venue, including the chairperson of the general meeting, chief executive officer, chief financial officer, company secretary, auditor, and those providing audio-visual support. During the CMCO and RMCO, where safe distancing requirements remain, public companies may conduct their general meetings in a fully virtual or hybrid manner, that is, physical presence in the general meeting with the option of remote participation for shareholders. Nevertheless, the SC announced that a general meeting conducted in states or districts under CMCO should be conducted in a fully virtual manner only where all shareholders are able to participate in the meeting online.[84] Despite the announcement made by

82 Hereinafter referred to as the SC.

83 Securities Commission, *Guidance Note*, April 18, 2020.

84 "Only Fully Virtual General Meetings to be Conducted in States Subject to Conditional Movement Control Order," Securities Commission, October 13, 2020, https://www.sc.com.my/resources/media-releases-and-announcements/only-fully-virtual-general-meetings-to-be-conducted-in-states-subject-to-conditional-movement-control-order-cmco.

the SC, from 2 January 2020 to 17 April 2020, only 85 general meetings have been conducted, representing a decrease of 23% compared to 2019.[85]

In view of MCO 2.0, the SC announced that public companies should conduct fully virtual meetings in areas under MCO 2.0 and CMCO. Hybrid or physical meetings may be conducted in areas under RMCO or areas not subjected to any movement restrictions.[86]

Extension of Time to Hold Annual General Meeting

Section 340(4) of the CA 2016 states that a company may apply to the Registrar to extend the periods within which to call for AGM, and the Registrar may extend such periods as he/she considers appropriate, upon being satisfied with the reasons provided. Thus, companies should utilize this provision to seek for extension of time in view of the pandemic. Hence, the CCM granted an extension of 3 months from the date the AGM was to be held. However, companies must apply for the extension of time, and the CCM will waive the RM100 fee. The SC and Bursa Malaysia also announced that AGMs are allowed to be deferred as long as application was made to CCM.[87] However, as AGMs are not compulsory for private companies, they are not eligible to apply for this extension. In that case, private companies will resort to written resolutions.

A Moratorium for Lodgement of Statutory Documents

The CCM granted a moratorium of 30 days from the end of the MCO to lodge all affected statutory documents. The moratorium is kept open-ended so that it will be pegged to the end of any extended MCO. This means that late lodgement fees are exempted.

85 Doreenn Leong, "Virtual AGM – A Necessary Reality," *Focus Malaysia*, April 20, 2020, https://focusmalaysia.my/mainstream/virtual-agm-a-necessary-reality/.
86 "MKN SOP for Capital Market and SC's Guidance on Virtual Meetings for Listed Issuers," Securities Commission, January 18, 2021, https://www.sc.com.my/resources/media-releases-and-announcements/mkn-sop-for-capital-market-and-scs-guidance-on-virtual-meetings-for-listed-issuers.
87 "Capital Market Regulators Grant Flexibility for Listed Issuers on AGMs and Issuance of Periodic Reports," Securities Commission, March 17, 2020, https://www.sc.com.my/resources/media-releases-and-announcements/capital-market-regulators-grant-flexibility-for-listed-issuers-on-agms-and-issuance-of-periodic-reports.

Extension of Time for Lodgement of Financial Statements

The CCM provided an extension of 3 months from the date the companies have to lodge their financial statements. Hence, companies must be aware of the Practice Directive No. 6 of 2020, which was revised on 15 April 2020. However, an application for the extension of time must still be made and sent to the CCM by email before 30 June 2020 to be eligible. Hence, the CCM will waive the application fee of RM100 for the extension of time.

As for Bursa Malaysia, it announced that public listed companies are granted an automatic 1-month extension for issuance of quarterly and annual reports for the Main and ACE Markets, semi-annual and annual audited financial statements for the LEAP Market, which were due on 31 March 2020 and 30 April 2020.[88]

Extension of "2020 Compliance Campaign"

The 2020 Compliance Campaign, which commenced on 1 January 2020, was initiated by the CCM with several objectives, namely, encouraging compliance with the provisions of the CA 1965 and CA 2016 to ensure that only active companies are registered in the CCM's records and that the information in CCM's database is up to date and available upon request by the public and stakeholders.

The CCM extended the deadline of the "2020 Compliance Campaign of the Companies Act 2016" from 30 April to 30 June 2020. In this campaign, the CCM provided a maximum compound reduction rate of 90% from the original value of the compound for certain common offences under CA 1965 and CA 2016.

Presumption of Insolvency

In view of the pandemic, the Companies (Exemption) Order (No. 2) 2020 and the Direction of the Minister under section 466(1)(a) of the CA 2016 were gazetted.[89] The Exemption Order and the Directive will take effect from 23 April 2020 to 31 December 2020. Under the Exemption Order, the Minister of Domestic Trade and Consumer

88 "Bursa Malaysia Announces Additional Relief Measures to Alleviate the Impact of COVID-19 on Capital Market Players," Bursa Malaysia, March 26, 2020, https://www.bursamalaysia.com/about_bursa/media_centre/bursa-malaysia-announces-additional-relief-measures-to-alleviate-the-impact-of-covid-19-on-capital-market-players.

89 On April 23, 2020.

Affairs[90] has exempted all companies from the application of the presumption of insolvency provision under section 466(1)(a) of the CA 2016.[91]

Furthermore, the Directive increases the statutory threshold for the presumption of insolvency from RM10,000 to RM50,000. Moreover, the time period for a company to comply with a notice of demand is extended to 6 months from 21 days. This was seen to ease the burden of the businesses resulting from the COVID-19 pandemic.[92] It will provide some relief to companies facing cash-flow problems during these trying times. The effect of the Direction is that a creditor may only issue a statutory demand against a company for a debt that is more than RM50,000, and the company neglected it for more than 6 months.

Nevertheless, section 466(1) of the CA 2016 provides that the Minister only has the power to prescribe the amount for the presumption of insolvency and not the power to extend the 21-day period. Section 615 of the CA 2016 only empowers the Minister to exempt all or any of the provisions of the Act.[93] It does not empower the Minister to amend any provision of the CA 2016. Thus, the validity of the Directive regarding the time period is questionable. In that case, a creditor may challenge the validity of the 6-month period and assert the validity of the 21-day period. Therefore, the Minister had acted ultra vires.[94] Thus, the court will have to determine the validity of the Directive. Since the Exemption Order and Directive came into effect on 23 April 2020, it did not go far enough in protecting those companies that were already suffering the consequences of COVID-19 from an earlier period, that is, before 23 April 2020. This is strange as the Government announced that MCO 1.0 took effect on 18 March 2020. The Government should have emulated the approach taken by Singapore by way of primary legislation, as can be seen in the COVID-19 (Temporary Measures) Act 2020, particularly in section 22. Malaysia should have grabbed its opportunity to do the same when the COVID-19 Act 2020 was enacted.

On the other hand, despite the measures taken by the Minister, it does not stop a creditor from seeking to wind up a company by resorting to section 466(1)(b) or (c) of

90 Datuk Alexander Nanta Linggi.

91 Pursuant to s 615(1) of the CA 2016.

92 Rahmat Lim & Partners, "COVID 19 Response: Changes to the Presumption of Insolvency Provision under Section 466(1)(a) of the Companies Act 2016," *Knowledge Highlights*, April 27, 2020, https://www.rahmatlim.com/media/8686/my_changes-to-presumption-of-insolvency-under-s-466-1-a-of-ca-2016.pdf.

93 Ranjit Singh, "Govt's Exemption Order on Debt Period Raises Questions," *Focus Malaysia*, April 23, 2020, https://focusmalaysia.my/mainstream/exclusive-govts-exemption-order-on-debt-period-raises-questions/.

94 Shamsul Bahrin Manaf, "Companies (Exemption) Order 2020 – Does Minister Possess the Power to Make Such Order?," *Mohanadass Partnership Newsletter*, April 24, 2020, http://mohanadass.com/download/articles/companies-exemption-order-2020-24-4-2020.pdf.

the CA 2016.[95] The former provision applies to circumstances where the creditor can prove to the satisfaction of the court that the company is indeed unable to pay its debts. The latter provision provides for circumstances where a creditor may commence legal proceedings, obtain a judgement, and thereafter seek to enforce the judgement by attaching the available assets of the company concerned. It is important to bear in mind that, in some cases, the creditors themselves may be facing financial difficulties and pressures from their creditors and see the debt recovery as an option to ease their concerns.

Another matter that remains unclear is if a debtor had received a statutory demand issued under the CA 2016 before the Exemption Order and Directive took effect. The question is whether the creditor will be able to present the winding-up petition after the expiration of 21 days.[96] Another concern is the winding-up petitions filed during the MCO 1.0 but before the announcement made by the CCM. This is because the MCO 1.0 commenced on 18 March 2020, and the announcement was made on 23 April 2020.

Lessons from Other Jurisdictions

United Kingdom

Pursuant to section 123(1)(a) of the Insolvency Act 1986, a company is deemed unable to pay its debts if, among other reasons, a creditor, to whom the company is indebted in a sum exceeding £750, serves a statutory demand requiring the company to repay the debt and the company has failed to repay that debt for 3 weeks thereafter. Under section 10 of the Corporate Insolvency and Governance Act 2020 (CIG),[97] creditors may not present a winding-up petition based on an unpaid statutory demand or an unpaid judgement debt in the relevant period, that is, between 1 March 2020 and 30 September 2020 unless the creditor has reasonable grounds for believing that COVID-19 has not had a financial effect on the company or the company's inability to satisfy the statutory demand or judgement debt was not caused by COVID-19.

95 "COVID-19: Interim "Immunity Booster" for Financially Distressed Companies," *Lawyers Who Know Asia*, *Christopher & Lee Ong*, April 2020, https://www.christopherleeong.com/media/3900/clo_covid19_interim_immunity_booster_financially_distressed_companies.pdf.

96 Lavinia Kumaraendran, and Sean Tan Yang Wei, "Temporary Measures Announced by the Companies Commission of Malaysia (SSM)," Thomas Philip, April 11, 2020, https://www.thomasphilip.com.my/articles/legal-alert-temporary-measures-announced-by-the-companies-commission-of-malaysia-ssm-1/.

97 Hereinafter referred to as CIG Act 2020.

The UK Government also amended its legislation to provide temporary relief to businesses affected by the pandemic.[98] Among the amendments is the temporary suspension of the wrongful trading provisions retrospectively from 1 March 2020 for 3 months to allow companies undergoing a rescue or restructuring process to continue to trade. Section 12(1) of the CIG Act 2020 provides that in determining for the purposes of section 214 or 246ZB Insolvency Act 1986, the contribution to a company's assets that it is proper for a person to make, the court is to assume that the person is not responsible for any worsening of the financial position of the company or its creditors that occurs during the relevant period. Section 12(2) CIG of the Act 2020 provides that the relevant period is the period that begins on 1 March 2020 and ends on 30 September 2020.

Singapore

The debt threshold in relation to insolvency was increased from SGD10,000 to SGD100,000 as provided by section 22(1)(a) COVID-19 (Temporary Measures) Act 2020, which was a tenfold[99] increase, unlike in Malaysia, which was fivefold. Hence, the increase in Malaysia may not have a significant impact on the meaning of unable to pay debts. This is because the amount is still low, and thus, many companies would still fall within the purview of being unable to pay their debts and be subjected to a winding-up process. The intention to increase the threshold is to save companies from being subjected to a winding-up process in light of the pandemic. Furthermore, the time frame to respond to a statutory demand is provided for under a primary legislation, that is, the Singapore Companies Act. As such, it was necessary for the amendment to the time frame to be enacted through an Act of Parliament. This was done through the passing of section 22(1)(b) of the COVID-19 (Temporary Measures) Act 2020 on 7 April 2020. This was not so in Malaysia, as discussed in the preceding section.

Furthermore, section 22(2) of the COVID-19 (Temporary Measures) Act 2020 provides that for the purpose of section 339(3) of the Companies Act, an officer of the company or an officer, the manager, or the custodian of the variable capital company is not to be treated as having no reasonable or probable ground of expectation of the company or variable capital company being able to pay a debt if the debt is incurred in the ordinary course of the company's or variable capital company's business;

98 Yoong Shin Min, and Ng Hooi Huang, "COVID-19: The Impact on Businesses, Relief Measures and Rescue Mechanisms," *Shook Lin & Bok, Legal Update*, April 1, 2020.

99 "COVID-19 Responses Across Asia: An Essential Guide," *King & Wood Mallesons*, May 28, 2020, https://www.kwm.com/en/sg/knowledge/downloads/covid-responses-across-asia-an-essential-guide-20200528.

during the prescribed period; and before the appointment of a judicial manager or liquidator of the company or variable capital company.

Australia

On 22 March 2020, the Treasurer, Josh Fryderberg, announced various temporary changes to the corporate insolvency laws to provide temporary relief for companies that were generally profitable and viable but now facing financial distress due to COVID-19. The aim of these measures was to ensure that these businesses could keep their head above water during the market downturn with a lifejacket in place for them until the crisis passes. Two approaches were taken, namely, on the presumption of insolvency and director's liability for wrongful trading.

Under sections 9 and 459E of the Corporations Act 2001 (CA),[100] the minimum debt threshold for creditors to issue a statutory demand against a debtor company is AUS$2,000. Under the changes brought about by Schedule 12, Part 2, section 26(1) of the Coronavirus Economic Response Package Omnibus Act 2020, the current minimum threshold is increased 10-fold to AUS$20,000. There was also an increase in the statutory time frame for a debtor company to respond to statutory demands from creditors. The time frame for a debtor company to respond was 21 days, whereas under the changes brought about by Schedule 12, Part 2, section 26(2) of the Coronavirus Economic Response Package Omnibus Act 2020, this will be extended to 6 months. These changes will be effective for a period of 6 months.

Also, section 588G of the CA 2001 imposes personal liability on directors who allow a company to trade while being insolvent. Hence, there is a duty on directors to prevent companies from trading when insolvent. If that is so, such a duty may put directors under immense pressure to make quick decisions to enter into an insolvency process to avoid any risk of the company trading while insolvent since they will be personally liable. This will put the company in a precarious position and affect all stakeholders.

Under the changes brought about by Schedule 12, Part 3, section 31 of the Coronavirus Economic Response Package Omnibus Act 2020, directors will be temporarily relieved of their duty to prevent insolvent trading with respect to any debts incurred in the ordinary course of the company's business. This will apply for a period of 6 months. The aim is to assist companies that are otherwise well-performing from going into liquidation just because of the COVID-19 outbreak and to make sure that companies have the ability to continue to trade through the outbreak with the aim of quickly returning to viability when the crisis has passed. However, this is not a blanket relief that applies across the board. This will only apply with respect to

100 Hereinafter referred to as CA 2001.

debts incurred in the ordinary course of the company's business. Therefore, cases of dishonesty and fraud by directors will still be subject to criminal penalties.

Reforms to Address the Implications

With regard to the Companies (Exemption) Order 2020, although it was done with good intention to mitigate the effect of COVID-19 on the companies, it must be balanced with the need to comply with the principles of the rule of law. Hence, section 466(1)(a) needs to be amended to give effect to the Companies (Exemption) Order 2020. It is recommended that the extension of 21 days to 6 months under section 466 (1) of the CA 2016 be done via amending legislation. Otherwise, the directive issued by the Minister will be challenged in the court on the grounds of ultra vires. Consequently, the company, its stakeholders, and creditors' interests will be affected.

A study must be carried out to identify the date or period when exactly the impact of COVID-19 started to affect Malaysia's economy significantly. Once the date is deduced, a legal solution should take effect from that date, even if it is retrospective. Currently, there are several dates an affected party has to bear in mind, that is, the date MCO 1.0 commences, the date the Exemption Order took effect, and the date the COVID-19 Act 2020 came into force. This is to ensure that only those companies that are struggling due to the COVID-19 pandemic are protected.[101] It is also to ensure that other companies do not misuse these temporary measures by the regulators. If the measures initiated by the regulators are not properly implemented, they may be abused by irresponsible directors, thus increasing the number of fraud cases.[102]

However, one major concern is proving that the difficulties the companies are currently facing are a direct consequence of the COVID-19 pandemic. Hence, to avoid such problems, there must be clear provisions regarding the timing of insolvencies and provide for a rebuttable statutory presumption.

It is to be noted that the CCM is currently drafting the Companies Amendment Act (2020) to introduce provisions to help companies with various financial problems, not just from the impact of the Covid-19 pandemic.[103] Nevertheless, at the

---

101 Nimalan Devaraj, and Janice Ooi, "COVID-19: Malaysia Takes Steps to Address Insolvency Concerns of Companies," Skrine, April 14, 2020, https://www.skrine.com/insights/covid-19-updates/covid-19-malaysia-takes-steps-to-address-insolvenc.

102 Nimalan Devaraj, and Janice Ooi, "COVID-19: Proposed Interim Reliefs for Financially Distressed Companies and Individuals?," Skrine, March 27, 2020, https://www.skrine.com/insights/covid-19-updates/covid-19-proposed-interim-reliefs-for-financially.

103 Harizah Kamel, "SSM Drafting New Companies Act for Better Protection," *The Malaysian Reserve,* June 26, 2020, https://themalaysianreserve.com/2020/06/26/ssm-drafting-new-companies-act-for-better-protection/#:~:text=THE%20Companies%20Commission%20of%20Malaysia,of%20the%20Covid%2D19%20pandemic.

time of writing this chapter, no further information was available. In view of the Emergency (Essential Powers) Ordinance 2021, which came into effect on 11 January 2021, Regulation 14(1) provides that there will not be any sitting by the Parliament till 1 August 2021. Thus, there will not be any legislative amendments to the CA 2016 till then.

Conclusion

At the time the CA 2016 was enacted, what the legislature had in mind was to ensure that the recommendations by the CLRC were taken into account and the developments are in tandem with the approaches taken in the United Kingdom, Australia, Singapore, and Hong Kong. The legislature must have opined that a good job was done, especially the fact that it took over 50 years to replace the CA 1965. Nonetheless, it would not have been in the wildest dream of anyone that we would be faced with the world's greatest enemy, that is, COVID-19. Hence, the CA 2016 had to withstand the onslaught of the pandemic. Additionally, companies were faced with an uphill task of complying with the requirements of the CA 2016. In some cases, they were successful and in some cases not. Fortunately, the regulators took swift action in initiating temporary measures to provide some form of flexibility in complying with the CA 2016. In certain aspects, the regulators did a remarkable job, and in some aspects, the initiatives are questionable and may be subjected to a test of validity at the courts. Thus, it is best to take a leaf from countries that have been successfully addressing these matters, namely the United Kingdom, Australia, and Singapore. Be that as it may, the measures initiated by the regulators are merely temporary. The regulators would have to think in a bigger picture and long-term results since the pandemic is still around, and no one knows when it will end. On that note, the COVID Act 2020 must also be re-examined. Certainly, the implications of the COVID-19 for the CA 2016 and companies are far-reaching, and they must be addressed. Otherwise, businesses will collapse, and the domestic economy will be severely affected.

Sunitha S. Sivakumaran

6 COVID-19 Pandemic and Competition Law

Introduction

The COVID-19 pandemic continues to have a devastating impact across the world. There has been a loss of many lives and a debilitated health status for many who survived. The pandemic and the consequent containment measures, particularly the Movement Control Order (MCO), have gravely affected the global economy by disrupting most sectors of the economy; manufacturing, tourism, and hospitality virtually ground to a standstill.

In order to survive the pandemic, firms are forced to relook at their business operations and find efficiencies wherever possible, including corporate restructuring. This corporate restructuring and firms exiting the marketplace have led to a rapid increase in unemployment, from 3.2% in December 2019 to 5.1% in May 2020.[1] The rise in unemployment has led to (i) lower consumer confidence as individuals are inclined to increase savings in these uncertain times and (ii) the reduction of disposable income in the case of households who have been directly impacted by the pandemic. Both of the above factors deflate demand.

Given the current difficult situation, many businesses would opt out for survival strategies to avoid a ruinous liquidation of their assets. They may be more open than they ordinarily would be to private buyouts and mergers or to collaborate and coordinate to share their resources and information.[2] The competition rules of Malaysia do not govern mergers and acquisitions, and there is no rule against "monopolization" as in the USA. It is, therefore, open to Malaysian enterprises to freely merge with or acquire other enterprises.

Business may also be tempted to initiate cooperation with other operators to overcome shared challenges in order to survive in the market. They may also be inclined to take advantage of the crisis by engaging in horizontal and vertical agreements. Such cooperation between competitors may lead to serious financial penalties for the participating firms in Malaysia. This is because the Competition Act 2010 (CA 2010) prohibits any horizontal or vertical agreement between enterprises insofar as the agreement has the object or effect of significantly preventing, restricting, or distorting competition in any market for goods or services.

1 "Economic and Financial Developments in the Malaysian Economy in the 3rd Quarter of 2020," BNM Quarterly Bulletin, November 13, 2020, https://www.bnm.gov.my/documents/20124/1067374/3Q2020_fullbook_en.pdf.

2 "The Covid-19 pandemic has prompted concerns that, while most businesses will act responsibly, some businesses might respond with anti-competitive conduct, e.g., by cartelizing or abusing a dominant position."

https://doi.org/10.1515/9783110723694-006

Businesses may also turn to their associations or representatives to lobby for aid and incentives. This frequency of contact may increase the risk of sharing sensitive data that may lead to anti-competitive conduct. In an attempt to maintain a certain level of profitability, they may fix prices, control market outlets or production, or attempt to partner with other similar businesses to allocate supply and distribution to different territories.

Whilst there have been losses in most sectors, there are those who have had significant growth, such as e-commerce, logistics, pharmaceuticals, and other health products. In the case of the pharma and healthcare industries, which have seen an increase in revenue, there is a possibility of an abuse of dominance. This is particularly so when the dominant business is producing a product that is essential and is highly sought by many. An excessive price increase for essential products or services may itself be regarded as an abuse of dominance.[3] For example, in the early days of the MCO, the price of face masks shot up from RM0.80 to RM 2.00 per unit (an increase of 150%). This came as a result of Pharmaniaga Berhad (Pharmaniaga) being the sole supplier to local public sector hospitals, i.e., a monopoly created by the procurement practice of the Ministry of Health. Following public and consumer organization complaints to the Ministry of Domestic Trade and Consumer Affairs (the Ministry), the price was reduced to RM 1.50, which is still a price hike of 87.5%. The Malaysian Competition Commission (MyCC) remained silent.[4]

From a competition law viewpoint, competition rules should be used to ensure a level playing field for all businesses,[5] especially during a crisis. There were no penalties imposed on Pharmaniaga. The Ministry merely agreed that the price is reduced to RM1.50 without explaining how this price was arrived at. The Ministry has also implemented a price control scheme on essential items such as dry foods, fresh food, drinks, and other products utilized for personal hygiene and health.[6]

---

3 Competition Ac 2010, s 10 prohibits conduct amounting to abuse of a dominant position in any market for goods or service. Amongst others, such conduct includes imposing excessive pricing, unfair trading conditions, or limiting or controlling market outlet or market access to the prejudice of consumers.

4 This is probably because in Malaysia, the Ministry may exercise its powers under the Price Control and Anti-Profiteering Act 2011 and the Price Control and Anti-Profiteering (Mechanism to Determine Unreasonably High Profit) Regulations 2018.

5 Vince Eng Teong See, "Competition Act 2010: Issues and Challenges," *European Journal of Law and Economics* 40, no. 3 (2015): 587–616, https://doi.org/10.1007/s10657-012-9344-1.

6 The Regulations 2018 prescribes a mechanism to determine unreasonably high profits by examining either (i) the mark-up percentage; or (ii) the margin percentage, of the goods and services sold. The price control mechanism can be implemented by the Ministry of Domestic Trade and Consumer Affairs (KPDNHEP) at any time during the MCO if there is indiscriminate hike in prices of goods. See "Domestic Trade Ministry Can Implement Price Control During MCO, Says Minister," *Malaymail*, April 18, 2020, https://www.malaymail.com/news/malaysia/2020/04/18/domestic-trade-ministry-can-implement-price-control-during-mco-says-ministe/1857913.

This chapter describes the Malaysian competition law and considers the matters that the MyCC has to address given the unprecedented situation regarding competition occasioned by the pandemic. Reference will also be made to measures that have been adopted by competition authorities in other jurisdictions.

Malaysian Law – Key Provisions of the Competition Act 2010

The CA 2010 deals with anti-competitive agreements and abuse of dominance but not with the control of anti-competitive mergers and acquisitions.[7] The CA 2010, therefore, is confined to the supervision of market behaviour but not of market structure. The Act applies to enterprises. An "enterprise" is defined as "any entity carrying on commercial activities relating to goods or services, and for the purposes of this Act, a parent and subsidiary company shall be regarded as a single enterprise if, despite their separate legal entity, both form a single economic unit within which the subsidiaries do not enjoy real autonomy in determining the actions of the subsidiaries on the market".[8] This definition is unlike that of company law, which is based on the concept of "separate legal entity". The definition is wide and includes, for example, companies, partnerships, individuals operating as sole traders, and state-owned corporations. The MyCC has made it clear that even government- linked companies are not immune when it imposed a financial penalty of RM10 million each for market allocation on Malaysia Airlines (MAS), a government-linked entity, and AirAsia.[9] The CA 2010 applies to all commercial activities within and outside Malaysia so long as the commercial activity transacted outside Malaysia has an effect on competition in any market in the country.[10]

The Second Schedule exempts specific "matters" from the prohibitions specified in Part II of the CA 2010. These include, at the time of enactment of the Act and currently: (i) any activity, directly or indirectly carried out in the exercise of governmental authority[11]; (ii) any activity conducted based on the principle of

7 This was a deliberate decision that was to develop the capital market to consolidate corporate players to face global competition; in effect to create national champions.

8 Competition Act 2010, s 2.

9 Infringement of Section 4(2)(b) of the CA 2010 by Malaysian Airline System Berhad, AirAsia Berhad and AirAsia X Sdn. Bhd. 31 March 2014 (No. MyCC.0001.2012). The MyCC imposed a financial penalty of RM10,000,000 on MAS and AirAsia, respectively.

10 For a discussion of the complexity of extraterritorial application of the CA 2010, see Nasarudin Abdul Rahman and Hanif Ahmat, *Competition Law in Malaysia* (Subang Jaya: Sweet & Maxwell, 2016), 69–72.

11 The CA 2010 does not define the term "in the exercise of governmental authority". In the EU case law, "an entity, public of private, which performs tasks of a public nature, connected with the

solidarity[12]; and (iii) any purchase of goods or service done for the purposes of offering goods and services as part of an economic activity.[13] It was made clear to Parliament that government-linked corporations were not excluded from the ambit of the CA 2010,[14] but they clearly would be when they are carrying out activities in the exercise of governmental authority. This will call for the MyCC to distinguish between purely commercial activity and activity in the exercise of governmental authority.

Chapter 1 Prohibition – Anti-Competitive Agreements

Section 4 of the CA 2010 prohibits horizontal and vertical agreements between enterprises where an agreement has the object or effect of significantly preventing, restricting, and distorting competition in any market for goods and services.[15] The term agreement is defined in a broad manner to include any form of contract (written and oral), arrangement, or understanding between enterprises, whether legally enforceable or not, and includes a decision by an association and concerted practice.[16] Concerted practice is defined as any form of coordination between enterprises that knowingly substitutes practical cooperation between them for the risks of competition.[17] The concept of "concerted practice" is adopted from European case law.[18] This usually involves some form of informal cooperation or collusion where parties enter into an informal arrangement or understanding and would include situations where

exercise of public powers or in the exercise of official authority" is exempted from the provisions of competition law. Alison Jones, Brenda Sufrin and Niamh Dunne, *EU Competition Law: Text Cases and Material* (Oxford: Oxford University Press, 2011), 127.

12 The CA 2010 does not define the term "solidarity". There is much EU case law on the term. In brief, it covers social functions that are inherently non-economic. Examples of some of these cases are Diego Cali v SPEG C343/95 [1997] ECR1-1547, Sodemare v Regione Lombardia C 70/95[1997] ECR-1 3395, Cisal v INAIL C 218/00 [2002] ECR1-691, AOK Bundeeverband v Ichthyol-Gesellschaft Cordes Hermani C 264,306,354 and 355/01 [2004] ECR-1 2493.

13 Competition Act 2010, s 3(1) and (2).

14 Malaysia, Perbahasan Dewan Rakyat, Bacaan Kedua, April 22, 2010, 146 (Y.B. Dato' Sri Isamil Sabri Yaakob).

15 Competition Act 2010, s 4(1).

16 Competition Act 2010, s 2.

17 Competition Act 2010, s 2.

18 Its meaning was first considered in Case 48/69 *Imperial Chemical Industries Ltd v Commission (Dyestuffs)* [1972] ECR 619. The court defined the term "concerted practice" as ". . .a form of coordination between undertakings which, without having reached the stage where an agreement properly so-called has been concluded, knowingly substitutes practical cooperation between them for the risks of competition" (para 64).

enterprises mirror or follow the price that is set by another competitor without being unilateral or independent.[19]

Horizontal agreements are those that apply to enterprises at the same level of the production or distribution chain.[20] The Act incorporates a mechanism under Section 4(2) to deem certain categories of horizontal agreements as having "the object of significantly preventing, restricting, or distorting competition". The categories of horizontal agreements covered under this provision are those that

a) fix purchase or selling prices or other traditional condition,
b) share market or sources of supply,
c) limit or control production, market outlets or access, technical or technological development or investment, or
d) perform an act of bid rigging.[21]

When assessing whether an agreement has the object of restricting competition, the MyCC will not only examine the actual common intention of the parties but will assess the aims of the agreement taking into consideration the surrounding economic context.[22] As for other horizontal conduct not falling within Section 4(2), the MyCC indicates that it will assess if the agreement has a trivial or significant impact on competition.[23] The MyCC has in its Chapter 1 Prohibition Guidelines provided a "safe harbor" by stating that anti-competitive agreements or decisions will not be considered as "significant" if the parties to the agreement are:

a) competitors who are in the same market and the combined market share of the parties to the agreement does not exceed 20% of the relevant market; or
b) not competitors, their individual market shares in any relevant market are not more than 25%.[24]

Vertical agreements refer to agreements by enterprises operating at a different level in the production or distribution chain.[25] The MyCC considers vertical agreements to be less harmful to competition compared to horizontal agreements.[26] This is because parties to a vertical agreement usually have a joint interest in ensuring that the final product or service is competitive as opposed to horizontal agreements,

19 Sharon Tan, "Malaysia: Overview," *The Asia Pacific Antitrust Review* 2015, February 20, 2015, https://globalcompetitionreview.com/review/the-asia-pacific-antitrust-review/the-asia-pacific-antitrust-review-2015/article/malaysia-overview.
20 Competition Act 2010, s 2.
21 Competition Act 2010, s 4(2).
22 Sharon Tan, "Malaysia: Overview."
23 MyCC Guidelines on Chapter 1 Prohibition Anti-Competitive Agreements, para 3.4.
24 MyCC Guidelines on Chapter 1 Prohibition Anti-Competitive Agreements, para 3.4.
25 Competition Act 2010, s 2.
26 MyCC Guidelines on Chapter 1 Prohibition Anti-Competitive Agreements, para 3.11.

which are between competitors operating at the same level in the production or distribution chain.[27]

The CA 2010, therefore, does not bar all cooperative agreements. It only bars collusive agreements that fall under Section 4(2), which are deemed to have "the object of significantly preventing, restricting, or distorting competition". Even if the collusive conduct has "the object of significantly preventing, restricting, or distorting competition", it may be granted an exemption if the criteria specified in Section 5 are met, in which case the enterprise may seek and obtain the exemption.

The MyCC has targeted cartel practices, mainly by trade associations such as the Cameron Highlands Floriculturist Association, Pan-Malaysia Lorry Owners Association, Sibu Confectionary and Bakery Association, and the General Insurance Association of Malaysia.[28] There has also been one market sharing case, namely the MAS-AirAsia case, which involved a collaboration agreement between Malaysian Airlines and AirAsia. This agreement was found to have the object of market sharing resulting in the withdrawal of some routes on which both airlines competed.[29]

A problem that the definition of the terms "agreement" and "enterprise" has posed the MyCC is that it leaves ambivalent the position of trade associations. A trade association that itself is involved in "commercial activity" would be covered by definition. What if a decision by a trade association that itself is not involved in commercial activity, but the decisions of which result in anti-competitive conduct by its members? In such instances, the MyCC has penalized the members who have complied with the anti-competitive decisions of their trade associations but refrained from sanctioning the trade association itself because Section 4(3) only provides that "Any enterprise which is a party to an agreement which is prohibited under this section shall be liable for infringement of the prohibition." There is no specification that the association itself shall be liable. The MyCC has sought an amendment to the CA 2010 to address this lacuna in the law.[30]

27 MyCC Guidelines on Chapter 1 Prohibition Anti-Competitive Agreements, para 3.11.

28 Information available at http://www.mycc.gov.my/legislation/case.

29 The High Court reinstated the decision of the MyCC, which imposed a fine of RM10 million each on MAS and AirAsia Bhd for breach of market-sharing prohibition under the CA 2010. See "High Court Reinstates RM10mil Fine Imposed on MAS and AirAsia," *The Star*, December 20, 2018, https://www.thestar.com.my/news/nation/2018/12/20/high-court-reinstates-rm10mil-fine-imposed-on-mas-and-airasia.

30 Proposed Amendments to the Act Definition: The definition of "enterprise" is widened to include the underlined words: "'enterprise' means any person, being an individual, a body corporate, an unincorporated body of persons or other entity, capable of carrying on commercial or economic activities relating to goods or services and for the purpose of this Act, a parent and subsidiary company shall be regarded as a single enterprise if, despite their separate legal entity, they form a single economic unit within which the subsidiaries do not enjoy real autonomy in determining their actions on the market". With this proposed amendment, the Act will apply to individuals (e.g. sole

Relief from Liability and Exemptions

Section 5 of the CA 2010 provides relief of liability for an enterprise that is a party to a prohibited agreement under Section 4. In principle, no activity is precluded from the application of Section 5 of the CA 2010,[31] including those specified in Section 4(2) as being deemed to have the object of significantly preventing, restricting, or distorting competition. The infringing enterprise has to establish that there are significant identifiable technological, efficiency, or *social benefits directly arising from the agreement*. In addition, it has to establish that the benefits could not reasonably have been provided by the parties to the agreement without the agreement having the anti-competitive effect, that the detrimental effect is proportionate to the benefits provided, and that the agreement does not allow the enterprise concerned to eliminate competition completely in respect of a substantial part of the goods or services.[32] All the above-mentioned conditions are to be read conjunctively and have to be met. These are onerous conditions to meet. In practice, there would have to be extremely convincing evidence to satisfy the MyCC that the benefits to competition outweigh the detriments.

The term "social benefits" is not defined anywhere in CA 2010, and the MyCC has yet to consider the meaning of the term. However, in economics, social benefit is the total benefit to society from producing or consuming a good/service.[33] The Organisation for Economic Co-operation and Development (OECD) glossary of statistical terms defines "social benefits" as "current transfers received by households intended to provide for the needs that arise from certain events or circumstances, for example, sickness, unemployment, retirement, housing, education or family circumstances".[34] Using such a definition, it would not be unreasonable to state that horizontal agreements between businesses may be deemed to provide "social benefits" when they are beneficial to consumers as a whole. In the context of the economic situation occasioned by COVID-19, where supply chain disruptions have led to a scarcity of goods, a level of collaboration between businesses with regard to procurement and sourcing could be beneficial to facilitate greater access to the market. This is especially true for essential products, including those required to specifically deal with healthcare, such as masks, gloves, sanitizers, and other medical necessities. These goods are currently in short supply and, due to the prevailing market dynamics, have seen an increase in prices. Should collaboration between businesses lead to a more

---

proprietors and partnerships) and not confined to legal entities so long as they are capable of carrying on commercial or economic activities.

31 S 5 of CA 2010 deals with relief of liability.

32 Competition Act 2010, s 5.

33 As defined in the glossary "Helping to Simplify Economics," accessed February 11, 2021, https://www.economicshelp.org/blog/glossary/social-benefit.

34 "Glossary of Statistical Terms." OECD, accessed February 11, 2021, https://stats.oecd.org/glossary/detail.asp?ID=2480.

efficient supply chain and/or manufacturing process, cost savings could be passed on to consumers in the form of lower prices. In the instance described above, businesses could argue that there is a "social benefit" from their collaboration; their collaboration would be in the consumers' interest.[35]

Alternatively, it could be that the "social benefit" is indirectly derived by facilitating the economic activity of a third party to produce essential goods or services at a lower cost and thereby benefit consumer welfare. Hence, an accommodative definition of "social benefit" would allow for a broader category of collaborations between enterprises to be permissible.

As noted earlier, SMEs contribute more than two-thirds of the country's employment.[36] Should these enterprises fail, the loss of jobs would be a devastating blow to the nation's economy. Unemployment will have immense economic and social costs, including:

- *Lower gross domestic product*
  The loss of employment would further exacerbate the negative multiplier effect as household consumption and business investment decrease.
- *Increase in social problems*
  Unemployment may lead to socioeconomic division, increased likelihood of substance abuse, mental illness and health complications, and an increase in crime. Individuals affected by prolonged employment often find themselves less desirable in the job market,[37] and this further reduces their likelihood of securing employment. Prolonged unemployment could result in other negative multiplier effects such as vandalism, delinquency, and alienation posing a challenge to national integration and social harmony.
- *Political instability*
  Periods of prolonged unemployment, specifically youth unemployment, could lead to political instability.[38]

---

35 Sunitha Sivakumaran and Skanda Jivan, "Competition Law in the New Normal," *European Competition Law Review* 41, no. 10 (2020): 500–508.

36 D Kanyakumari, "Malaysia's Unemployment Rate Is Also Now the Highest in a Decade," *CNA*, May 8, 2020, https://www.channelnewsasia.com/news/asia/malaysia-unemployment-rate-highest-in-decade-covid-19-mco-12715022. The article reported that Department of Statistics' chief statistician Mohd Uzir Mahidin said: "The unemployment rate in March 2020 increased to 3.9 per cent, highest since June 2010 when the unemployment rate was at 3.6 per cent."

37 Rand Ghayad and William Dickens, "What Can We Learn by Disaggregating the Unemployment Vacancy Relationship?" *Public Policy Briefs*, no. 12–3 (October 2012): 1–13, http://dx.doi.org/10.2139/ssrn.2285075.

38 Therese F. Azeng and Thierry U. Yogo, "Youth Unemployment, Education and Political Instability: Evidence from Selected Developing Countries 1991–2009," *Households in Conflict Network (HiCN) Working Paper 200* (2015), accessed February 12, 2021, https://gsdrc.org/document-library/youth-unemployment-education-and-political-instability-evidence-from-selected-developing-countries-1991-2009/.

It is submitted that the term "social benefit" needs to be interpreted such as to facilitate production that helps sustain enterprises and, consequently, employment. The special circumstances occasioned by the COVID-19 pandemic calls for an accommodative approach.

Exemptions

The MyCC can either grant an individual exemption[39] or a block exemption,[40] and for such exemptions may impose conditions and obligations that it considers appropriate.[41] In the case of an individual exemption, it is up to the parties to demonstrate the claimed benefits according to the criteria set out in Section 5 of the Act.[42]

The annual fee payable for filing an application for an individual exemption is RM50,000. In addition, an annual fee becomes payable once the exemption is granted (= RM25,000 × the number of years for which the exemption is granted). In the case of a block exemption, the application fee is RM100,000 (excluding disbursement) and an annual fee of RM50,000 (excluding disbursement) × the number of years for which the exemption is granted.[43] In light of the current situation, the MyCC may consider waiving the fee.

---

39 Competition Act 2010, s 6(2).

40 Competition Act 2010, ss 8(1) and 8(2).

41 S 6(4) of the CA 2010 states: "The individual exemption granted by the Commission may be – (a) subject to any condition or obligation as the Commission considers it appropriate to impose; and (b) for a limited duration as specified in the order." S 6(5) provides: "An individual exemption may provide for it to have effect from a date earlier than that on which the order is made." And s 8(4) states: "The Commission in granting the block exemption may impose any condition or obligation subject to which a block exemption shall have effect."

42 MyCC Guidelines on Chapter 1 Prohibition – Anti-Competitive Agreements, para 5.2 states that the infringing enterprise has to establish that "(a) there are significant identifiable technological, efficiency or social benefits directly arising from the agreement; (b) the benefits could not reasonably have been provided by the parties to the agreement without the agreement having the effect of preventing, restricting or distorting competition; (c) the detrimental effect of the agreement on competition is proportionate to the benefits provided; and (d) the agreement does not allow the enterprise concerned to eliminate competition completely in respect of a substantial part of the goods or services".

43 Information available at MyCC's website, accessed February 22, 2021, https://www.mycc.gov.my/exemption-application-fees.

Chapter 2 Prohibition – Abuse of Dominance

Just like the provision on anti-competitive agreements, Section 10 provides for a general prohibition against abuse of a dominant position with a non-exhaustive list of specific instances of abuse. Section 10 of the CA 2010 is a transplant of the provisions of article 102 of the Treaty on the Functioning of the European Union (EU) and its case laws. Teong says that:

> The intent and purpose of such provisions is to create a level-playing field, whether competitors at the same level or between two enterprises operating at two different levels of productions or distribution chain. This is to ensure that competitors will not be excluded from the market through anti-competitive means, leaving the market with fewer players and thus fewer competitive choices for consumers, to the detriment of consumers.[44]

Section 10(1) lays down the prohibition of engaging independently or collectively in any conduct which could amount to an abuse of dominant position in the relevant market. Section 10 of the CA 2010 has adopted the EU jurisprudence on abuse of dominant position. Thus, a finding of abuse is possible not only when the enterprise itself independently abuses its dominant position but also when it does so in concert with other dominant players.[45]

The dominant position is defined in Section 2 of the Act as a situation where one or more enterprises attains a significant market power capable of adjusting prices, outputs or trading terms, without effective constraint from competitors, that is, they are able to do so without incurring any loss. Section 10(2) provides a non-exhaustive list of conduct that would amount to an abuse of dominant position. It includes practices such as:

a) directly or indirectly imposing an unfair purchase or selling price or other unfair trading conditions on a supplier or customer;
b) limiting or controlling production, market outlets or market access, technical or technological development, or investment, to the prejudice of customers;
c) refusing to supply to particular enterprises or group or category of enterprises;
d) applying different conditions to equivalent transactions with other trading parties to an extent that may
   (i) discourage market entry or expansion or investment by an existing competitor; or
   (ii) force from the market or otherwise seriously damage an existing competitor which is no less efficient than the enterprise in a dominant position; or
   (iii) harm competition in any market in which the dominant enterprise is participating or in any upstream or downstream market;

44 Vince Teong, "Competition Act 2010: Issues and Challenges," 602.
45 Vince Teong, "Competition Act 2010: Issues and Challenges," 602.

e) forcing conditions in a contract that have no connection with the subject matter of the contract; or
f) any predatory behaviour towards competitors; or
g) buying up scarce supplies of goods or services where there is no reasonable commercial justification.

Section 10(3) of the Act provides a defence: a dominant enterprise is not precluded from engaging in conduct that has reasonable commercial justification or represents a reasonable commercial response to the market entry or market conduct of a competitor, the so-called meeting the competition defence.[46] The defence will have to be raised in response to the MyCC's allegations of an abuse of dominant position. The onus of proof of the reasonable commercial justification or response lies on the dominant enterprise.[47] Proving reasonable commercial justification or response may not be a straightforward task. Reliance on COVID-19 and its aftermath is in itself inadequate as it has to be based on how the market structure itself has been affected for the enterprise concerned and its competitors.

A dominant enterprise should be punished for any anti-competitive behaviour that impedes the control of the epidemic and hampers economic recovery, including unfair unilateral price hikes, tying, predatory behaviour, and discriminatory conduct. It is important to protect consumers and other market players from unfair, unconscionable, and unjust commercial practices. Most jurisdictions have either issued a cautionary note or recommendation discouraging such conduct.

As a rule of thumb, the MyCC, before identifying the type of abuse, would first have to consider whether the enterprise is dominant. The MyCC has stated that it will consider a market share above 60% as indicative that an enterprise is dominant.[48] This figure is on the higher end of the scale amongst jurisdictions around the world but is similar to that of Singapore. However, Section 10(4) of the Act makes it clear that market share is "not conclusive as to whether that enterprise occupies, or does not occupy, a dominant position".[49] Apart from market share, there are other factors that would be taken into consideration in assessing whether an

46 The MyCC has provided some examples of situations where such a defence could be relied on: (i) refusing to sell to a buyer who did not pay for past purchase, (ii) refusing to grant access to a dominant enterprise's infrastructure that is already being used to capacity, (iii) offering a loyalty rebate that is related to the reduced costs of supplying a particular customer, and (iv) meeting a competitor's price even though the price may be below cost in the short term. MyCC Guidelines on Chapter 2 Prohibition – Abuse of Dominant Position, para 5.2.

47 Sharan Tan, "Malaysia: Overview," 11.

48 MyCC Guidelines on Chapter 2 Prohibition – Abuse of Dominant Position, para 2.2.

49 MyCC Guidelines on Chapter 2 Prohibition – Abuse of Dominant Position, para 2.12. For example, even if an enterprise has high market share, it would not be considered dominant if it is not in a position to increase price above the current level due to the possibility of new entrants or imports.

enterprise is dominant. These include the degree of product differentiation, barriers to entry, and countervailing buyer power.[50]

Penalties

An enterprise that is found to have infringed the Act (i.e. engaged in anti-competitive agreements or has abused its dominant position) may be subject to financial penalties of up to 10% of the worldwide turnover of the enterprise over the period of infringement.[51] This penalty is higher than that in other jurisdictions where the penalty imposed is limited to a specified maximum number of years.[52] The MyCC has issued a set of Guidelines on Financial Penalties,[53] which explains how the appropriate fine will be determined and the factors that may be taken into account in any particular case.[54] The Guidelines specify a set of aggravating factors[55] and a non-exhaustive list of mitigating factors, including "co-operation by the enterprise in the investigation".[56]

Section 61(a) of the CA 2010 also provides general penalties for persons who obstruct the MyCC's investigations by giving false or misleading information, evidence, or documents and destroys or alters the record. The general penalties cover body corporate and non-body corporate.[57] The penalty could involve a term of imprisonment and/or a fine.[58]

---

50 MyCC Guidelines on Chapter 2 Prohibition – Abuse of Dominant Position, paras 2.18–2.20.
51 Competition Act 2010, s 40(4).
52 For example, in Singapore, under s 69(4) of the Singapore Competition Commission Act 2004, the financial penalty may not exceed 10% of such turnover of the business of the undertaking in Singapore for each year of infringement, up to a maximum of 3 years. The fine is limited to 10% of the overall annual turnover of the company.
53 MyCC Guidelines on Financial Penalties available at https://www.mycc.gov.my/sites/default/files/pdf/newsroom/Guildline-on-Financial-Penalties.pdfhttps://www.mycc.gov.my/sites/default/files/pdf/newsroom/Guildline-on-Financial-Penalties.pdf
54 MyCC Guidelines on Financial Penalties, para 3.2.
55 MyCC Guidelines on Financial Penalties, para 3.4.
56 MyCC Guidelines on Financial Penalties, para 3.5.
57 Elaine Law Soh Ying, "Overview of Competition Law in Malaysia," *Mondaq*, February 18, 2016, https://www.mondaq.com/antitrust-eu-competition-/467510/overview-of-competition-law-in-malaysia.
58 Competition Act 2010, s 61(b).

Responses and Measures

Horizontal Agreements – Crisis Cartels

Crisis cartels, as the term implies, are used broadly to describe collaborations or joint actions taken by competitors during and as a result of an economic crisis. These agreements may have as their object to reduce overcapacity or agree on prices to prevent undertakings from going bankrupt or leaving the market. However, a business may be reluctant to cooperate due to the risk of competition law enforcement; it acts as a deterrent. Crisis-related collaborations between private sector firms that are not approved by the state, and which restrict competition (e.g. whether to fix prices, set quantities, set market shares, limit production, rig bids, and even share competitive data) are deemed illegal under the CA 2010. Cartels that are enforced or directed by the state (or exempted by the relevant competition authority) are beyond the reach of antitrust enforcement.[59] Permitting crisis cartels may involve exchanging information (e.g. sales data, capacity data, and demand data for rationing purposes), sharing of distribution networks, and pooling of staff. These while well-intentioned are likely to be illegal as it decreases the incentives to compete and reduces the decision-making independence of the parties. The purpose for coordination between competitors relates to alleviating shortages and ensuring the continuity of supply of essential goods and services.

In most jurisdictions, the law against cartels incorporates three elements: prohibition, exemption, and penalty. There are two principles that govern the approach adopted by countries towards prohibiting the anti-competitive conduct of cartels. Under a per se prohibition, cartelistic behaviour is per se illegal. Under a *rule of reason* approach, cartelistic behaviour may be permitted to some extent, but sufficient regulation is exercised to prevent any harm induced by such activities. Any collaboration between competitors needs to be examined to ensure that it does not infringe competition law.

In the EU, the European Court of Justice (ECJ) has indicated the acceptance of crisis cartels in emergency situations in cases of force majeure. The ECJ, in the case of *Compagnie Royal Asturienne des Mines SA and Rheinzink GbmH v the Commission*,[60] held that an agreement of long duration between competitors concerning the supply of goods constitutes a violation of the prohibition of anti-competitive agreements. However, such an agreement could be allowed in certain circumstances if the object was to avoid emergency situations in cases of force majeure. This

---

59 Shanti Kandiah, "Covid-19 and Crisis Cartels – Can Cartels Be Good for Recovery?," *The Star*, April 2, 2020 https://www.thestar.com.my/business/business-news/2020/04/02/covid-19-and-crisis-cartels–can-cartels-be-good-for-recovery.

60 Judgment of the Court (Fourth Chamber) of 28 March 1984. *Compagnie Royale Asturienne des Mines SA and Rheinzink GmbH v Commission of the European Communities*. Case C-29/83.

judgement indicates that there may be limited scope for such arrangements if the circumstances are so exceptional that it can be considered a real crisis.

There are other instances where such coordination between competitors has been permitted. The parties concerned had invoked art 101(3) of the Treaty of the Functioning of the EU[61] to justify their conduct. The parties in the following sectors,[62] (synthetic fibres, Dutch bricks, and Irish beef) suffered declines in demand which led to issues of structural overcapacity. In each case, rival undertakings agreed to reduce capacity in an agreed and concerted way, rather than allow market forces to remedy the problem.

Crisis cartels are not a new feature. During the last century, such cartels have also appeared in times of crisis, with examples being the nineteenth-century German crisis, the post-war era Japanese crisis, the US crisis during the great depression of the 1930s, and the South East Asian financial crisis in 1997.

Does the COVID-19 situation warrant the formation of "crisis cartels"? Competition regulators around the world have issued statements concerning the application of competition law in their respective jurisdictions during the current crisis. The US and EU competition authorities[63] were quick to pledge they would not enforce the cartel laws against companies collaborating to deal with supply disruptions during the corona crisis. Both the US federal antitrust authorities, the Department of Justice and the Federal Trade Commission (see Joint Statement, 24 March 2020), and the European Commission (see Temporary Framework Communication, 8 April 2020) have stated that, exceptionally, they will offer rapid guidance to businesses seeking clarification as to the compatibility of COVID-19-related business cooperation with competition law.

Broadly, in line with similar announcements made by other authorities (dealt with in ensuing discussion), these agencies have made it clear that collaborative activities between manufacturers, distributors, or purchasers (such as research and development, technical know-how or asset-sharing arrangements, information exchanges, joint production, transportation, storage, or purchasing agreements) may be compatible with competition rules where:

---

61 The balancing of anti-competitive effects is conducted exclusively within the framework laid down by art 101(3) TFEU. The EU's guidelines examine the four conditions of art 101(3) TFEU (i) efficiency gains; (ii) fair share for consumers; (iii) indispensability of the restrictions; and (iv) no elimination of competition.

62 EU's reaction to historical crises in the markets for synthetic fibres (Commission Decision 84/380/EEC), Dutch bricks (Commission Decision 94/296/EC) and – most importantly – Irish beef (Case C-209/07).

63 Antitrust: Joint statement by the European Competition Network (ECN) on application of competition law during the Corona crisis, *Antitrust Case Law e-Bulletin*, March 23, 2020. The UK and a few member states had been even quicker. For example, the Dutch ACM head Martijn Snoep already made similar statements on 19 March in the press presentation of its 2019 annual report.

- the firms are working to benefit consumers by increasing output, or overcoming shortfalls, of vital products and services (such as medication, medical equipment, transport, food, energy, and broadband); and
- the arrangements are limited in scope and duration to that which is required during the period of the epidemic.

Therefore, it seems that many forms of coordination that would not be acceptable in normal situations become not only possible but necessary, especially when they are justified in the context of joint efforts to address the immediate needs of the pandemic. This is especially true when it comes to joint efforts for the production or distribution of essential goods or directly linked to the health sector.[64]

The OECD states that the term crisis cartel has been used in two ways: to a cartel between private firms that are not approved by the state or to an agreement between firms that a government body sanctions during a period of economic distress. The first type of crisis cartel may contravene the competition law of the jurisdiction in question, while the second type of crisis cartel may well require an exemption from that law.[65] Therefore, it is for the competition authorities to decide how much priority to give to cartel enforcement and whether that priority should change over the business cycle.

In Israel, its competition authority has issued a short statement addressing the possibility of cooperation between competitors in this imminent "time of crisis". It stressed that such cooperation would remain subject to the competition rules. The decisions will depend on the specific circumstances of the case in question.[66] The Hong Kong Competition Commission has stated that while it will continue its operations to enforce the Competition Commission Ordinance 2015, which remains in effect during the COVID-19 outbreak, the Commission also recognizes that there could

64 Jonathan Watson, "The Challenge of Covid-19 for Competition Rules," Internal Bar Association, September 22, 2020, https://www.ibanet.org/Article/NewDetail.aspx?ArticleUid=9DC34AA3-CB52-4F2F-B110-11413A42306E.

65 "OECD Policy Roundtables Crisis Cartels," 2011 DAF/COMP/GF(2011) 11, accessed February 12, 2020, http://www.oecd.org/daf/competition/cartels/48948847.pdf.

66 The ICA emphasizes that the terms of the Block Exemption, which include the demonstration of economic necessity and a competitive analysis showing lack of significant harm to competition, continue to apply. **Nonetheless, and most importantly, the ICA notes that one of the considerations to be taken in the framework of the competitive assessment under the Block Exemption is the continued existence of effective competition is the long run, where business entities are currently unable to operate regularly.** Thus, collaborations that allow such struggling competitors to continue to exist will not be seen by the ICA as collaborations "whose objective is to reduce or prevent competition", and will not be deemed illegal for that reason alone. The ICA also recognizes that, in this time of crisis, more collaborations may fall within the framework of the Block Exemption than would normally be the case. Hersog Fox and Neeman, "Israeli Competition Authority Addresses Covid-19 Pandemic," *Lexology*, April 19, 2020, https://www.lexology.com/library/detail.aspx?g=03fb8071-c8d3-4273-b386-9fc3921e4cfb.

be a need for additional cooperation between businesses in certain industries on a temporary basis. The UK Competition and Markets Authority has also relaxed some elements of competition law to help supermarkets work together to ensure the security of supplies of essential products and services, such as groceries. However, it has also warned that it "will not tolerate unscrupulous business exploiting the crisis as a 'cover' for non-essential collusion".[67]

Jurisdictions such as Australia and New Zealand have granted exemptions. The exemptions have been termed as interim or provisional authorization. In Australia, to protect the supply of essential goods, services, medicines, and equipment to respond to the COVID-19 pandemic and facilitate hardship relief, the Australian Competition and Consumer Commission has temporarily authorized (i.e. granted statutory immunity) coordination between competitors in a number of industries that might otherwise contravene Australia's competition laws, including cartel laws. The New Zealand Government amended the Commerce Act 1986 to make an authorization for competitor collaboration more workable in COVID-19 conditions. The authorization is available where social benefits (generally economic efficiencies) exceed anti-competitive detriments. The Competition Agency of Canada has also stated that competitor collaborations aimed at short-term responses to the COVID-19 crisis that are in the public interest will generally not be subject to scrutiny from the Bureau provided that they are good-faith collaborations that do not go further than needed.[68] Regulators have provided for a process by which firms can request informal guidance from the Bureau on such collaborations has been established.

It is evident that most jurisdictions have acknowledged the need for cooperation and coordination between enterprises. Some authorities have considered granting exemptions, while a few have created a process by which enterprises can request informal guidance on collaborations.[69] The competition regulators in the UK[70] and China[71] have also provided clear guidelines as to when will such an exemption be granted.

67 "Coronavirus (COVID 19) and application of the UK Competition Law," *Lexis Nexis*, March 26, 2020, https://www.lexisnexis.co.uk/legal/news/coronavirus-covid-19-application-of-uk-competition-law

68 "Competition Bureau Statement on Competitor Collaborations During the COVID-19 Pandemic," Competition Bureau Canada, April 20, 2020, https://www.canada.ca/en/competition-bureau/news/2020/04/competition-bureau-statement-on-competitor-collaborations-during-the-covid-19-pandemic.html.

69 As in New Zealand and Canada.

70 Nick Pimlott, "Competition Law and Covid 19 – Where Are We Now?," *Fieldfisher*, April 7, 2020, https://www.fieldfisher.com/en/insights/competition-law-and-covid-19-%E2%80%93-where-are-we-now.

71 Jet Deng and Ken Dai, "Covid-19: Chinese Antitrust Regulators Have Taken Actions," *Mondaq*, May 11, 2020, https://www.mondaq.com/china/operational-impacts-and-strategy/930528/covid-19-chinese-antitrust-regulators-have-taken-actions.

Abuse of Dominant Position

Abuse of dominant position is a central concern of competition law, and consequently, all competition law regimes have measures that seek to control the exercise of such power. Competition law does not per se punish the existence of a dominant position or its creation. Only the abuse by dominant firms is subject to antitrust screening. Besides providing guidance on possible collaborations, most competition authorities have also sent a clear message that they will not permit enterprises to strategically use the excuse of the economic crisis to implement anti-competitive practices such as abuse of market power and pricing abuses by dominant enterprises.

For example, the Korean Fair Trade Commission launched a formal investigation regarding market abuses connected to the COVID-19 pandemic. Fifty-nine distributors were caught hoarding 4.49 million face masks and about 100,000 bottles of hand sanitizer in warehouses.[72] The government passed a law imposing heavier fines on companies that tried to profit from the coronavirus outbreak.[73] The new regulation will punish anyone or a company that engages in the hoarding of face masks by imposing a prison sentence of a maximum of 2 years or a maximum fine of 50 million won ($42,108).[74]

Another example would be South Africa. The Competition Act 1998 of South Africa prohibits excessive pricing. The Minister of Trade, Industry and Competition has published specific regulations to deal with price gouging by "dominant" suppliers during this period. These regulations prohibit dominant suppliers from charging excessive prices for certain specified goods and services (mainly basic food and consumer items; medical and hygiene supplies; and emergency and emergency clean-up products and services). The regulations provide that "a material price increase" by a dominant supplier of specified critical medical equipment and basic consumer goods, which does not correspond to or is not equivalent to an increase in cost, or which increases the net margin or mark-up on the product or service above the average margin or mark-up in the 3-month period, will be a "relevant and critical factor" in determining whether the price is "excessive" in terms of the Competition Act.[75]

In Japan, although the Japan Fair Trade Commission (JFTC) has not launched any investigation in relation to COVID-19, it has requested that trade associations

---

72 "59 Distributors Caught Hoarding 4.5 Million Masks: Police," *Yonhap New Agency*, March 4, 2020, https://en.yna.co.kr/view/AEN20200304005900315.

73 Lee Han-soo, "Korea to Impose Tougher Penalties Against Face Mask Hoarding," *Korea Biomedical Review*, February 4, 2020, https://www.koreabiomed.com/news/articleView.html?idxno=7363.

74 Lee Han-soo, "Korea to Impose Tougher Penalties Against Face Mask Hoarding," *Korea Biomedical Review*, February 4, 2020, https://www.koreabiomed.com/news/articleView.html?idxno=7363.

75 Michael-James Currie and John Oxenham, "The South African Competition Tribunal Publishes Its Written Reasons to Penalize a Pharmaceutical Chain for Excessive Pricing," *Concurrences*, July 7, 2020, https://www.concurrences.com/en/bulletin/news-issues/july-2020/the-south-african-competition-tribunal-publishes-its-written-reasons-to.

notify their members that a tying sale of unnecessary products with face masks can be a violation of the competition law.[76] If the JFTC formally initiates an investigation against a case in relation to COVID-19, the investigation may lead to a cease-and-desist order and a surcharge order.

The EU has also issued a joint statement. The statement identifies excessive pricing as a particular area of concern stressing that: "it is of utmost importance to ensure that products considered essential to protect the health of consumers in the current situation (e.g., face masks and sanitising gel) remain at competitive prices".[77] It was stressed that "a crisis is not a shield against competition law enforcement and the EC will stay even more vigilant than in normal times if there is a risk of virus-profiteering".[78]

Competition authorities have also stressed that a dominant enterprise will not be exempted from any form of abuse of dominant position. The responses have either been in the form of a new law, regulation, or notification as in South Korea, South Africa, and Japan.

However, there are jurisdictions where the competition authorities have not taken any action with regard to excessive pricing. For example, in Singapore, there has been no report of any investigations in relation to any action taken by the Competition and Consumer Commission of Singapore under the abuse of dominance provisions. This is because the Price Controller appointed by the Ministry of Trade and Industry has powers under the Price Control Act 1950 to enter premises of any trader, manufacturer, or producer and to examine books, accounts, or other documents and require parties to furnish information in relation to explain their business. In this regard, the Price Controller has recently exercised its powers to require sellers of surgical masks who have sold these masks at higher-than-normal prices to explain the basis of their selling prices, including their cost price

---

76 "Covid-19 Pandemic: The Reactions of Competition Authorities to the Covid-19 Pandemic – An IBA Contribution," IBA Antitrust Committee, International Bar Association, June 2020, file:///C:/Users/tadnan/Downloads/Antitrust-June-2020-Covid19-Matrix.pdf.

77 George S. Cary, Maurits J. F. M. Dolmans, Bruce Hoffman, Thomas Graf, Leah Brannon, Richard Pepper, Henry Mostyn, Alexis R. B. Lazda, Savannah Haynes, Kristi Georgieva, Jan Przerwa, "Exploitative Abuses, Price Gouging & COVID-19: The Cases Pursued by EU and National Competition Authorities," *Concurrences* April 30, 2020, https://www.concurrences.com/en/bulletin/special-issues/competition-law-covid-19-en/exploitative-abuses-price-gouging-covid-19-the-cases-pursued-by-eu-and-national-en.

78 George S. Cary, Maurits J. F. M. Dolmans, Bruce Hoffman, Thomas Graf, Leah Brannon, Richard Pepper, Henry Mostyn, Alexis R. B. Lazda, Savannah Haynes, Kristi Georgieva, Jan Przerwa, "Exploitative Abuses, Price Gouging & COVID-19: The Cases Pursued by EU and National Competition Authorities," Concurrences April 30, 2020, https://www.concurrences.com/en/bulletin/special-issues/competition-law-covid-19-en/exploitative-abuses-price-gouging-covid-19-the-cases-pursued-by-eu-and-national-en.

and profit margins.[79] If these businesses fail to respond to the request for information, they may be fined up to S$10,000 for a first offence and up to S$20,000 for second and subsequent offences. However, other than the issuance of these letters, the authorities may only take further action (e.g. penalties for pricing above fixed prices set by law) under the Price Control Act if the goods in question have been designated as price regulated goods.

Therefore, should the MyCC relax enforcement of some of the competition rules to accommodate the challenges brought about by the COVID-19 pandemic? The MyCC has yet to announce any clarification pertaining to the enforcement of competition law during and subsequent to the MCO.

Conclusion

Although Malaysia's competition rules prohibit horizontal and vertical anti-competitive agreements (as provided for in Part I of the CA 2010) and abuse of a dominant position (as specified in Part II of the CA 2010), there are two areas that permit flexibility. One is the requirement that an exemption is permissible if the specified four cumulative conditions in Section 5 of the Act are met. The other is when an enterprise is caught for an infringement under Section 4, it may apply for relief under Section 5 of the Act. In both instances, the enterprise concerned will have to provide compelling evidence to satisfy the MyCC that the benefits to competition outweigh the detriments.

Competition law also prohibits the abuse of dominant position. However, the dominant enterprise is not precluded from engaging in conduct that has reasonable commercial justification or represents a reasonable commercial response, the so-called meeting the competition defence. Given the situation, the MyCC should issue a notice stating the circumstances in which such a defence may be considered.

It is imperative that the MyCC exercises its advocacy and enforcement functions as prescribed under Section 16 of the Competition Commission Act 2010. The MyCC's advocacy function is not limited to merely educating the public but also includes providing advice and considering and making recommendations to the Malaysian Government on reforms to the competition laws. The MyCC is well placed to assist the Government in ensuring that the regulations under consideration do not unduly restrict competition. As for its enforcement powers, the MyCC should provide clear guidelines[80] regarding

---

79 "Covid-19 Pandemic: The Reactions of Competition Authorities to the Covid-19 Pandemic – An IBA Contribution," IBA Antitrust Committee, International Bar Association, June 2020, file:///C:/Users/tadnan/Downloads/Antitrust-June-2020-Covid19-Matrix.pdf.

80 The MyCC may issue an announcement, public recommendations, guidelines. It may also issue warnings or statements regarding excessive pricing that will have a dissuasive effect on enterprises from engaging in price gouging, particularly if such soft warnings are complemented by investigations into collective price fixing.

the circumstances under which an enterprise that is a party to such an agreement may relieve its liability for infringement. This is to ensure that Section 5 is not utilized as a free pass for businesses to engage in conduct that could harm consumers.

Given the troubling circumstances brought about by the pandemic, it is vital that the MyCC clearly communicates how the principles of competition law enforcement will apply in the context of the crisis so that there is clarity on what is permitted and prohibited in these such circumstances. This communication will also increase (i) the consumers' awareness of potential exploitation and (ii) the reputational risks for enterprises if they are found to have engaged in anti-competitive practices. The communication can be in any form and should also stipulate the duration for which it will be in force.

Shanthy Thuraisingham and Danusha Rachagan

7 Discussions on Human Rights and the Rule of Law in the COVID-19 Reality

Introduction

The COVID-19 pandemic has created devastating health and socio-economic problems in societies around the world. Further, the virus has had an unequal impact on groups and, unfortunately, it has been found that the poor and vulnerable have been more acutely affected.[1] As countries tried to manage the pandemic, several policy measures have had to be taken by the respective governments, directly impacting people's human rights. Adopting effective responses to the pandemic whilst upholding human rights is the sensitive task that governments have had to embark on, in this global health crisis. Governments have empowered authorities to impose restrictions on individual freedoms and movement. This is done by suspending constitutional norms and by using directions that bypass the usual parliamentary scrutiny. However, it is double jeopardy as the pandemic itself has created significant health-related and socio-economic impacts on different groups in society; and the policy response has in some instances also negatively impacted human rights.[2] It has been said that the disruption caused by the pandemic has not only damaged human rights but also created an environment for human rights abuses to take place freely under the pretext of coronavirus protection measures.

The Secretary General of the Council of Europe, Marija Pejčinović Burić, issued a toolkit for governments across Europe on respecting human rights, democracy and the rule of law during the COVID-19 crisis. The Secretary General said:

> The virus is destroying many lives and much else of what is very dear to us. We should not let it destroy our core values and free societies. The major social, political and legal challenge facing our member states will be their ability to respond to this crisis effectively, whilst ensuring that the measures they take do not undermine our genuine long-term interest in safeguarding Europe's founding values of human rights, democracy and the rule of law.[3]

---

1 J.A. Patel, F.B.H. Nielsen, A.A.Badiani, S. Assi, V.A. Unadkat, B. Patel, R. Ravindrane, and H. Wardle, "Poverty, Inequality and COVID-19: The Forgotten Vulnerable," *Public Health* 183 (June 2020): 110–111, https://doi.org/10.1016/j.puhe.2020.05.006.

2 "Law, Justice and Development Week, COVID-19 and Human Rights: Impacts and Lessons Learned," The World Bank, November 17, 2020, https://www.worldbank.org/en/events/2020/10/07/ljdweek2020-covid-19-and-human-rights.

3 Michael Cross, "Governments Warned on Rule of Law During Covid-19 Lockdown," *The Law Society Gazette*, April 8, 2020, https://www.lawgazette.co.uk/law/governments-warned-on-rule-of-law-during-covid-19-lockdown/5103816.article.

https://doi.org/10.1515/9783110723694-007

The toolkit is designed to help ensure that measures taken by the European member states to restrain the spread of the virus remain proportional to the threat posed by the spread of the virus and are also limited in time.

According to the McKinsey report,[4] the measures introduced by countries around the world to limit the reach of the virus have affected human rights in three main areas:

1. It limits on personal movement. This includes physical distancing, imposing lockdowns, restricting public gatherings and quarantine.
2. Health information and reporting. This includes COVID-19 testing, temperature testing, health surveys and collection of data by public authorities.
3. Health tracing. This includes manual and automated tracking and contact-tracing mechanisms and apps, by both public and private companies.

This chapter examines the challenges that countries face in times of emergency in relation to their constitutional framework, the imposition of restrictive measures such as lockdowns and data collection to curb the spread of the virus, and the challenging balance to uphold and fulfil human rights obligations and the rule of law. It focuses on two key areas that impact human rights in times of a crisis or emergency:

1. Derogation of Human Rights in times of emergency – respect for the rule of law and democratic principles in times of emergency, including limits on the scope and duration of emergency measures and to avoid potentially disproportionate measures.
2. Fundamental human rights standards, including freedom of expression, privacy, and data protection.

Limitations and Derogations of Human Rights in Time of Emergency

Though human rights put people in center stage, however, in times of crises it is often the first casualty. For governments confronted with civil wars, military coup. insurgencies, economic crises, natural disasters, and similar threats, the pressures to restrict individual liberties can be irresistible. International law scholars have

4 Daniel Mikkelsen, Henning Soller, and Malin Strandell-Jansson, "How Can European Companies Best Prevent Measures Intended to Control the COVID-19 Pandemic from also Undermining Data Privacy and Security? Privacy, Security, and Public Health in a Pandemic Year," McKinsey & Company, June 15, 2020, https://www.mckinsey.com/business-functions/risk/our-insights/privacy-security-and-public-health-in-a-pandemic-year.

long recognised that "the response of a state to a public emergency is an acid test of its commitment to the effective implementation of human rights".[5]

Emergency powers provide a situation in which governments are authorised within limited boundaries to be able to put through special powers that it would normally not be permitted to do, primarily for the safety and protection of their citizens. Most democracies have a range of special powers available to respond to emergencies that threaten safety, property, or the integrity of the state. The normal workings of legislative and executive powers that have been established by a country's constitution are set aside when these special powers are approved and put in place. What these special powers do is to confer broad regulation-making powers in an official within the executive government. Once these special powers are triggered, the executive government is authorised to make regulations with respect to whatsoever is believed to be necessary to respond to the emergency. The vulnerability of this is that it is free from normal processes of parliamentary scrutiny.[6]

A derogation of a right or an aspect of a right is its complete or partial elimination as an international obligation.[7] Derogation "refers to the legally mandated authority of states", who are otherwise bound by the obligations of treaties or constitutions, "to suspend certain civil and political liberties, in response to crises" and "can be justified solely by the concern to return to normality".[8] Derogations are a type of "escape clause" found in many accords.[9]

Human rights are often the first casualties of a crisis. Hence, the concept of derogation can be traced back to governments that recognised "flexibility in the face of unpredictability".[10] Governments also appreciated the need for limitations to invoke and maintain states of emergency that would uphold the democratic order.[11]

---

5 Dominic McGoldrick, "The Interface Between Public Emergency Powers and International Law," *International Journal of Constitutional Law* 2, no. 2 (April 2004): 380–429, https://doi.org/10.1093/icon/2.2.380.

6 H. P. Lee, Michael W. R. Adams, Colin Campbell and Patrick Emerton, *Emergency Powers in Australia* (Cambridge: Cambridge University Press, 2019).

7 Joan Hartman, "Derogations from Human Rights Treaties in Public Emergencies," *Harvard International Law Journal* 22, no. 1 (Winter 1981): 1–52.

8 Emilie M. Hafner-Burton, Laurence R. Helfer and Christopher J. Fariss, "Emergency and Escape: Explaining Derogations from Human Rights Treaties," *International Organization* 65, no. 4 (October 2011): 673–707.

9 Laurence R. Helfer, Flexibility in International Agreements, in Interdisciplinary Perspectives on International Law and International Relations 175, 186 (Jeffrey L. Dunoff & Mark A. Pollack eds., 2013).

10 Dominic McGoldrick, "The Interface Between Public Emergency Powers and International Law," *International Journal of Constitutional Law* 2, no. 2 (April 2004): 380–429, 383, https://doi.org/10.1093/icon/2.2.380.

11 Oren Gross and Fionnuala Ní Aoláin, *Law in Times of Crisis: Emergency Powers in Theory and Practice* (Cambridge: Cambridge University Press, 2006), 365–420.

Human rights are the fundamental principles which underpin all societies where there is rule of law and democracy.[12] Under international human rights law, countries can limit the exercise of most human rights if it is necessary to protect the rights of others or collective interests. The exceptional circumstances brought by the COVID-19 pandemic has led to more extensive restrictions globally, on both scope and length of time, of human rights than in usual times.

Today, against this backdrop, it is even more essential that policy responses be firmly grounded in human rights, and that governments comply with the obligation to respect and protect human rights.

Carl Schmitt as the theorist who claimed that a state of emergency is the moment that shows who in a country is the sovereign. Legislators and laws, even the constitution, may be set aside when the true sovereign, typically a President or Prime Minister, declares a state of emergency.[13]

For example, in Malaysia, the country's constitutional monarch, declared a nationwide state of emergency on 12 January 2021 at the Prime Minister's request. This is the first of its kind for more than 50 years, the last being in 1969 when there were racial riots in Malaysia. Prime Minister Muhyiddin Yassin asserted that the emergency declaration was definitely not a coup but the Covid-19 pandemic was pushing Malaysia's healthcare system to the brink of collapse. He averred the emergency was implemented because it would allow the police and military to have extra powers to battle the pandemic. "It's more about holding on to power, but the mechanism would not have been possible without the pandemic being there," said Bridget Welsh, an honorary research associate with the University of Nottingham's Asia Research Institute in Malaysia.[14] The concern often is that when a leader in a country is not able to maintain his or her power, there is reliance on emergency powers to help maintain power. The unique political situation in Malaysia is that after an unexpected shift in political alliances brought down the ruling government, the King appointed Muhyiddin Prime Minister in February 2020, ushering in a new ruling coalition of parties without holding a general election.

Some human rights treaties allow for the more far-reaching option of a country to derogate from some of its obligations during a situation of crisis. This applies to other than so-called non-derogable rights under the UN-level International Covenant

12 "Human Rights: Handbook for Parliamentarians No. 26," Office of the United Nations High Commissioner for Human Rights (OHCHR) and the Inter-Parliamentary Union (IPU), (2016), accessed February 23, 2021, https://www.ohchr.org/documents/publications/handbookparliamentarians.pdf.

13 Martin Scheinin, "COVID-19 Symposium: To Derogate or Not to Derogate?," *OpinoJuris*, April 6, 2020, http://opiniojuris.org/2020/04/06/covid-19-symposium-to-derogate-or-not-to-derogate/.

14 Zsombor Peter, "Motivation Behind Malaysia's State of Emergency Questioned," *Voice of America*, January 14, 2021, https://www.voanews.com/east-asia-pacific/motivation-behind-malaysias-state-emergency-questioned.

on Civil and Political Rights (ICCPR, see article 4) and the American Convention on Human Rights (see article 27) and the European Convention on Human Rights (ECHR, see article 15). Article 4 of the ICCPR permits countries to derogate temporarily from some of their ICCPR obligations in times of public emergency. This means that in certain circumstances, a country can suspend ICCPR obligations. Article 4(1) reads:

> In time of public emergency which threatens the life of the nation and the existence of which is officially proclaimed, the States Parties . . . . . . may take measures derogating from their obligations . . . . to the extent strictly required by the exigencies of the situation, provided that such measures are not inconsistent with their other obligations under international law and do not involve discrimination solely on the ground of race, colour, sex, language, religion or social origin.

When a government decides to derogate temporarily from some of their ICCPR obligations in times of public emergency with powerful presence of police and other security personnel, numerous challenges can surface, including the perception of bias, disparate use of force or the use of excessive force and other human rights issues. There is also a probability that some governments may exploit the use of emergency powers to consolidate executive authority at the detriment of the rule of law by stifling dissent and undermining democratic institutions, especially where courts and other oversight bodies struggle to perform due to COVID-related restrictions.

European Court of Human Rights defined "other public emergency threatening the life of the nation" as "an exceptional situation of crisis or emergency which affects the whole population and constitutes a threat to the organised life of the community of which the State is composed".[15] The international law is structured around the principle of state supremacy. This ensures the independence of countries. Internally, countries have control on the lawful use of physical force. The country's powers, nonetheless, are not without limits. International human rights conventions impose various conditions and only under these conditions that governments may derogate human rights.

Many derogable rights can be limited without the need to resort to derogation. This simply means that it can be done by proportionate measures prescribed by law to protect public health, such as the right to life. The principle of derogation is itself subject to the principle of proportionality.[16] Therefore, often it is hard to understand why derogation would be required in respect of a right that could be limited by proportionate measures. To further illustrate this point, we just have to take a look at a country's constitution to ascertain if it provides freedom of movement, which is a

15 Lawless v. Ireland [1961] ECHR 2, App no. 332/57 (A/3).

16 Sarah Joseph, "A Timeline of COVID 19 and Human Rights: Derogations in Time of Public Emergency," *Griffith News*, May 5, 2020, https://news.griffith.edu.au/2020/05/05/a-timeline-of-covid-19-and-human-rights-derogations-in-time-of-public-emergency.

derogable right. It may be limited, aside from derogation, by proportionate measures designed to protect certain interests such as public health and the rights of others. The same applies to the freedom of assembly and freedom of association. Many of the lockdown measures have, in fact, impacted those three rights.[17] The difference between valid derogation and the limits could be revoked if derogations somehow incorporate a more respectful notion of proportionality, giving the country more scope to interfere with human rights than under the ordinary limitation clauses.[18]

Derogation is the tool provided under international human rights law to allow countries to deal with public emergencies, such as the COVID-19 pandemic. Many countries have resorted to domestic emergency powers, either nationally or on a regional or local basis. Such powers typically entail rule by decree, that is, the executive assuming law-making powers that normally belong to the elected Parliament. In addition to such a power shift, in most cases, they also allow deviation from constitutionally protected fundamental rights. Emergency powers always carry a higher probability of being abused, often for political purposes such as curtailing dissent, dissolving Parliament, postponing elections or cementing the powers of a dictator.

Due to the risk of abuse, the safe course of action is to insist on handling the crises through normal applicable powers and procedures and in full compliance with human rights. This however has not been followed by a vast number of countries.

The UK introduced what is generally termed "emergency powers" and called it "major incident" but has not declared a state of emergency. The Government managed to convince Parliament to pass legislation allowing additional powers in just a few days.[19] The UK Government's additional powers must be renewed by Parliament after 6 months and will expire completely after a period of 2 years. Unlike the UK, Spain's state of emergency is valid for only 30 days. This however is renewable for another 30 days on the expiration of the first 30 days.

Legally declaring a state of emergency basically allows exceptional powers in extraordinary circumstances. It gives powers to authorities who are not legally elected by the people. This generally is also taken to mean that the mechanism is supposed to prevent such powers from being passed in normal times. If a state of emergency is not declared, this "quarantining effect" of the special powers is lost.

---

17 Sarah Joseph, "A Timeline of COVID 19 and Human Rights: Derogations in Time of Public Emergency," *Griffith News*, May 5, 2020, https://news.griffith.edu.au/2020/05/05/a-timeline-of-covid-19-and-human-rights-derogations-in-time-of-public-emergency.

18 Audrey Lebret, "COVID-19 Pandemic and Derogation to Human Rights," *Journal of Law and the Biosciences* 7, no. 1 (January–June 2020): 1–15, https://doi.org/10.1093/jlb/lsaa015.

19 Alan Greene, "State of Emergency: How Different Countries Are Invoking Extra Powers to Stop the Coronavirus," *The Conversation*, March 31, 2020, https://theconversation.com/state-of-emergency-how-different-countries-are-invoking-extra-powers-to-stop-the-coronavirus-134495.

Instead, countries can pretend that the exceptional measures they have invoked are perfectly compatible with the normal legal framework.

Malaysia's right to derogate is allowed under article 153 of the Constitution of Malaysia. Unfortunately, Malaysia does not have a strong legal and policy framework to protect human rights. One example of this is its lack of participation in the United Nations treaties relevant to equality of rights. It is a party to only three of the major human rights treaties: CEDAW (Committee on the Elimination of Discrimination Against Women), Committee on the Rights of the Child, and CRPD (Committee on the Rights of Persons with Disabilities) and that too is subject to considerable reservations. Malaysia is yet to join many others like the ICCPR and the International Covenant on Economic, Social and Cultural Rights, International Convention on the Elimination of Racial Discrimination, among others. Also, it is impossible for Malaysians whose human rights have been compromised to file complaints and pursue remedies through the relevant complaint procedures as Malaysia has not signed up to the Optional Protocols to CEDAW and CRPD to which it is a party. This goes to show the vulnerability of Malaysians who would like to bring an action in international courts for violation of their human rights.

Another important limitation is that the treaties to which Malaysia is a party do not have direct application but rather must be implemented through the country's legislative bodies. Interestingly, in recent times the courts have created a precedent of direct application of international treaties to which Malaysia is a party in reaching decisions on fundamental rights cases, as demonstrated in the pregnancy discrimination case of Noorfadilla[20] in which CEDAW was applied.[21]

Further, it is interesting to point out that the Philippine President Rodrigo Roa Duterte is reported to have sought Congressional approval to takeover unspecified privately owned utilities and businesses, expanding on existing COVID-19 emergency measures such as checkpoints, lockdowns, and strict quarantines at home already in place.[22] China is reportedly continuing propaganda to control the narrative of its successful government responses in contrast to other countries, without including coverage on the full scope of leadership decision-making's impacts on delays in responses, lack of transparency, and the silencing of whistle-blower doctors such as Li Wenliang.[23] This is difficult to reconcile with the protection of human rights.

---

20 *Noorfadilla bt Ahmad Saikin v Chayed bin Basirun & Ors* [2012] 1 MLJ 832.

21 Accessed February 23, 2021, https://www.equalrightstrust.org/ertdocumentbank/concl.pdf.

22 Martin Petty and Neil Jerome Morales, "Philippine President Seeks Powers Over Firms, Supplies, Funds to Avert Crisis, Emerging Markets," *Reuters*, March 23, 2020, https://www.reuters.com/article/us-health-coronavirus-philippines-idUSKBN21A0GG.

23 Jabin T. Jacob, 'To Tell China's Story Well': China's International Messaging During the COVID-19 Pandemic," *China Report* 56, no. 3 (2020): 374–392, https://doi.org/10.1177/0009445520930395.

In a resolution addressing COVID-19, the Inter-American Commission warned the American states on the risk of excessive measures:

> Even in the most extreme and exceptional cases in which suspension of certain rights may become necessary, international law lays down a series of requirements such as legality, necessity, proportionality and timeliness, which are designed to prevent measures such a state of emergency from being used illegally or in an abusive or disproportionate way, causing human rights violations or harm to the democratic system of government.[24]

The principle of proportionality requires a continuous evaluation of the strict necessity of derogatory measures. This is what countries must do when they review on a regular basis, the need to extend their measures. As doing so will demonstrate that human rights are not suspended, and emergency powers will be controlled. It is best that a government decides to maintain the usual form of normalcy, that is, fight the pandemic within the framework of permissible limitations that are proven necessary and proportionate in pursuit of a legitimate aim. In its recent statement on COVID-19, the Human Rights Committee reiterated the "temporary basis" of countries' exceptional emergency powers. It is critical that parliaments and national judges are in the capacity to scrutinize the "necessity" and "proportionality" of governmental measures.[25]

There are few who doubt that this health crisis is an emergency threatening the life of the nation. If countries have the discretion to determine the emergency, then the international human rights courts will have to in the end scrutinize the need for the measures adopted to overcome the pandemic by applying the "principle of proportionality". It has been said that countries must pay attention to vulnerable populations to ensure they are not disproportionally affected by the measures taken. In other words, they are not suffering hardship in disproportionate measures. In their scrutiny, international courts would rely on different indicia to determine if, at the time they were adopted, less severe measures could have achieved the same results. The duration of those measures will also be considered.[26]

As stated earlier, it has always been understood that emergency powers carry a serious risk of being abused and often for political purposes such as restraining dissent, dissolving parliament, postponing elections, or cementing the powers of a would-be dictator. Therefore, in light of the risk of abuse, the safe course of action is to insist on the principle of normalcy. This means to handle a crisis through normally applicable powers and procedures. There is also a need to insist on full adherence with human rights. This would then mean introducing new necessary and proportionate restrictions upon human rights based on emergency needs cre-

24 Lebret, "COVID-19 Pandemic and Derogation to Human Rights," 1–15.
25 Scheinin, "COVID-19 Symposium."
26 Lebret, "COVID-19 Pandemic and Derogation to Human Rights," 1–15.

ated by the pandemic. It was articulately captured by Alan Greene[27] in a recent blog post, where he said officially declaring a state of emergency and notifying international institutions about measures that derogate from some of their human rights treaty obligations may have the positive effect of humanising emergency powers by constraining the country to express their emergency measures under the terms of necessity, proportionality, pressure of the situation, temporality, and a commitment to human rights as a framework for legitimate emergency measures.[28]

In *A and Others v the United Kingdom*[29] and *Osman Kavala v Turkey*,[30] the European Court of Human Rights held that the emergency legislation at issue had been used by the respondent Governments in bad faith for purposes other than those initially claimed, even for the purposes of impeding the work of human rights defenders and cramping the application of the Convention. Mindful of this danger, the court adopted a strict interpretation of any restrictions imposed on human rights during public emergencies. They delimited the State Parties' power, whereby not only the respect of non-derogable rights in article 15(2) of the European Convention had to be ensured always, but also the respect of all other Convention rights to a minimum extent.

In the present situation, the International Court is no difficulties finding that there is an actual and imminent public emergency threatening the life of the nation. What will be difficult for governments is to prove whether the extraordinary measures taken during the COVID-19 period have been an adequate and that proportionate response to the situation were taken under the circumstances.

It is important to remember the words of António Guterres, UN Secretary-General, April 2020:

> This is a time when, more than ever, governments need to be open and transparent, responsive and accountable to the people they are seeking to protect.[31]

---

27 Alan Greene, "States Should Declare a State of Emergency Using Article 15 ECHR to Confront the Coronavirus Pandemic," *Strasbourg Observers*, April 1, 2020, https://strasbourgobservers.com/2020/04/01/states-should-declare-a-state-of-emergency-using-article-15-echr-to-confront-the-coronavirus-pandemic/.

28 Scheinin, "COVID-19 Symposium."

29 [GC] – 3455/05, Judgment 19.2.2009 [GC], [24], 186–190.

30 Application no. 28749/18, December 10, 2019, 15–16.

31 "United Nations Human Rights Appeals 2021," Office of the High Commissioner, United Nations Human Rights, accessed February 23, 2021, https://www.ohchr.org/Documents/Publications/AnnualAppeal2021.pdf.

Fundamental Human Rights Standards

Privacy

Privacy is said to form the basis of our freedom and data protection is the pillar behind our right to privacy. There cannot be data privacy without data protection.

However, the COVID-19 pandemic is revealing data and technology together can be used to protect human health. For example, the Coronavirus tracing apps, temperature sensing drones, phone apps to monitor social distancing, tech giants sharing smartphone location and mobility data have been introduced to prevent the spreading of the virus. There is, therefore a clear and urgent need to collect, use, and share information to manage the spread of COVID-19. As governments across the world consider a track and trace response, technology companies raced to produce phone applications to trace us to discover if we have been in contact with someone suspected of carrying or of having COVID-19. The question then has to be, which do we value more, our health or our privacy?

As governments grapple with the best way to track and trace cases of the coronavirus, human rights groups are concerned about the increasing intrusion of government surveillance and what it will mean for the rights to privacy and human rights generally. Collecting information about people is nothing new. Governments have done it before. For example, the Malaysian Government requires its citizens to have a personal identification card, Mykad, with personal details such as date of birth, race and other information included. Also, governments have long conducted population data gathering in the form of a census. The difference now is that there are more forms of data that can be collected in a measurable and quantifiable way, which could then be analysed, stored and processed.[32]

Contract tracing is not a new tool. It has been used to control the spread of infectious diseases before, for example, it has been used successfully in efforts to contain Ebola, SARS, MERS, tuberculosis and other disease outbreaks. It is now in most countries a critical part of the fight against COVID-19. Contact tracing enables a targeted approach: rather than imposing a blanket society-wide lockdown, authorities are able to isolate those potentially infected.

The Australian Government has gone to great lengths to reassure citizens their data will be protected, and their privacy assured if they use the COVIDSafe app. It has introduced new public health information legislation to protect privacy, which comes on top of protections under the Biosecurity Act, and published a privacy impact assessment. University of New South Wales faculty of law senior lecturer Katharine Kemp says that the Government is collecting more

32 Rosalyn Page, "COVID-19 and the Privacy Problem," *CMO*, May 11, 2020, https://www.cmo.com.au/article/679047/covid-19-privacy-problem/.

data than they require.[33] So, how do we know unless is challenged in the courts at the end of the pandemic?

The Australian app is based on Singapore's TraceTogether app, which was launched in late March 2020 and has been released as "open-source" code so that it can be used by other countries. There is a high take-up rate of the app in Singapore, approximately 78%, on the assurance by the Government that the information will not be used unless a person has been in close contact with another who is diagnosed with Covid-19. However, in January 2021, a government minister said in Parliament that the police can use TraceTogether data for criminal investigations, and hence back-tracked on the earlier promise. This has eroded the confidence of the Singapore population in the privacy of their personal data.

In contrast, Germany has put privacy ahead of analytics and follows the Google/Apple approach. Although it had initially supported the centralised approach to data gathering, it reversed its approach in reaction to widespread privacy concerns. This change of direction marked a major blow to a homegrown-standardisation effort, called PEPP-PT, that had been aggressively backing centralisation while insisting it was preserving privacy by not tracking location data.[34]

Unfortunately, certain nations have introduced contact tracing and data storage methods that have been highly criticised in Western countries. For example, in South Korea, authorities used location data from cell phones, credit-card transactions, and CCTV footage to identify potentially infected persons. As noted by Jung Ki-suck, the former director of the Centres for Disease Control and Prevention, "people [in South Korea] are OK with their privacy being infringed for the wider public interest".[35]

Taiwan introduced geo-blocking, which has won global praise for its effective action against the coronavirus. The country rolled out a mobile phone-based "electronic fence" that uses location tracking to ensure people who are quarantined stay in their homes. Further, photo tracking was introduced in Poland to confirm that people in quarantine are in their homes. China is using public heat sensors to detect if a person has fever, while heat mapping is being used in the UK and Italy to confirm that people are social distancing. In Singapore, Taiwan, Russia, and Australia location or Bluetooth tracking for mobile phones have been introduced to support the tracing of COVID-19 cases.

---

33 Graham Greenleaf and Katharine Kemp, "The COVIDSafe Bill: Privacy Protections Improved, But More Needed," *UNSW Sydney Newsroom*, May 5, 2020, https://newsroom.unsw.edu.au/news/business-law/covidsafe-bill-privacy-protections-improved-more-needed.

34 Jeffrey L. Turner, "Privacy vs. Security in the Post-Pandemic World," *The National Law Review*, June 12, 2020, https://www.natlawreview.com/article/privacy-vs-security-post-pandemic-world.

35 Michelle Yun, "How Taiwan Is Containing Coronavirus – Despite Diplomatic Isolation by China," *The Guardian*, March 13, 2020, https://www.theguardian.com/world/2020/mar/13/how-taiwan-is-containing-coronavirus-despite-diplomatic-isolation-by-china.

China is also a much-cited example for the use of facial recognition, biometric data, location tracking and other data to generate health-status colour codes. The Government introduced an app-driven access system to help ensure adherence to local regulations. This is the green-amber-red health-code system hosted by Alibaba's mobile payments app and Tencent's messaging app WeChat. Using both self-reported data and data from authorities, the app segments users into three colour codes: green (healthy), amber (contact with an infected individual), and red (symptomatic or tested positive). Those with green classifications can travel freely, whereas those with amber or red classifications may face travel restrictions and quarantine or isolation requirements. An analysis by *The New York Times* of one of the apps indicated that it appeared to share information with police authorities.[36] Even the basis on which the colour codes are assigned is unclear, and the lack of transparency has been criticised. These are just some of the ways technology is being used to increase surveillance of citizens in the name of protection and at the expense of human rights. Then again, when does protection become an infringement on human rights?

Roseann Rife, East Asia research director at Amnesty International, told *Devex* that in times of crisis, people are more likely to consent to expanded state powers due to widespread public fear and she believes this is being taken advantage of. She said:

> Governments in Southeast Asia and across the world have been using COVID-19 as an excuse to widen their powers and to implement lasting and potentially dangerous restrictions on human rights . . . Independent media and civil society play a key role in helping to differentiate between necessary restrictions on rights and freedoms, on one hand, and arbitrary and abusive power grabs, on the other.[37]

However, restrictions on data protection rights should only be of legislative nature that means it is issued by the parliament, and not decided unilaterally by the executive branch. This legal nature of the restriction is protected by article 52(1) of the Charter of Fundamental Rights of the European Union, article 8(2) of the European Convention of Human Rights, and, more recently, article 23 of the General Data Protection Regulation (GDPR).

Restrictions of certain rights, from a legal perspective need to be in line with the GDPR six principles:

36 Paul Mozur, Raymond Zhong and Aaron Krolik, "In Coronavirus Fight, China Givés Citizens a Color Code, with Red Flags: A New System Uses Software to Dictate Quarantines and Appears to Send Personal Data to Police, in a Troubling Precedent for Automated Social Control." *The New York Times*, March 1, 2020, https://www.nytimes.com/2020/03/01/business/china-coronavirus-surveillance.html?smid=em-share.

37 Lisa Cornish, "Tracking COVID-19: What Are the Implications for Privacy and Human Rights?," *Devex*, May 15, 2020, https://www.devex.com/news/tracking-covid-19-what-are-the-implications-for-privacy-and-human-rights-97101.

- *Lawfulness, fairness, and transparency* – it is important to have the power to collect the data and be transparent as to the type of data collected and the reason for collecting it.
- *Purpose limitation* – only personal data for a specific purpose can be collected. This purpose must be clearly stated, and data can only be collected for as long as necessary to complete that purpose.
- *Data minimisation* – they can only process the personal data that they need to achieve its processing purposes.
- *Accuracy* – this is integral. The GDPR states that "every reasonable step must be taken" to erase or rectify inaccurate or incomplete data.
- *Storage limitation* – there is a requirement to delete personal data when it is no longer necessary.
- *Integrity and confidentiality* – this is the only principle that deals explicitly with security. The GDPR states that personal data must be "processed in a manner that ensures appropriate security of the personal data, including protection against unauthorised or unlawful processing and against accidental loss, destruction or damage, using appropriate technical or organisational measures".[38]

However, the above is said to be not at all exhaustive, and it has been recommended that it also must be:
- of an exceptional nature;
- imposed for a limited duration in time (temporary);
- not applied retroactively;
- subject to clear and defined conditions (criteria of "foreseeability").[39]

Accountability

Australian Human Rights Commissioner Edward Santow emphasised the importance at this time to define and understand where the boundaries existed for the breach of surveillance. He said: "In extreme situations like we face now with the COVID-19 pandemic, governments do have greater flexibility to take robust measures to address the

38 Luke Irwin, "The GDPR: Understanding the 6 Data Protection Principles," *IT Governance*, June 30, 2020, https://www.itgovernance.eu/blog/en/the-gdpr-understanding-the-6-data-protection-principles.

39 Florencio Travieso, "Digital Privacy and Covid-19: Between a Paradox and a Hard Place," *The Conversation*, November 17, 2020, https://theconversation.com/digital-privacy-and-covid-19-between-a-paradox-and-a-hard-place-136418.

public health emergency." Santow said, "And that can include restrictions on some human rights which would not be allowed in normal circumstances."[40]

UN Secretary-General António Guterres on 23 April 2020 averred that the Covid-19 pandemic provided some countries with an excuse to adopt oppressive measures for reasons other than the pandemic. He warned that the outbreak risks becoming a human rights crisis.[41]

The question/discussions should revolve around the following:

1. How long is "temporary"?
2. The use of algorithms and artificial intelligence can enable the processing of enough data from users to predict the spread of the pandemic. A global pandemic could, in principle, convince people to accept a certain level of restriction in their civil liberties that could imply a surveillance regime. A logical trade-off must take place between civil liberties, security and public health. Pivotal to this discussion is the compromise between individual privacy and the need to protect public health. Generally, what is acceptable is short-term restrictions of individual liberty being enacted to protect the long-term interests of communities.
3. What can states do with the data collected?
4. The telecommunication companies have access to individuals' data, and the high-tech industry has the tools to process it, and the state must oversee how it is processed and respected. As a precaution, contract-tracing phone apps should be voluntary, guaranteeing users anonymity, data collected should only be needed for the tracing, data retention should be limited to the actual measures, and access to the privileged data should only be given to specific people.[42]

Conclusion

Following the 9/11 attacks, the terms of the debate shifted to another dualistic choice, though a basically different one: privacy vs. security. Interestingly, with practically no debate, security won. Privacy experts[43] are concerned that the extra technological possibilities created during the COVID-19 pandemic will remain after the end of the

40 Cornish, "Tracking COVID-19."

41 "UN Chief Warns against Repressive Measures amid Coronavirus Crisis," *Euractiv*, April 23, 2020, https://www.euractiv.com/section/global-europe/news/un-chief-warns-against-repressive-measures-amid-coronavirus-crisis/.

42 Florencio Travieso, "Digital Privacy and Covid-19: Between a Paradox and a Hard Place," *The Conversation*, November 17, 2020, https://theconversation.com/digital-privacy-and-covid-19-between-a-paradox-and-a-hard-place-136418.

43 David P. Fidler and Lawrence O. Gostin, *Biosecurity in the Global Age: Biological Weapons, Public Health, and the Rule of Law* (Stanford: Stanford University Press, 2008).

pandemic, such as what happened after the 9/11 attacks in the USA.[44] Therefore, governments implementing contact tracing measures should ensure the temporary character of the measures for them to be proportionate to the aim.[45] It is hoped that world leaders, as they continue to discuss joint action to contain and eliminate the spread of the virus, will consider the need to avoid long-term harm to the rule of law principles and fundamental freedoms.

A survey by a polling group found that two-thirds of people in a Council of Europe member state are in favour of government phone tracking to help tackle the COVID-19 pandemic. Does that mean that we should all be willing to allow privacy breaches if they might save lives?[46]

Alessandra Pierucci, Chair of the Council of Europe's Data Protection "Convention 108" Committee, said it very much depends on the way the questions in surveys are submitted. She said if we ask people whether they would prefer to save their life or their privacy, it could be predicted that the answer would be obvious. She said the point is that we should not believe that we are obliged to choose either health or privacy. She went on to say that we should put ourselves into a mental attitude, which is based on the reconciliation of fundamental rights. In that circumstance, she said the answer could be what we want, and we can have both health and privacy. This is not to mention that there are certain rights such as health, where the sacrifice is more self-evident for people. Other rights, such as the right to privacy, whose attrition, at least in the near future, could be less foreseeable but still very serious in terms of consequences for individuals' liberties.[47]

It was said that the most important component needed to prevent the overuse of personal data is a clear definition of the specific purpose, processing and use of it. In this instance, the purpose is to prevent the spread of the virus and curtail the pandemic. It was empathetically said that any other use, for example, commercial or law enforcement, should not be allowed. What is also crucial, Pierucci said was that if special measures are taken in an emergency, like the one we are facing now, it is always important to ensure that these special measures only last as long as the emergency lasts and no longer. Some countries may use this for a prolonged time to suit their own needs such collection of data to find out a whistle-blower. So, it is

44 G. Alex Sinha, "NSA Surveillance Since 9/11 and the Human Right to Privacy," *Loyola Law Review* 59, no. 4 (August 2013): 861–946.

45 Hannah van Kolfschooten and Anniek de Ruijter, "COVID-19 and Privacy in the European Union: A Legal Perspective on Contact Tracing," *Contemporary Security Policy* 41, no. 3 (May 2020): 478–491, https://doi.org/10.1080/13523260.2020.1771509.

46 Alessandra Pierucci, "Data Protection and Privacy," interview by Charles Amponsah, *Council of Europe*, accessed February 3, 2021, video 10:44, https://www.coe.int/en/web/portal/covid-19-health-and-privacy.

47 Alessandra Pierucci, "Data Protection and Privacy," interview by Charles Amponsah, *Council of Europe*, accessed February 3, 2021, video 10:44, https://www.coe.int/en/web/portal/covid-19-health-and-privacy.

important that to prevent further and unexpected use and abuse of data, it should also be erased once the objective has been achieved and the emergency is over.

The effectiveness of these measures, which must be evaluated first, is very much based on the social acceptability and transparency of these tools and on trust rather than on oppression. It is also crucial that there is minimisation of data. This must be ensured, and it means avoiding the processing of any unnecessary data. It is therefore opting for the processing of proximity data rather than location data. This has a more sensitive connotation and it is better to implement solutions that provide for the storing of data in the individuals' devices.

An important question to address is also when will we know that these potentially unprecedented levels of scrutiny will be lifted after the pandemic? We run the risk that some countries might want to continue with high levels of scrutiny indefinitely for their other benefits. There are two elements that must be recalled. First and foremost, even in an emergency, human rights should never be suspended. Human rights can be derogated by law, and only if it is strictly necessary to face the emergency and only ensuring the essence of fundamental rights. Secondly, it is important to ensure that, once the emergency is over, the exceptional measures that were taken are abandoned and that things go back to the usual data protection regime. It is extremely important, therefore that from the very beginning that procedures are contemplated and that mechanisms are in place to ensure that the ordinary data protection regime is again restituted once the emergency is over. That is why the law and the role of the legislature should not only foresee its limits but also the means and procedures to go back to the full expression of fundamental rights.

However, the current global pandemic which is now seeing the various mutation of the virus giving rise to new variants and the questionable effectiveness of the vaccine added to the need for herd immunity, makes one realise that this emergency will go on for some time. This heightens the fear of the derogation of human rights and privacy of personal data for yet a long while.

Considering the UN Personal Data Protection and Privacy Principles, the UN Secretary-General's policy brief on human rights and COVID-19, and relevant health and humanitarian standards, data collection, use, and processing countries in their operations should, at a minimum:

1. Be lawful, limited in scope and time, and necessary and proportionate to specified and legitimate purposes in response to the COVID-19 pandemic. The brief went on to emphasise that while some of these measures may prove effective in containing the outbreak, governments should ensure these tools are implemented with full transparency and accountability. Governments should also ensure they commit to a swift reversal when the crisis is over.
2. Ensure appropriate confidentiality, security, time-bound retention and proper destruction or deletion of data.

3. Warrant that any data exchange adheres to applicable international law, data protection, and privacy principles and is evaluated based on proper due diligence and risk assessments.
4. Have in place mechanisms and procedures to ensure that measures taken regarding data use are justified by and in accordance with the principles and purposes, and cease as soon as the need for such measures is no longer present.
5. Be completely transparent always.[48]

As Senator Maria Cantwell wrote in April 2020, in her opening remarks for a paper hearing by the Senate Committee on Commerce, Science, and Transportation on the role of Big Tech during the pandemic, "Rights and data surrendered temporarily during an emergency can become very difficult to get back".[49]

Right now, the temptation is very strong to do "whatever is necessary".[50] Few countries have frameworks in place to support these extraordinary measures in ways that are fast, secure and in compliance with existing privacy and data protection regulations. As a result, many countries have passed laws specifying how data collection will be restricted to a certain population, for what time, and for what purpose.

If we accept government data tracking, the surveillance necessary to curtail Covid-19 could become a permanent fixture in our lives. It's an unknowable tradeoff.

"Do you give up a little liberty to get a little protection?"[51]

48 "Joint Statement on Data Protection and Privacy in the COVID-19 Response," World Health Organization, November 19, 2020, https://www.who.int/news/item/19-11-2020-joint-statement-on-data-protection-and-privacy-in-the-covid-19-response.
49 Sue Halpern, "Can We Track COVID-19 and Protect Privacy at the Same Time?," *The New Yorker*, April 27, 2020, https://www.newyorker.com/tech/annals-of-technology/can-we-track-covid-19-and-protect-privacy-at-the-same-time.
50 Demetri Sevastopulo, James Politi and Miles Johnson, "G7 Countries Vow to Do 'Whatever is Necessary' to Support Global Economy," *Financial Times*, March 17, 2020, https://www.ft.com/content/571f51e0-67b3-11ea-800d-da70cff6e4d3.
51 Turner, "Privacy vs. Security in the Post-Pandemic World."

Priya Sharma

8 COVID-19 and Trafficking of Migrant Workers for Forced Labour

Introduction

As the world faces the COVID-19 pandemic, it continues to have widespread impacts on workforces globally. They are disproportionately at risk from the impact of the pandemic due to several reasons, including exploitative labour systems.

Most recently, Malaysia's Top Glove, a leading manufacturer of disposable rubber gloves, had a detention order imposed on its products by the United States (US) Customs and Border Protection (CBP).[1] The CBP further banned imports of palm oil products from Sime Darby Plantation, one of Malaysia's largest palm oil producers,[2] and Felda Global Ventures Holdings Berhad, a global, diversified, and sustainable integrated agri-business leader. These orders were based on an allegation and evidence of forced labour in the manufacturing process, which revealed multiple International Labour Organization (ILO) indicators of forced labour, including "debt bondage, excessive overtime, retention of identification documents, and abusive working and living conditions".[3]

The examples above demonstrate the seriousness of the issue amid the COVID-19 pandemic. As trafficking in person thrives on chaos and desperation in communities already ravaged by poverty, one can be sure that these communities will be even more vulnerable to violence, abuse, and exploitation in the wake of this massive, worldwide economic and social disruption. For such migrant workers trapped in this country, perpetrators within the trafficking chain, including recruiters, private employment agencies, outsourcing companies, and employers, will find ways to keep them trapped in exploitative, forced labour situations.

1 Liz Lee, "Amid Virus Crisis, U.S. Bars Imports of Malaysia's Top Glove over Labour Issues," *Reuters*, July 16, 2020, https://www.reuters.com/article/us-top-glove-usa/amid-virus-crisis-us-bars-imports-of-malaysias-top-glove-over-labor-issues-idUSKCN24H0K2.
2 "U.S. Blocks Palm Oil Imports from Malaysia's Sime Darby over Forced Labour Allegations," *Reuters*, December 31, 2020, https://www.reuters.com/article/us-malaysia-sime-darby-usa-idUKKBN2941FY.
3 Liz Lee, "Amid Virus Crisis, U.S. Bars Imports of Malaysia's Top Glove over Labour Issues."

https://doi.org/10.1515/9783110723694-008

Trafficking in Persons (TIP) Report

In 2020, the Trafficking in Persons (TIP) Report by the US Department of State ranked Malaysia at the tier 2 Watch List.[4] The TIP Report is an annual report issued by the US Department of State to monitor and combat human trafficking worldwide through the US Tier Ranking System.[5] The report divides nations into tiers 1, 2, 2 Watch List, and 3 based on their compliance with standards outlined in the US domestic legislation, Trafficking Victims Protection Act of 2000 (TVPA).[6] The four tiers[7] are founded on the "3P" Paradigm, which is a framework based on the 3P Anti-Trafficking Policy Index, evaluating governmental anti-trafficking efforts in the three main policy dimensions (3Ps) – Prosecution, Protection, and Prevention.[8]

The "3P" paradigm framework is established by the requirements of the Protocol to Prevent, Suppress, and Punish Trafficking in Persons Especially Women and Children[9] (Palermo Protocol), supplementing the United Nations Convention against Transnational Organized Crime (UNCTOC).[10] The Palermo Protocol marked a momentous milestone in international efforts to stop the buying and selling of people. It is the first global legally binding instrument with the most comprehensive and internationally

4 "2020 Trafficking in Persons Report: Malaysia," US Department of State, accessed February 17, 2021, https://www.state.gov/reports/2020-trafficking-in-persons-report/malaysia/.

5 "2020 Trafficking in Persons Report: Malaysia," US Department of State, accessed February 17, 2021, https://www.state.gov/reports/2020-trafficking-in-persons-report/malaysia/.

6 United States of America: Victims of Trafficking and Violence Protection Act of 2000, Public Law 106–386 [H.R. 3244], October 28, 2000, https://www.refworld.org/docid/3ae6b6104.html.

7 Under the U.S. Department of State's "*Tier-Placements*", Tier 1 Countries whose governments fully comply with the TVPA's minimum standards; Tier 2 Countries whose governments do not fully comply with the TVPA's minimum standards, but are making significant efforts to bring themselves into compliance with those standards; Tier 2 Watchlist Countries whose governments do not fully comply with the TVPA's minimum standards, but are making significant efforts to bring themselves into compliance with those standards and (a) the absolute number of victims of severe forms of trafficking is very significant or is significantly increasing; or (b) there is a failure to provide evidence of increasing efforts to combat severe forms of trafficking in persons from the previous year; or (c) the determination that a country is making significant efforts to bring themselves into compliance with minimum standards was based on commitments by the country to take additional future steps over the next year; Tier 3 Countries whose governments do not fully comply with the minimum standards and are not making significant efforts to do so.

8 "Human Trafficking: An Overview," United Nation Office on Drugs and Crime (UNODC), (2008), accessed February 18, 2021, https://www.unodc.org/documents/human-trafficking/2008/Human Trafficking-AnOverview.pdf.

9 Protocol to Prevent, Suppress and Punish Trafficking in Persons, Especially Women and Children, Supplementing the United Nations Convention against Transnational Organized Crime, November 15, 2000, https://www.ohchr.org/en/professionalinterest/pages/protocoltraffickinginpersons.aspx.

10 United Nations Convention against Transnational Organized Crime: Resolution / adopted by the General Assembly, January 8, 2001, https://www.refworld.org/docid/3b00f55b0.html.

agreed definition of trafficking in persons.[11] The protocol aims to "facilitate convergence in national approaches regarding the establishment of domestic criminal offences that would support efficient international cooperation in investigating and prosecuting trafficking in persons cases".[12] Hence, the protocol calls upon governments worldwide to implement this instrument into their own legislation to prevent and combat trafficking in persons. The Palermo Protocol serves as a core reference to the Anti-Trafficking in Persons and Anti-Smuggling of Migrants Act 2007[13] (ATIPASMA 2007) and informs its objectives. A review of the Hansard reveals that the act is a manifestation of the Government's determination to execute Malaysia's international obligations to address the crime of human trafficking and "directly meet the requirements of the Palermo Protocol".

Employing the doctrinal legal research methodology and using the "3P" paradigm framework as the benchmark, this chapter evaluates Malaysia's approach to the prosecution of traffickers of migrant workers for forced labour offences and the elements necessary to make out the offence of "trafficking in persons". This is done by critically analysing the specific provisions under the ATIPASMA 2007 and related legislation, investigating judicial interpretation and application of these legislative provisions in case law, and comparing them to international prescribed standards under the Palermo Protocol.

"Prosecution" under the "3P" paradigm framework emphasizes that an effective criminal justice response to human trafficking should treat the prosecution of cases as seriously as other grave crimes such as kidnapping and rape, and all perpetrators of human trafficking should be held criminally accountable by governments, including intermediaries aware of the intended exploitation.[14] Under the benchmark, governments should enact domestic laws making human trafficking a criminal offence. Governments are required to criminalize all forms of human trafficking, vigorously investigate and prosecute cases of human trafficking, and convict and sentence guilty parties with prison sentences that are adequately stringent to deter the crime and sufficiently reflect the dreadful nature of the offense.[15]

Statistically, the 2020 TIP Report demonstrates a decrease in the number of case investigations in Malaysia compared to previous years. The Government was reported to have conducted only 277 case investigations in 2020, a decrease compared

---

11 Ann T Gallagher, "Human Rights and the New UN Protocols on Trafficking and Migrant Smuggling: A Preliminary Analysis," *Human Rights Quarterly* 23, no. 4 (2001): 975, 1004.

12 United Nations Convention against Transnational Organized Crime and the Protocols Thereto, November 15, 2000, https://www.unodc.org/unodc/en/organized-crime/intro/UNTOC.html.

13 Anti-Trafficking in Persons and Anti-Smuggling of Migrants Act 2007 (Act 670), an Act to prevent and combat trafficking in persons and smuggling of migrants and to provide for matters connected therewith.

14 UNODC, "Human Trafficking: An Overview," 31.

15 UNODC, "Human Trafficking: An Overview," 31.

to 281 investigations in 2019 and 398 investigations in 2017. Of the 277 investigations, 80 cases were for the trafficking of migrant workers for forced labour as compared to 123 cases of forced labour in 2018. The Government convicted 20 individuals in 2020 as compared to 50 individuals in 2019. However, as a result of the merging of migrant smuggling offences and human trafficking offences under the ATIPASMA 2007, this figure may have also included convictions for migrant smuggling.[16] Overall, between 2014 and 2018, Malaysia secured 140 human trafficking convictions despite launching more than 1,600 investigations and identifying almost 3,000 victims.[17]

Criminalization and Prosecution of Trafficking in Persons Offences

Pursuant to the Palermo Protocol, the definition of "trafficking in persons" took the following form:

> "Trafficking in persons" shall mean the recruitment, transportation, transfer, harbouring or receipt of persons, by means of the threat or use of force or other forms of coercion, of abduction, of fraud, of deception, of the abuse of power or of a position of vulnerability or of the giving or receiving of payments or benefits to achieve the consent of a person having control over another person, for the purpose of exploitation.' Exploitation shall include, at a minimum, the exploitation of the prostitution of others or other forms of sexual exploitation, forced labour or services, slavery or practices similar to slavery, servitude or the removal of organs.[18]

The protocol further requires countries to ensure that the conduct contained in article 3 is criminalized in their domestic legislation.[19]

The criminalization and prosecution of trafficking in persons is provided in Part III of the ATIPASMA 2007, sections 12, 13, and 14. For ease of reference, these sections are reproduced below.

Section 12: Offence of trafficking in persons. "Any person, who traffics in persons not being a child, for the purpose of exploitation, commits an offence and shall, on conviction, be punished with imprisonment for a term not exceeding fifteen years, and shall also be liable to fine."

Section 13: Offence of trafficking in persons by means of threat, force, etc. "Any person, who traffics in persons not being a child, for the purpose of exploitation, by one or more of the following means: (a) threat; (b) use of force or other forms of coercion; (c) abduction; (d) fraud; (e) deception; (f) abuse of power; (g) abuse of the

---

16 US Department of State, "2020 Trafficking in Persons Report: Malaysia."

17 "Human Trafficking Court Nets Few Scalps in First Year," *MalaysiaKini*, September 4, 2019, https://www.malaysiakini.com/news/490582.

18 Palermo Protocol, art 3(a).

19 Palermo Protocol, art 5(a).

position of vulnerability of a person to an act of trafficking in persons; or (h) the giving or receiving of payments or benefits to obtain the consent of a person having control over the trafficked person, commits an offence and shall, on conviction, be punished with imprisonment for a term not less than three years but not exceeding twenty years, and shall also be liable to fine."

Section 14: Offence of trafficking in children. "Any person, who traffics in persons being a child, for the purpose of exploitation, commits an offence and shall, on conviction, be punished with imprisonment for a term not less than three years but not exceeding twenty years, and shall also be liable to fine."

Based on the above offences created by the Palermo Protocol[20] and as incorporated into ATIPASMA 2007, there are three main aspects to the crime of trafficking in persons. Firstly, there must be an "act" (The Actus Reus). Secondly, the act above must be by way of "coercion" (The Means). Thirdly, the "act" and "means" must have been carried out for the purpose of "exploitation" (The Purpose). Trafficking in person, therefore, occurs when a perpetrator takes any one of the enumerated "actions" and then employs the "means" of "coercion" for the "purpose" of compelling the victim to provide commercial sex acts or labour or services.[21] The three elements are discussed below in detail.

(a) The Actus Reus

Following the elements of the crime as outlined in the Palermo Protocol, the trafficking in persons cycle can be described as a well-organized business that is divided into three consecutive stages. The first actus reus element, the "acts" element, can be satisfied through one of the following five acts: (i) recruitment, (ii) transportation, (iii) transfer, (iv) receipt, or (v) harbouring of a person.[22] This includes recruitment of potential candidates for employment abroad, or transferring of recruited workers to their assigned jobs abroad, or the receipt or harbouring of migrants in order to put them to work under coercive, exploitative, or forced labour conditions.[23]

According to Section 2 of the ATIPASMA 2007, "trafficking in persons" means "all actions involved in acquiring or maintaining the labour or services of a person

20 Art 3 of the Palermo Protocol further explains that trafficking in persons has three constituent elements: (1) An act (what is done); (2) The means (how it is done); and (3) Exploitative purpose (why it is done).

21 UNODC, "Human Trafficking: An Overview."

22 Palermo Protocol, art 3(a).

23 "Trafficking for Forced Labour; How to Monitor the Recruitment of Migrant Workers" (A Training Manual) International Labour Organisation, (2005), accessed February 17, 2021, https://ec.europa.eu/anti-trafficking/sites/antitrafficking/files/how_to_monitor_the_recruitment_of_migrants_1.pdf.

through coercion, and includes the act of recruiting, conveying, transferring, harbouring, providing or receiving a person for the purposes of this Act". When the act was enacted in 2007, the definition under Section 2 dealt only with the means deployed. The term "trafficking in persons" meant certain specified acts like the recruiting, transporting, transferring, harbouring, providing, or receiving of a person for the purpose of "exploitation".

Recruitment is considered to mean: advertising and offering to prospective migrants job opportunities in another location or country, selecting applicants, and transferring the selected applicants to jobs abroad by using force, coercion, deception, or fraud.[24] It may imply a direct contractual relationship linking the recruiter to the worker, or it may be an act of brokerage linking a user abroad to the worker.[25] Transporting involves moving or relocating a person to another place in order to exploit them. A trafficked person may travel normally and lawfully, with a passport, if they're crossing a border any mode of transportation. Alternatively, the trafficker may force them to travel illegally and/or in unsafe, risky ways to prevent exposure.[26]

"Transfer" involves facilitating of trafficking by individuals in transit countries and occurs when the trafficked person is transferred from one person to another.[27] "Providing" includes giving to another individual. "Receiving" consists of taking by force, trading something for the power to control, and "Harbouring" comprises isolation, confinement, and monitoring of these migrant workers. Harbouring or receiving occurs when a human trafficker hides or houses a trafficked person and keeps them under control in order to exploit them.[28]

In *Choong Loke Kian & Anor v Public Prosecutor (Choong Loke Kian & Anor)*,[29] following *PP v Nam Oitthantip (Nam Oitthantip)*,[30] the High Court held that a description of the act needs to be shown to establish trafficking in person offence. As such, "how the victim was brought from Thailand, transported to the Pearl View Hotel, tricked, forced to work, guarded, controlled, accepted, searched for by customers, persuaded and so on was relevant in determining the actus reus of trafficking in person".[31] Similarly, in *Public Prosecutor v Boon Fui Yan (Boon Fui Yan)*,[32] the High Court held that the act of bringing the victims from Pekan Depot to the Rantau Panjang amounted to an act of "transporting" within the definition of "trafficking in persons" under ATIPASMA 2007.

24 ILO, "Trafficking for Forced Labour; How to Monitor the Recruitment of Migrant Workers."
25 ILO, "Trafficking for Forced Labour; How to Monitor the Recruitment of Migrant Workers."
26 ILO, "Trafficking for Forced Labour; How to Monitor the Recruitment of Migrant Workers."
27 ILO, "Trafficking for Forced Labour; How to Monitor the Recruitment of Migrant Workers."
28 ILO, "Trafficking for Forced Labour; How to Monitor the Recruitment of Migrant Workers."
29 [2012] MLJU 221.
30 [2008] 5 CLJ 285.
31 *Choong Loke Kian* [2012] MLJU 221.
32 [2015] MLJU 999.

In such circumstances, one should be mindful that abusive circumstances of each stage of the trafficking in persons cycle do not have to be achieved cumulatively for a situation of trafficking to exist. Coercion and exploitation can occur at a later stage of the trafficking cycle upon commencing work, while the recruitment and transport of the migrant worker have been as concurred upon before departure.[33] The trafficking in persons cycle and its stages are therefore fluid. It is not necessarily the case that every recruited and transported migrant will end up in a forced labour situation. It may also be the case that despite having been recruited and transported in a regular and legal manner, a migrant worker finds him/herself working under forced labour conditions. In some situations, many migrant workers who end up in forced labour situations have migrated of their own volition and become victims during their journey or at their destination.[34]

In 2010, ATIPASMA 2007 amended the definition of "trafficking in persons." The term was expanded to include "*all actions involved in acquiring or maintaining the labour or services*".[35] The proposed amendment came in response to the TIP Report in 2010, which revealed that many Malaysian labour outsourcing companies recruited excess workers, who were then often subject to conditions of forced labor.[36] Numerous migrant workers in plantations, construction sites, textile factories, and employed as domestic workers throughout Malaysia experienced restrictions on movement, deceit, and fraud in wages, passport confiscation, or debt bondage, which are practices indicative of trafficking. Several Malaysian employers reportedly did not pay their foreign domestic workers 3–6 months' wages in order to recoup recruitment agency charges, making them vulnerable to trafficking.[37]

However, despite the amendment to the definition, legal issues surrounding the recruitment of migrant workers through outsourcing of companies, contract for labour, and private recruitment agencies remain a factor contributing to abusive conditions arising in the trafficking in person cycle.

For example, an employer can also be a labour contractor who provides workers for labour to various individuals or companies. Known as outsourcing agencies, they could be both a recruitment agent as well as an employer. Section 2(1) of the Employment Act 1955[38] defines a "contractor for labour" as "a person who contracts with a principal, contractor or sub-contractor to supply the labour required for the

33 ILO, "Trafficking for Forced Labour; How to Monitor the Recruitment of Migrant Workers."

34 Gary Craig, "'Cunning, Unprincipled, Loathsome': The Racist Tail Wags the Welfare Dog," *Journal of Social Policy* 36, no. 4 (October 2007): 605–623, https://doi.org/10.1017/S0047279407001201.

35 ATIPASMA 2007, s 2.

36 "Trafficking in Person Report 2010: Malaysia," US Department of State, accessed February 17, 2021, https://2009-2017.state.gov/j/tip/rls/tiprpt/2010//index.htm.

37 "Trafficking in Person Report 2010: Malaysia," US Department of State, accessed February 17, 2021, https://2009-2017.state.gov/j/tip/rls/tiprpt/2010//index.htm.

38 Employment Act 1955 (Act 265) is the principal legislation that governed the employment practice and employer-employee relationship in Malaysia.

execution of the whole or any part of any work which a contractor or sub-contractor has contracted to carry out for a principal or contractor, as the case may be". The act lays out a definition of a "contractor for labour" as a means of enhancing accountability for employers who are responsible for employing foreign migrant workers. This is particularly relevant in a context where outsourcing agencies or labour brokers often double up as employers and where accountability becomes difficult due to a web of complex contractual relationships between contractors and subcontractors and employers.[39]

The main concern here is that outsourcing of the management of migrant workers to agencies shields principal employers from accountability for workplace harms, exploitation and excludes migrant workers from company grievance procedures because the worker works for a company that is not his/her employer. Further complications arise where both the contractor for labour and the company avoid responsibility due to lack of direct contractual relationship.[40]

However, in March 2019, the Government enforced a ban on Malaysia-based outsourcing companies following numerous complaints of cheating and abuse of workers' rights. The Government required current employees of outsourcing companies to transfer their employment directly to the company they were performing work for or face deportation after 31 March 2019.[41]

In its place, the recruitment of migrant workers is now managed by private employment agencies. Private recruitment agencies in Malaysia are currently regulated under the Private Employment Agencies Act 1981 (PEAA).[42] The act is administered by the Ministry Of Human Resource (MOHR) and provides for the licensing of any person or company that "acts as an intermediary" between employers and workers for the placement of these workers in local positions or overseas. Private employment agency "means a body corporate which is incorporated under the Companies Act 2016 [Act 777] and is granted a licence under this Act to carry on recruiting activity".[43] The PEAA 1981 was amended in August 2017 to increase the Government's ability to regulate the recruitment activities of private employment agencies. It is

---

39 "Situation and Gap Analysis on Malaysian Legislation, Policies, and Programmes and the ILO Forced Labour Convention and Protocol," International Labour Organization, accessed February 17, 2021, https://www.ilo.org/asia/projects/WCMS_650658/lang-en/index.htm.

40 Zuraini Ab Hamid, Siti Fazilah Abdul Shukor and Ashgar Ali Ali Mohamed, "Rights of Migrant Workers Under Malaysian Employment Law," *Journal of East Asia and International Law* 11, no. 2 (November 2018): 359–360, https://doi.org/10.14330/jeail.2018.11.2.05.

41 US Department of State, "2020 Trafficking in Persons Report: Malaysia."

42 Private Employment Agencies Act 1981 (Act 246), an Act to regulate private employment agencies in Malaysia.

43 Private Employment Agencies Act 1981, s 3.

meant to better regulate migrant workers' recruitment and prevent trafficking in persons and forced labour resulting from practices of middlemen or agents.[44]

Despite these efforts, it has been argued that managing foreign labour hiring under the PEAA 1981 does not resolve the problem, as the act still uses third parties to recruit workers. As stated earlier, a private employment agency is a body corporate and is granted a licence to carry on recruiting activity. "Recruiting" means activities which have been carried on by any person, including advertising activities, as intermediaries between an employer and a job seeker to:

a) offer to look for an employment, offer an employment or obtain an employment, for a job seeker; or
b) offer to look for an employee, *offer an employee* or obtain an employee, for an employer.'[45]

It has been argued that the phrase "offer an employee" allows the private employment agency to provide their own employees instead of workers to be employed by the employer of the work place. The phrase therefore attempts to transform private employment agencies into "contractors for labour", allowing them to supply their "own employees" instead of workers, who once accepted shall be employees of the employer of the workplaces.[46]

In support of this argument, the Malaysian Employers Federation (MEF) Executive Director, Datuk Shamsuddin Bardan, recently stated that MEF is of the view that third parties should not be allowed to be involved in recruitment, whether it is through outsourcing companies or the PEAA 1981.[47] The problem is escalated with the fact that a private employment agency may impose a placement fee as specified in the First Schedule on any job seeker or non-citizen employee upon the acceptance of an offer of employment by them.[48] According to the First Schedule, allowable placement fees imposed on migrant workers are capped to not more than 1 month of basic wages.[49] However, the act does not define what comprises a "placement fee". As a result, the majority of migrant workers in Malaysia end up paying fees to recruitment agents in Malaysia as well as to recruitment agents in their

44 "Malaysia's Private Employment Agencies (Amendment) Act to Be Enforced Next Month," Human Resources Online, January 8, 2018, https://www.humanresourcesonline.net/malaysias-private-employment-agencies-amendment-act-to-be-enforced-next-month.

45 Private Employment Agencies Act 1981, s 3.

46 Charles Hector, "Private Employment Agencies (Amendment) Bill 2017 – Sneaking in 'contractor for labour' system? Local Worker suffers?," accessed February 25, 2021, http://charleshector.blogspot.com/2017/07/private-employment-agencies-amendment.html?m=1

47 Ng Min Shen, "No 3rd Parties in Recruitment," *The Malaysian Reserve*, October 30, 2018, https://themalaysianreserve.com/2018/10/30/no-3rd-parties-in-recruitment/.

48 Private Employment Agencies Act 1981, s 14B.

49 Private Employment Agencies Act 1981, First Schedule.

home country, which has been documented to contribute to the workers' vulnerability to debt bondage and forced labour.[50] Therefore, the Malaysian Trade Union Congress, trade unions, and civil society groups have called for the abolition of this contractor for labour system, stressing that all workers at any workplace must be direct employees of the factory/workplace employers.[51]

It was suggested that the private employment agencies, who find employers for workers looking for employment and find employees for employers needing workers, should merely be a service provided for a one-off stipulated fee. Moreover, since domestic laws fail to clarify the employer's obligation for "employees supplied" by the "contractor for labour", if the "contractor for labour" system is to continue in any form whatsoever, these groups argue that there must be clear provisions in law defining the "employer obligations" of the supplier, and the "employer obligations" of employers who use these "supplied employees". It must be noted that a "supplied employee" of another and not an employee of the workplace have no rights to demand better rights or better working conditions from the workplace employer. Once "supplied", most of these "employees of the supplier" unwittingly end up under total control of the employer of the workplace, with no right to demand better rights.[52]

(b) The Means

Under the Palermo Protocol, the actus reus of the trafficking in persons offence must be committed through the "means of the threat or use of force or other forms of coercion, of abduction, of fraud, of deception, of the abuse of power or of a position of vulnerability or of the giving or receiving of payments or benefits to achieve the consent of a person having control over another person, for the purpose of exploitation".[53] In evaluating the term "coercion", it is necessary to assess the other means listed in the protocol to provide clarity to the intended scope of "coercion" in relation to, or opposition to, other methods which may be used to exploit victims of human trafficking. The listed means under the protocol as stated above include "threat or use of force or other forms of coercion, of abduction, of fraud, of

50 US Department of State, "2020 Trafficking in Persons Report: Malaysia."
51 "Review of Labour Migration Policy in Malaysia," International Labour Organization, (2016), accessed February 18, 2021, https://www.ilo.org/wcmsp5/groups/public/—asia/—ro-bangkok/documents/publication/wcms_447687.pdf.
52 "Review of Labour Migration Policy in Malaysia," International Labour Organization, (2016), accessed February 18, 2021, https://www.ilo.org/wcmsp5/groups/public/—asia/—ro-bangkok/documents/publication/wcms_447687.pdf.
53 Palermo Protocol, art 3(a).

deception, of the abuse of power or of a position of vulnerability or of the giving or receiving of payments or benefits".

One form of coercion anticipated by the drafters of the Palermo Protocol is, therefore, the concept of "threat or use of force". However, it is also clear from the wording (threat or use of force or other forms of coercion) that coercion may include approaches or conduct outside of force. From the plain meaning of the text, the clear inclusion of "use of force" can be interpreted to deal with situations of physical force. Similarly, the inclusion of "other forms of coercion" as a separate and distinct *means* implies an intention by the drafters to include non-physical forms of force, such as psychological force or pressure. The notion of coercion as psychological in nature was articulated in the *travaux préparatoires*[54] ". . .it was suggested that the article should focus on the coercive (physical and psychological) nature of such trafficking which is in effect the characteristic that determines the nature and degree of danger of the crime . . .".[55]

According to Section 2 of the ATIPASMA 2007, the means of acquiring or maintaining the labour or services of a person, including the act of recruiting, conveying, transferring, harbouring, providing, or receiving a person, must be by way of coercion. The definition in Section 2 provides for "coercion" in three circumstances: "(a) threat of serious harm to or physical restraint against any person; (b) any scheme, plan, or pattern intended to cause a person to believe that failure to perform an act would result in serious harm to or physical restraint against any person; or (c) the abuse or threatened abuse of the legal process".

Several cases are examined to investigate the judicial approach in interpreting coercion. In *Boon Fui Yan*,[56] the alleged trafficked victims claimed that they were coerced to work as masseuses at the accused's beauty salon. The trial court held that the prosecution established all ingredients of the trafficking in persons definition under Section 2 and convicted the accused. On appeal, the High Court held that the alleged trafficked victims were not forced or coerced based on the fact that there was no restraint of movements or communications imposed on them. This was attributed to the fact that they were free to move and held mobile phones of their own. There was additionally no evidence of any attempt to escape from the accused. As such, the element of coercion was not established.

In the case of *Public Prosecutor v Benedict Chai Jun Siang (Benedict Chai Jun Siang)*[57] an appeal was made by the prosecution against the decision of the learned

---

54 "Travaux Préparatoires of the negotiations for the elaboration of the United Nations Convention against Transnational Organized Crime and the Protocols," UN Doc A/55/383/Add.1 UN, 3 November 2000. (Travaux Préparatoires).

55 "Travaux Préparatoires of the negotiations for the elaboration of the United Nations Convention against Transnational Organized Crime and the Protocols," UN Doc A/55/383/Add.1 UN, 3 November 2000. (Travaux Préparatoires).

56 *Boon Fui Yan* [2015] MLJU 999.

57 [2017] MLJU 577.

Sessions Court to acquit the respondent of three charges under ATIPASMA 2007 without calling for his defence. Ravinthran Paramaguru J allowed the appeal and the respondent was ordered to enter his defence at the Sessions Court. In arriving at this decision, the judge considered testimony by the alleged victims that they had no valid travel documents and were threatened by their handlers with repercussions on account that they would have no place to run on the small island of Labuan without any valid travel documents. The judge also considered the fact that just because the alleged victims were not under total restraint did not mean that they were not exploited, emphasizing that all circumstances of the case must be considered.[58]

The accused was acquitted and the prosecution appealed against the decision of the learned Sessions Court Judge. The High Court held that there was insufficient evidence to prove coercion. The combined evidence of prosecution and defence witnesses indicated that the movement of the alleged victims was not restrained by the accused. They were free to go in and out of their respective quarters as the keys to both premises were inside the premises, and the premises could be opened anytime.

The above case demonstrates an inconsistency towards the interpretation and application of the term "coercion". Traditionally, in *Boon Fui Yan*,[59] the High Court is seen adopting a narrow approach, limiting coercion to cases of actual or physical threat or physical restraint, including restraint of movement and communication. Although Ravinthran Paramaguru J. in *Benedict Chai Jun Siang*[60] took a broad approach in interpreting the term "coercion" by taking into account fraud and psychological, mental, and emotional threats when directing the respondent to enter his defence, the High Court's decision on appeal once again limited "coercion" to restraint of movement and communication, demonstrating a return to the narrow approach.

Such a narrow approach has severe implications. Firstly, it excludes situations involving mental, emotional, and physiological intimidation and coercion, which may not be as visible as cases of actual or physical threat. Upon a more detailed examination of the definition of coercion, it is clear that the term "coercion" means "threat of serious harm to OR physical restraint".[61] "Or" typically signifies a disjunctive list, meaning satisfying any one condition in the list is sufficient. Under the modern approach, courts look at the words of a statute in their context, considering such external factors as legislative intent, textual meaning, and legal norms when interpreting a statutory provision. The meaning of "or" therefore depends on the statute's purpose.[62]

58 [2020] MLJU 261.

59 *Boon Fui Yan* [2015] MLJU 999.

60 *Benedict Chai Jun Siang* [2017] MLJU 577.

61 ATIPASMA 2007, s 2.

62 John Middleton, "Statutory Interpretation: Mostly Common Sense?" *Melbourne University Law Review* 40, no. 2 (2017): 626.

The core purpose of ATIPASMA 2007 is threefold: to combat trafficking in persons by ensuring that traffickers are apprehended, their cases investigated, prosecuted, found guilty, and appropriately punished; to protect and support victims of trafficking; to set up legal and administrative mechanisms for the prevention of trafficking. As explained above, the act is a manifestation of the Government's determination to execute Malaysia's obligations under the Palermo Protocol.[63] Since the Palermo Protocol informs the objectives of the ATIPASMA 2007, the protocol must be relied on as a core reference. Based on this analysis, it is argued that "*or*" under (a) and (b) above suggests that the harm is not limited to physical harm and includes psychological coercion. Additionally, "harm" may also include psychological harm as intended by the Palermo Protocol.[64]

Such a narrow judicial approach to coercion is also inconsistent with the Palermo Protocol, which demonstrates that two important features of "coercion" can be drawn out from the act of trafficking; coercion as an act of force or active pressure, and coercion that includes non-physical forms of force and threats, particularly the use of psychological pressure.[65] The broader definition under the protocol is aimed to cover particular cases of child trafficking where adults use their power over children to force them into exploitative work and prevent them from escaping. It is also essential to effectively prosecute traffickers who abuse adult victims by using fear, psychological manipulation, and spiralling debt to prevent them from seeking help. Although the victims may not be physically restrained, they may be affected by psychological coercion.

For example, in *Boon Fui Yan*[66] above, together with the absence of restraint of movement and communication, the High Court found that the retention of passport per se is not a coercion or compulsion/force within the meaning envisaged under ATIPASMA 2007. The court found that there was no evidence that the alleged victim had wanted to leave the place of employment, let alone escape or neither did she request for the return of her passport or that the accused had refused to return it. Consequently, the court decided that there was no valid reason to accept the alleged victim's claim that she was afraid to escape because the accused retained her passport.

The case above demonstrates the failure of the court to consider the psychological impact of retaining identification documents. Instilling fear in the victims is a major method of control utilized by traffickers over their victims. Retaining passports is a clear example. This serves as a form of psychological intimidation and

63 Federal, *Parliamentary Debates*, House of Representatives, May 9, 2007, 30.
64 "Abuse of a Position of Vulnerability and Other "Means" Within the Definition of Trafficking in Persons," UNODC, (2013), accessed February 18, 2021, https://www.unodc.org/documents/human-trafficking/2012/UNODC_2012_Issue_Paper_-_Abuse_of_a_Position_of_Vulnerability.pdf.
65 UN, "Travaux Préparatoires."
66 *Boon Fui Yan* [2015] MLJU 999.

coercion[67] as trafficking victims are aware that if they escape and are arrested by immigration officers without proper identification documents, they may be classified as illegal immigrants and liable to prosecution and punishment under the Immigration Act.

Secondly, the narrow approach of the term "coercion" has severe implications on how potential trafficking in person victims are treated by the law. This is especially so after the merging of Anti-Trafficking in Persons and Anti-Smuggling of Migrants into one legislation.

In 2010, the ATIPASMA 2007 introduced new offences related to 'migrant smuggling' which it defines as "arranging, facilitating or organizing, directly or indirectly, a person's unlawful entry into or through, or unlawful exit from, any country of which the person is not a citizen or permanent resident either knowing or having reason to believe that the person's entry or exit is unlawful".[68] The then Minister of Home Affairs, Dato' Seri Hishammuddin bin Tun Hussein, announced that the amendments to the ATIPASMA 2007 were made in recognition of the fact that human trafficking and migrant smuggling were "closely linked and interlinked, particularly in the context of exploitation of foreign labour and migrants".[69] The new law, therefore, introduces a new category of the illegal immigrant – smuggled persons. This group is treated no differently than other types of illegal entrants. Unlike victims of trafficking, they are not immune from prosecution for illegal entry, unlawful residence, or procurement of fraudulent travel or identity documents.

Migrant smuggling occurs when a person voluntarily enters into an agreement with a smuggler to gain illegal entry into a foreign country and is moved across an international border. As such, the distinction between trafficking in person and migrant smuggling under the ATIPASMA 2007 rests on the interpretation of "all actions involved in acquiring or maintaining the labour or services of a person through coercion". In differentiating between a victim of trafficking in person and a smuggled migrant, an investigating officer would need to determine whether the situation encompassing his/her entry involved "coercion" for the purposes of acquiring or maintaining that person's labour or services.

Due to the onerous burden of proving coercion and the narrow interpretation of the concept by the courts excluding mental, emotional, and psychological coercion, it is submitted this will ultimately result in victims of trafficking in persons being treated as smuggled migrants, translating into illegal migrants and criminals in breach of immigration laws subject to deportation instead of being treated as victims of trafficking

---

67 "Trapped: The Exploitation of Migrant Workers in Malaysia," Amnesty International, (2010), accessed February 18, 2021, https://www.amnesty.org/download/Documents/36000/asa280022010en.pdf.

68 ATIPASMA 2007, s 2.

69 "Human Trafficking Laws to be Tightened Soon," *Malaysiakini*, June 18, 2010, www.malaysiakini.com/news/134962.

in person entitled to protection under Part IV of the Act. This could essentially make it more likely that victims of human trafficking will be treated as undocumented migrants and be subject to deportation.

This was indeed the danger that the drafters of the Palermo Protocol attempted to avoid when it was suggested at the fourth session of the Ad Hoc Committee that coercive practices should include (physical and psychological) nature of trafficking, highlighting that these characteristic "determines the nature and degree of danger of the crime, helping to separate trafficking in persons from the smuggling of migrants".[70]

According to Human Right Watch (HRW), this approach demonstrates that, counterintuitively, the ATIPASMA 2007 is not designed to address human trafficking and people smuggling.[71] Instead, the act can only be impactful with a small group of migrants who can prove coercion as per the narrow approach. The HRW further concluded that the act in its present form contravenes "international best practice", which demonstrates that a focus on smuggling "is likely to damage efforts to counter trafficking because it shifts the emphasis from countering exploitation of individuals, the hallmark of trafficking, to controlling immigration".[72]

Likewise, Aegile Fernandez of Tenaganita claims that within the act, the distinction between trafficking in persons and smuggling of migrants is unclear, and therefore it would be "difficult for the various enforcement agencies to differentiate between the two".[73] The act, rather than stopping trafficking, would result in trafficking victims getting "lost in the crowd" of irregular migrants and would significantly weaken Malaysia's already ineffective systems for identifying and prosecuting the crime of trafficking in persons.[74]

(c) The Purpose

The ATIPASMA 2007 requires that "trafficking in persons" is an offence when it includes the action and means that would result in the "exploitation" of the trafficked victims. Exploitation is given a prominent place in the definition of "human

---

70 UN, "Travaux Préparatoires."

71 Phil Robertson, "Malaysia: Letter to the Prime Minister Regarding Amendments to the Anti-Trafficking in Persons Act," *Human Rights Watch*, September 8, 2010, https://www.hrw.org/news/2010/09/08/malaysia-letter-prime-minister-regarding-amendments-anti-trafficking-persons-act.

72 Phil Robertson, "Malaysia: Letter to the Prime Minister Regarding Amendments to the Anti-Trafficking in Persons Act," *Human Rights Watch*, September 8, 2010, https://www.hrw.org/news/2010/09/08/malaysia-letter-prime-minister-regarding-amendments-anti-trafficking-persons-act.

73 Richard Loo Wai Hoong, "Separate Act Needed for Migrant Worker Smuggling," *Malaysiakini*, August 7, 2010, https://www.malaysiakini.com/news/139479.

74 Richard Loo Wai Hoong, "Separate Act Needed for Migrant Worker Smuggling," *Malaysiakini*, August 7, 2010, https://www.malaysiakini.com/news/139479.

trafficking" as seen in the Palermo Protocol. It is identified as the specific aim of the crime of trafficking: all human trafficking is for the purpose of exploitation. However, while the protocol lists some examples of exploitation, including slavery, servitude, or forced labour, it does not define the term itself.[75] The protocol makes several additional references to exploitation: in the preamble, noting (in the context of a statement of purpose) the existence of a range of international instruments "to combat the exploitation of persons"; in connection with its provision on the irrelevance of consent[76] and in a provision requiring States Parties to address the demand that fosters "all forms of exploitation of persons".[77] A review of the *Travaux Préparatoires* reveals that although there was a lack of desire to define "exploitation" in itself, a number of states suggested that forms of exploitation to be listed in the protocol should be explicitly defined. However, the United Nations Office on Drugs and Crime (UNODC) Model Law Against Trafficking in Persons notes that while exploitation is not explicitly defined in the protocol, this concept is generally associated with particularly harsh and abusive conditions of work, or "conditions of work inconsistent with human dignity".[78]

Similarly, the ATIPASMA 2007 does not define "exploitation" but instead provides an open-ended list of examples that includes, at a minimum, "the exploitation of the prostitution of others or other forms of sexual exploitation, forced labour or services, slavery or practices similar to slavery, servitude or the removal of organs".[79] The final element, "*for the purpose of*" is evident in the offences created in sections 12, 13, and 14, which provides the basis for identifying the mens rea aspect of the offence. The crime of trafficking in person is made out under the ATIPASMA 2007 once the relevant elements of act and purpose are made out along with an intention to exploit.

The issue of exploitation was expounded in *Siti Rashidah Razali & Ors v PP (Siti Rashidah Razali & Ors)*.[80] In this case, the accused were caught harbouring several Burmese nationals, allegedly for the purpose of exploitation. The court interpreted the term "exploitation" under Section 2 and concluded that for there to be "exploitation" the means that led to the exploitation must have been "by way of coercion, force or suppression, among other things".[81] In this case, the findings of the High Court revealed that the accused harbouring the Burmese illegal migrants were not

75 Marija Jovanovic, "What Is Exploitation in the Context of 'Modern Slavery'? A Legal Proposal," *openDemocracy*, December 4, 2020, https://www.opendemocracy.net/en/beyond-trafficking-and-slavery/what-is-exploitation-in-the-context-of-modern-slavery-a-legal-proposal/.

76 Palermo Protocol, art 3(b).

77 Palermo Protocol, art 9(5).

78 UNODC, "Model Law Against Trafficking in Persons," UN Sales No. E.09.V.11 (2009), 36.

79 ATIPASMA 2007, s 2(1).

80 [2011] 6 MLJ 417.

81 [2011] 6 MLJ 417, page 7.

considered as exploiting them as there was no element of coercion, force, or suppression against them as they were free to move indoors or out of their home without being restrained, bound or locked and none of the appellants used force or intimidation to leave the house.

The court held that the charges were defective, and the accused should have been charged for an offence under section 56(1)(d) of the Immigration Act 1959[82] for harbouring illegal immigrants in the premise. The offense was proven under the act, and the court revoked the conviction and sentence of the appellants under sections 12 and 14 of the ATIPASMA 2007 and substituted with the conviction under section 51(d) of the Immigration Act 1959.

In *Benedict Chai Jun Siang*,[83] the High Court found that since "coercion" was not established under the second element of "means" on the basis that there was no restraint on freedom of movement or communication, "there was no need to go on to consider the third element of 'exploitation' under the Act",[84] thereby affirming the test to prove "exploitation" as per *Siti Rashida's* case.

The High Court in *Siti Rashida's* case, sentenced all four appellants to 9 months imprisonment, and each was fined RM120,000.00 or 6 months imprisonment if defaulted.[85] In comparison, on conviction, Section 12 of the ATIPASMA 2007 imposes imprisonment for a term not exceeding fifteen years and fine, whereas Section 14 of the ATIPASMA 2007 imposes imprisonment for a term not less than 3 years but not exceeding 20 years, and fine. In this case, appeals by the appellants on conviction and sentence under sections 12 and 14 of the ATIPASMA 2007 were allowed, and conviction and sentence were changed to section 56(1)(d) of the Immigration Act 1959. As seen above, it is likely that the outcome will not adequately represent the totality of harm endured by the victim. This tendency is further evidenced when civil society and media reported cases of forced labour that were charged as disparate labour law and penal code violations instead of criminal cases of human trafficking.[86]

It is submitted that, in the absence of a cohesive definition of "exploitation", relying on the narrow approach of coercion to determine exploitation may be detrimental to conveying the actual severity of the offence and may lead to a less than suitable outcome for the aggrieved party. When *means* such as coercion are identified in a situation, there is an additional question as to what level of "seriousness" is required to constitute a situation of human trafficking versus a situation of a lesser exploitative

82 Immigration Act 1959/63 (Act 155), an Act relating to immigration.

83 *Benedict Chai Jun Siang* [2020] MLJU 261.

84 *Benedict Chai Jun Siang* [2020] MLJU 261, page 5.

85 *Siti Rashidah Razali* [2011] 6 MLJ 417.

86 "2019 Trafficking in Persons Report: Malaysia," US Department of State, accessed February 17, 2021, https://www.state.gov/reports/2019-trafficking-in-persons-report-2/malaysia/.

form. Indeed, non-coercive mechanisms such as offers can be exploitative of a weaker party's vulnerabilities and circumstances in the transaction. However, this in itself does not constitute coercion as defined for criminal law purposes.[87]

Constructing coercion as a broad concept to determine exploitation, therefore, risks undermining the integrity of the law as well as its effectiveness in implementation, as seen in *Rashida's case*. The lack of clear perimeters inadvertently results in courts inaccurately classifying victims as "predatory economic migrants", who willingly use the services of smugglers, or as "criminals", who engage in unlawful activities.[88]

Forced Labour as a Form of Exploitation

The Palermo Protocol cites several exploitative situations that would fall under the umbrella term of labour trafficking, including forced labour, slavery or slave-like practices, and servitude. In addition, debt bondage is generally accepted as a form of labour trafficking.[89] While "forced labour" is not defined in the protocol itself, references are made to other international treaties under which these terms have been defined. However, when adopting definitions from treaties created in other contexts, the definitions must be interpreted in a manner consistent with the purpose of the treaty importing the terms. Malaysia ratified the ILO Convention on Forced Labour 1930[90] (Forced Labour Convention) on 11 November 1957. The Forced Labour Convention provided the first global understanding of forced labour through its definition of "forced labour" as "all work or service which is exacted from any person under the menace of any penalty, and for which the said person has not offered himself voluntarily".[91] The Convention defined forced labour as an act of compulsion and intimidation and commanded all state parties to take the necessary preventative measures to counter this activity.[92]

Four important elements can be distinguished when reading this definition: "work or service performed", "any person", "penalty", and the "voluntary offer". The Committee of Experts gave further guidance on these elements in one of their reports concerning the application of C. 29 in 2002. The element of "all work or

87 "The Concept of 'Exploitation' in the Trafficking in Persons Protocol," UNODC, (2015), accessed February 18, 2021, https://www.unodc.org/documents/congress/background-information/Human_Trafficking/UNODC_2015_Issue_Paper_Exploitation.pdf.

88 Marija Jovanovic, "What Is Exploitation in the Context of 'Modern Slavery'? A Legal Proposal."

89 Palermo Protocol, art 3(a).

90 Convention Concerning Forced or Compulsory Labour (ILO No 29), opened for signature 28 June 1930, 39 UNTS 55 (entered into force on 1 May 1932) (Forced Labour Convention).

91 Forced Labour Convention, art 2(1).

92 Forced Labour Convention, art 1(1).

service" includes all types of work, service, and employment, without distinction of the industry or sector, and it includes legal but also illegal employment.[93] The element of "any person" means that there is no distinction between adults or children and nationality. Furthermore, it is irrelevant that a person is a national of the country in which the forced labour has been identified.[94]

The phrase "menace of any penalty" relates to both criminal sanctions and different forms of coercion such as threats, violence, and non-payment of wages. The Committee of Experts feels that the phrase "menace or penalty" must be interpreted broadly. It "need not only be in the form of penal sanctions", but the "loss of rights or privileges" is also a probable situation of "menace or penalty" (e.g. promotion, transfer, and housing).[95]

With reference to the element of "voluntary offer" the Committee of Experts noted that work accepted under the menace of a penalty is not work accepted voluntarily. The question in this regard raised two pertinent questions: Firstly, is the consent to work freely given?, and secondly, is the worker able to revoke his/her consent?[96] These are crucial issues to be considered as it is difficult to determine whether a worker voluntarily entered a forced labour situation. Workers often enter into a situation by their own choice only to find out later that they are not free to withdraw themselves from the labour situation or that they withdraw their consent to work, which they possibly gave involuntarily or unknowingly.

According to this approach, therefore, forced labour is said to involve the use of sexual, physical, and psychological violence; prevent the individual's movement; create a debt of bondage (a condition where an employee is supposed to work to pay off debt, which keeps on increasing due to the food and shelter he/she is given, which is charged by the exploiter at a very high rate); involve a refusal to pay employees; and involve the confiscation of legal identification documents.[97]

---

93 "Combating Forced Labour: A Handbook for Employers and Business," International Labour Organization, (2015), accessed February 18, 2021, http://www.ilo.org/wcmsp5/groups/public/—ed_norm/—declaration/documents/publication/wcms_101171.pdf.

94 "Combating Forced Labour: A Handbook for Employers and Business," International Labour Organization, (2015), accessed February 18, 2021, http://www.ilo.org/wcmsp5/groups/public/—ed_norm/—declaration/documents/publication/wcms_101171.pdf.

95 "Forced Labour and Human Trafficking: Casebook of Court Decision," International Labour Organization, May 6, 2009, 12, https://www.ilo.org/global/topics/forced-labour/publications/WCMS_106143/lang–en/index.htm.

96 "Forced Labour and Human Trafficking: Casebook of Court Decision," International Labour Organization, May 6, 2009, 12, https://www.ilo.org/global/topics/forced-labour/publications/WCMS_106143/lang–en/index.htm.

97 "Human Trafficking and Forced Labour Exploitation: Guidelines for Legislation and Law Enforcement," International Labour Organization, January 1, 2005, https://www.ilo.org/global/topics/forced-labour/publications/WCMS_081999/lang–en/index.htm.

The ATIPASMA 2007 does not define exploitation but instead provides an open-ended list of examples that includes forced labour. As a legal concept, forced labour is not defined in any legislation in Malaysia, although it is a form of exploitation criminalized under ATIPASMA 2007. In his Explanatory speech in the House of Representatives, Dato' Seri Mohamed Nazri bin Abdul Aziz, the then Minister in the Prime Minister's Department, stressed that "forced labour" is not defined for the fear that "it will narrow that meaning of the concept."[98] As such, forced labour was intentionally left undefined to remain wide in its scope.[99]

As forced labour has not been defined by legislation in Malaysia, judges have attempted to define the concept. In *Boon Fui Yan,*[100] the court stated that, in its ordinary meaning, forced labour "must mean some form of force or compulsion on the worker to continue working. Under this ingredient, there must be evidence to show that the worker was forced to remain or prevented by some form of coercion."[101] When addressing the issue on appeal, the court was of the view that the Sessions Court Judge was wrong to find that the fact of long hours of work, the unilateral retention and deferment of salaries, the very limited off days and cramped accommodations constituted "exploitation" within the meaning of the act. The court found that these facts of poor working conditions may fairly be regarded as exploitative in the "social sense" but are clearly not sufficient to be concluded as forced labour.

In *Mohamad Nizam Mohamad Selihin & Anor v Public Prosecutor (Mohamad Nizam Mohamad Selihin & Anor),*[102] the thrust of the appeal to the High Court was based on the alleged non-payment of salaries and the physical abuse for the purpose of proving the exploitation of the victim in accordance with the provision of Section 2 of act. In its findings, the High Court was of the view that the issue of non-payment of salaries came within the definition of "forced labour or services" under Section 2 of the ATIPASMA 2007.

Conversely, in the case of *Public Prosecutor v Siti Madinah bt Ilias Khan (Siti Madinah bt Ilias Khan),*[103] the High Court, referred to the "Word, Phrases & Maxims" (Legally & Judicially Defined) by Anandan Krishnan volume 7 at page 366, where the term "forced labour" is defined as "Any factor which deprives a person of a choice of alternatives and compels him to adopt one particular course of action may properly be regarded as 'force' and if labour or service is compelled as a result of

98 Federal, *Parliamentary Debates*, House of Representatives, 9 May 2007, 10 (Dato' Seri Mohamed Nazri bin Abdul Aziz, Minister in the Prime Minister's Department).

99 Federal, *Parliamentary Debates*, House of Representatives, 9 May 2007, 10 (Dato' Seri Mohamed Nazri bin Abdul Aziz, Minister in the Prime Minister's Department), 7.

100 *Boon Fui Yan* [2015] MLJU 999.

101 *Boon Fui Yan* [2015] MLJU 999, 8.

102 [2018] MLJU 1624.

103 [2017] MLJU 879.

such 'force' it would be 'forced labour'."[104] In the final analysis, the court found that there was no evidence of forced labour or services, nor had the alleged victim suffered any physical injuries through physical abuse, as per the charge. In the upshot, the appeal was dismissed, and the decision of the trial judge was affirmed.

In any case, the Employment Act 1955, which is applicable to migrant workers, deals with factors that are considered indicators of forced labour, such as contract substitution, excessive overtime, withholding of wages, debt bondage, abusive working and living conditions.[105] For example, pursuant to section 60A(4)(a) of the act, limitations on overtime are to be decided via independent regulation, the "Employment (Limitations on Overtime Work) Regulations" which places a monthly ceiling of 104 h on the quantity of time a person may be asked to work in excess of their normal working hours, in exceptional circumstances.

Nevertheless, despite indicators under the Employment Act 1955, it is clear that the absence of a coherent definition of forced labour with specific indicators and clear illustrations and examples have resulted in several problematic issues. Firstly, the understanding of forced labour is limited and may be restricted to extreme cases, failing to disregard the significance of non-visible indicators of forced labour and psychological coercion. Indeed, how does one distinguish between facts of poor working conditions being regarded as exploitative in the "social sense" as opined by the court in *Boon Fui Yan*[106] and poor working conditions being regarded as "forced labour" as determined by the High Court in *Mohamad Nizam Mohamad Selihin & Anor*[107] or as specified under the ATIPASMA 2007?

The perplexity around forced labour and sub-standard working conditions, including poor working conditions, non-payment of salaries, and physical injuries as indicators are clear.[108] In its report, the ILO found that while there is a standardized procedure (SOP) to identify trafficking victims, procedures on identification, referral, and remedies particularly for forced labour cases is lacking at the moment. The SOP, however, does not provide illustrations and examples for each indicator of forced labour. In addition, in cases where workers are considered to be free to move within and beyond work premises, enforcement agencies are inclined to negate any other ill-treatment the worker suffered. In this case, emphasis on freedom of movement, without considering other less obvious indicators of forced labour, is likely to

104 [2017] MLJU 879, page 5.

105 Employment Act 1955, s 60A(4). The Act is applicable to migrant workers as it is applicable to "Any person, irrespective of his occupation, who has entered into a contract of service with an employer under which such person's wages do not exceed RM 2,000 a month . . . or engaged in manual labour . . . or engaged as a domestic servant."

106 *Boon Fui Yan* [2015] MLJU 999.

107 *Mohamad Nizam Mohamad Selihin* [2018] MLJU 1624.

108 ILO, "Situation and Gap Analysis on Malaysian Legislation, Policies, and Programmes and The ILO Forced Labour Convention and Protocol."

negatively influence a finding of forced labour.[109] The existence of psychological coercion in the forms of threat or debt bondage is often disregarded or not given due consideration in cases where there is freedom of movement, demonstrating a lack of conceptual clarity of forced labour, a lack of knowledge and skills in identifying indicators of forced labour, and a lack of comprehension of the impact of coercion in the context of forced labour.[110]

In the absence of a coherent definition of forced labour, proving the element of coercion becomes central to making a case of trafficking of migrant workers for forced labour under the ATIPASMA 2007. The required proof of coercion sets the bar very high and, in some cases, will be unattainable for forced labour cases as described above.[111] Coercion, as defined by the act and interpreted by case law, does not acknowledge that forced labour could occur using abuse of vulnerabilities and deception. It also does not clearly include psychological coercion, which is a powerful coercive practice, and while the definition in (b) refers to *"any scheme, plan, or pattern intended to cause a person to believe that failure to perform an act would result in serious harm to or physical restraint against any person"*,[112] it could be subject to misinterpretation as explained earlier.

The COVID-19 Pandemic Exacerbates the Problem

The COVID-19 pandemic is severely impacting migrant workers, making them even more vulnerable to traffickers who are exploiting global uncertainties to gain profits. Most countries in the world have implemented partial or total border closures. While this can be warranted by the necessity to protect public health, migrant workers are disproportionately affected by the border closures, finding themselves trapped in foreign countries.[113] This places them at higher risk of exploitation. They experience increased violence at the hands of their traffickers and are forced to keep working in unsafe, forced labour conditions. Traffickers detain their documents, therefore hindering the ability to access social protection benefits and health care. Workplace in-

109 ILO, "Situation and Gap Analysis on Malaysian Legislation, Policies, and Programmes and The ILO Forced Labour Convention and Protocol."

110 ILO, "Situation and Gap Analysis on Malaysian Legislation, Policies, and Programmes and The ILO Forced Labour Convention and Protocol."

111 ILO, "Situation and Gap Analysis on Malaysian Legislation, Policies, and Programmes and The ILO Forced Labour Convention and Protocol."

112 ATIPASMA 2007, s 2.

113 Christopher Johnson, "How are human traffickers taking advantage of the pandemic?," *Reuters*, 18 October 2020, How are human traffickers taking advantage of the pandemic? | Reuters.

spections are ceased in many places, leading to fewer opportunities to report labour crimes such as forced labour.[114]

The pandemic and lockdowns has further affected the capacity of governments and NGOs to provide essential services to victims of forced labour trafficking. NGOs and charities are coping with less funding and struggling with increased need for their services. Consequently, survivors and victims are deprived access to rehabilitation, welfare, and support services vital to their recovery.[115]

Moreover, as law enforcement's efforts are focused on the prevention of COVID-19's spread, the ability to respond to cases of forced labour trafficking is significantly reduced.[116] The justice system is not invested in proactive investigations to identify forced labour trafficking and the court systems have slowed down, fostering more impunity and denying victims the support and justice they need. Outreach from the police and labour inspectors have diminished drastically and the lockdowns have reinforced the isolation of victims, further reducing their chances of being identified. As such, focus is diverted from deterring traffickers and supporting victims, while vulnerable migrant workers already living in dangerous circumstances are at greater risk of being trapped in exploitative, forced labour situations.[117]

Conclusion

There are significant weaknesses in the prosecution of traffickers of migrant workers for forced labour offences under the ATIPASMA 2007. Critical analysis exposes inadequacies in the legislative framework and ambiguity in judicial interpretation and application of legislative provisions in case law, thereby demonstrating a failure to "vigorously investigate and prosecute cases of human trafficking" as required by the "Prosecution" aspect of the "3P" paradigm framework and the Palermo Protocol.[118]

The need for harmonization and clarity in the definition of coercion and the concepts of exploitation and forced labour is becoming increasingly evident as actors at different levels of the trafficking of migrants for forced labour cycle realize the

114 Christopher Johnson, "How are human traffickers taking advantage of the pandemic?," *Reuters*, 18 October 2020, How are human traffickers taking advantage of the pandemic? | Reuters.

115 Christopher Johnson, "How are human traffickers taking advantage of the pandemic?," *Reuters*, 18 October 2020, How are human traffickers taking advantage of the pandemic? | Reuters.

116 UNODC, "Impact of the Covid-19 Pandemic on Trafficking in Persons," accessed on February 25, 2021, https://www.un.org/ruleoflaw/wp-content/uploads/2020/05/Thematic-Brief-on-COVID-19-EN-ver.21.pdf.

117 UNODC, "Impact of the Covid-19 Pandemic on Trafficking in Persons," accessed on February 25, 2021, https://www.un.org/ruleoflaw/wp-content/uploads/2020/05/Thematic-Brief-on-COVID-19-EN-ver.21.pdf.

118 UNODC, "Human Trafficking: An Overview."

limitations as a result of lack of coordination with international prescribed standards under the Palermo Protocol and international instruments. This includes the inadequate guidance for judges in deciding cases and ineffective law enforcement training, operations, and coordination, resulting in fewer cases being investigated, fewer victims being identified, and fewer perpetrators being brought to justice.

It is undeniable that the above predicament will only become more problematic in today's context. However, whilst the Covid-19 pandemic poses significant challenges, it could also be the catalyst for change if governments choose to act with urgency to improve the laws, hold traffickers accountable, and strengthen the protection afforded to migrant workers trapped in forced labour situations. Combating the trafficking of migrant workers for forced labour at this time must remain a priority despite this global disruption. The law has to therefore keep up with the times, and the concepts discussed above must be clarified, unmistakably identified, illustrated, and explicated if it is to have a significant impact in solving the problem of trafficking of migrant workers for forced labour into Malaysia.

Ridoan Karim

9 The Importance of Legal Services During the COVID-19 Pandemic

Introduction

Legal services have always been considered an essential profession in modern civilization. The need for legal services in the COVID-19 era becomes more evident than ever before. The world drastically requires volunteer lawyers, legal counsellors, and judges around the legal profession to respond to the increasing legal concerns emerging from the pandemic and make suggestions to address those necessities. Legal services in this pandemic must address social justice, civil rights, and criminal justice issues. Legal and regulatory actions can ensure effective disaster responses and preserve fundamental human necessities. In this pandemic, events so far have called for a greater involvement of legal professions to address issues relating to insurance claims, evictions, medical and employment benefits. Acknowledging the necessity, legal practitioners in numerous nations serve as front-line responders[1] to ensure justice even in this pandemic.[2] The lawyers and judges are working remotely and operating virtual court hearings using different technical platforms, such as Zoom and Teams.[3]

By the time the courts return to their regular schedule, thousands of unemployed and homeless people would require legal help to defend their rights.[4] It is essential to work together amid this global crisis to ensure that everyone can overcome the pandemic effects with their needs met and their rights intact. Hence, all legal and judicial stakeholders, including the courts, bar associations, legal service organizations, national legal aids, and various legal support committees, must come together to resolve all legal issues arising from COVID-19.[5]

1 In times of catastrophe and pandemic, lawyers generally are not considered as key responders. Instead, the legal community provides assistance not just shortly after the devastation but for months and even years into the future. After the headlines move on, the lawyers carry on.

2 Belinda Bennett and Terry Carney, "Pandemic Preparedness in Asia: A Role for Law and Ethics?," *Asia-Pacific Journal of Public Health* 23, no. 3 (2011): 419–30, https://doi.org/10.1177/1010539511408411.

3 UNDP, "Ensuring Access to Justice in the Context of COVID-19," 2020, https://www.undp.org/content/undp/en/home/librarypage/democratic-governance/access_to_justiceandruleoflaw/ensuring-access-to-justice-in-the-context-of-covid-19-/.

4 Nelli Golubeva, Illia But, and Pavlo Prokhorov, "Access to Justice Due to the Covid-19 Pandemic," *Ius Humani. Law Journal* 9, no. 2 (2020): 47–64, https://doi.org/10.31207/ih.v9i2.243.

5 Tania Sourdin, Bin Li, and Donna Marie McNamara, "Court Innovations and Access to Justice in Times of Crisis," *Health Policy and Technology* 9, no. 4 (2020): 447–53, https://doi.org/10.1016/j.hlpt.2020.08.020.

https://doi.org/10.1515/9783110723694-009

This chapter outlines diverse factors and strategic contributions to guaranteeing equity and justice for all with regard to COVID-19. It stresses the significance of legal services to maintaining the standard of the rule of law and securing the application of universal human rights, including the right to equality before the courts and a fair trial. The research utilizes the qualitative method of data collection and focuses primarily on an exploratory literature review. The study further encompasses the doctrinal discussions on whether the legal profession can be considered an "essential service" in this pandemic. This chapter highlights some of the key aspects of legal services and addresses the short-, medium-, and long-term impact of the crisis. Such a challenge to ensure justice, distributional equity, and liberal standards can never be achieved without the support of conventional legal services. This chapter also highlights how the COVID-19 pandemic changed the national legal and judicial practices and analysed the importance of encompassing the innovations arising in this crisis and incorporating technological shift into the legal service.

Digitization of the Legal Services During the Pandemic: Prospects and Challenges

Legal and judicial services have struggled for a long time to choose between preserving their widely regarded traditional litigation approach and modernizing it with the immense technological advances.[6] Different nations managed to adopt reforms for modernizing the national courts.[7] Many of the advancements in recent decades have been introduced gradually to incorporate modern reforms. Judges are becoming more acquainted with the procedures of digitalizing evidence, filing cases electronically, and making pleas online.[8] The courts had also previously allowed virtual cross-examinations in exceptional cases, although this has been restricted to rare occasions.[9] The technological advances and its utilization in the

6 Agnieszka McPeak, "Disruptive Technology and the Ethical Lawyer," *University of Toledo Law Review* 50 (2019).

7 There is growing recognition of e-justice system for improving access to justice, for example: the trans-border European Union e-CODEX, British Columbia's eCourt project, Italian Trial Online, Ontario's Integrated Justice Project (IJP), English and Welsh Money Claim Online, Ontario's Court Information Management System (CIMS), the White Paper on the Trial of Beijing Internet Court etc.

8 Giampiero Lupo and Jane Bailey, "Designing and Implementing E-Justice Systems: Some Lessons Learned from EU and Canadian Examples," *Laws*, 2014, https://doi.org/10.3390/laws3020353.

9 Giampiero Lupo and Jane Bailey, "Designing and Implementing E-Justice Systems: Some Lessons Learned from EU and Canadian Examples," *Laws*, 2014, https://doi.org/10.3390/laws3020353.

legal services are inevitable as it offers a transparent, accessible, and effective operation of the judiciary system.[10]

Nevertheless, even minor changes in the judiciary can create severe challenges in the litigation process. Issues due to poor Internet access, troubleshooting, or technology unfamiliarity among parties, have caused obstructions, delays, and dilemmas.[11] There have also been many concerns in the past about the use of technology for full-virtual hearings – including whether people can accept such technological changes in court proceedings or even whether the legal service holders can reasonably perform.[12]

Notwithstanding, the COVID-19 pandemic has exhibited how quickly the world can change and how crucial it is for professionals to prepare and adapt to the new normal. The legal services have also transformed in this COVID-19 pandemic, and customary lawyers adapted themselves to modernization. It is unrealistic that legal services stay unchanged in the increasingly and constantly changing world and continue the conventional ways of doing things. More prominent utilization of electronic evidence by courts in civil and criminal procedures can help conquer a portion of the limitations forced by the COVID-19 emergency. For instance, the expanded utilization of videoconferencing can help take the evidence from witnesses without proceeding to court. It will also reduce the backlogs of cases after COVID-19. Hence, courts around the world have adopted several technological changes and transformed the litigation process in this COVID-19 pandemic.

On 24 March 2020, in *Fowler v Commissioners for Her Majesty's Revenue and Customs*,[13] the UK Supreme Court made history when it conducted a case entirely through videoconferencing after deciding to close the court premises for the public due to the spread of COVID-19. This promising beginning to video judgements has left legal counsellors scrambling to adjust rapidly to the digitalization process. Consequently, firms and chambers have distributed guidelines on moving towards virtual trials while maintaining social distancing.[14]

---

10 Gasco-Hernandez M and Jimenez-Gomez CE, "Information and Technology in Open Justice," *Social Science Computer Review* 38, no. 3 (2020): 247–51, https://doi.org/10.1177/0894439318810781.
11 C Popotas, "COVID-19 and the Courts. The Case of the CJEU," *Access to Justice in Eastern Europe* 3, no. 2–3 (2020): 160–71, https://doi.org/10.33327/ajee-18-3.2-3-n000033.
12 C Popotas, "COVID-19 and the Courts. The Case of the CJEU," *Access to Justice in Eastern Europe* 3, no. 2–3 (2020): 160–71, https://doi.org/10.33327/ajee-18-3.2-3-n000033.
13 [2018] EWCA Civ 2544.
14 Richard Susskind, "Technology Is Key to Stopping Coronavirus Wiping Out Law Firms," The Times, 2020, https://www.thetimes.co.uk/article/technology-is-key-to-stopping-coronavirus-wiping-out-law-firms-5kd307zlk.

Similar to the UK, the courts in Malaysia have also begun to conduct their proceedings virtually.[15] On 23 April 2020, the Malaysian Court of Appeal had its first virtual court session, broadcasted live on the judiciary's website.[16] Individuals from the general population were welcome to watch the judges at work. Besides, another tax case of Malaysia had its complete virtual preceding during the pandemic. The case included four witnesses to provide shreds of evidence distantly and virtually before the Special Commissioner of Income Tax.[17] Recognizing that virtual court proceedings are part of the new normal, Malaysian legal advisers have devised a protocol identifying the standard operating procedure of distant court hearings and providing guidelines for the court, the legal experts, and the parties.[18]

The restrictions created due to the pandemic have also put an enhanced focus on elective styles of execution of documents, such as the signing of an agreement by digital signature to complete transactions in a timely manner.[19] In Malaysia, e-marks and computerized signatures on contracts are legally recognized by the Electronic Commerce Act 2006 and the Digital Signature Act 1997.[20] Notwithstanding the context in which most of today's business exchanges can be executed electronically as they are legally permitted to have an effect and are enforceable under the current legal framework (except for those types of transactions which requires notarization or attestation), many clients still prefer the traditional form of contract execution.[21] Nonetheless, there is a considerable increase in smart and digital contracts with the introduction of new social distancing standards due to COVID-19.[22]

---

15 Nevertheless, judicial and legal services are not included in the list of essential services according to the Infectious Disease Prevention and Control Act 1988. Therefore, in time of the Movement Control Order (MCO), the courts and offices of advocates and solicitors remain closed.

16 "Portal Rasmi Pejabat Ketua Pendaftar Mahkamah Persekutuan Malaysia," 2020, http://www.kehakiman.gov.my/ms.

17 Although the trial was held on virtual platforms, the regular court rules continued to apply throughout the proceedings. The trial lasted for 2 days and consisted of four witnesses who demonstrated evidences through a videoconferencing platform. It was eventually quite successful, and all the parties involved (including the Malaysia Inland Revenue Board) contributed significantly to this crucial phase in "virtualizing" court trials.

18 Jafri Malin Abdullah et al., "A Critical Appraisal of COVID-19 in Malaysia and Beyond," *Malaysian Journal of Medical Sciences* 27, no. 2 (2020), https://doi.org/10.21315/mjms2020.27.2.1.

19 Although E-SIGN becomes a popular medium for executing documents, it is necessary to note that different jurisdictions provide distinct rules to ensure that every e-signature complies with the existing laws.

20 Heejin Kim, "Globalization and Regulatory Change: The Interplay of Laws and Technologies in E-Commerce in Southeast Asia," *Computer Law and Security Review* 35, no. 5 (2019), https://doi.org/10.1016/j.clsr.2019.03.009.

21 Zibin Zheng et al., "An Overview on Smart Contracts: Challenges, Advances and Platforms," *Future Generation Computer Systems* 105 (2020), https://doi.org/10.1016/j.future.2019.12.019.

22 Ahmad Idzam, Idza Hajar, and Heather Yee, "COVID-19- The Use and Recognition of E-Signature in Malaysia," 2020, https://www.zulrafique.com.my/article-sample.php?id=1149.

Meanwhile, in the United States of America, the rapid spread of COVID-19 expedited the reform of legal services guidelines to enhance accessibility to equity and justice. The American Bar Association (ABA) appointed a task force and a team consisting of prominent legal practitioners to examine the technologies which may allow legal service professionals to operate effectively and remotely.[23] The ABA believes that legal services will undergo changes due to COVID-19, and the ramifications will have adverse effects if technological development could not be further stepped up. Legal trendsetters are working to create mobile apps that enable individuals from the general public to apply for remote dispute resolution. Besides, legal technologists have built software to help American people decide if they are eligible for coronavirus-related government incentives under the new regulations.[24] In the USA, judges live-streamed the virtual court hearings and proceedings to impact the broader legal community through innovation and adaptation.[25] The US courts not only approve remote deposition but also practically allow virtual testimony in court.

Similarly, the vast majority of European nations and their courts are conjuring exceptional measures to retain the legal services and operations during COVID-19. Judges and others in the legal service are ensuring justice through videoconferencing and telecommunications. The new emergency legislation emphasises that whatever happens, justice must be served.[26] The prioritization of cases additionally addresses the critical issues relating to commercial, civil, and criminal litigations and seeks to achieve justice by ensuring social and economic stability.[27]

The hearings in Europe rely on the preference of the judiciary when it comes to urgent matters. Specifically, the critical issues that have so far been approved for trials in the courts throughout Europe are related to the investigations and prosecutions in criminal cases, civil law enforcement in relation to child custody, security matters, promissory note and check claims, privacy, data protection, and insurance claims.[28] Non-urgent matters and their hearings are generally postponed.

---

23 Katharina Pistor, *Law in the Time of COVID-19* (Columbia Law School, 2020).

24 "Government Response to Coronavirus, COVID-19," 2020, https://www.usa.gov/coronavirus.

25 "The ABA Coronavirus (COVID-19) Task Force," 2020, n.d., https://www.americanbar.org/advocacy/the-aba-task-force-on-legal-needs-arising-out-of-the-2020-pandem/.

26 Marco Velicogna, "Cross-Border Civil Litigation in the EU: What Can We Learn from COVID-19 Emergency National e-Justice Experiences?," *SSRN Electronic Journal*, 2020, https://doi.org/10.2139/ssrn.3737648.

27 Marco Velicogna, "Cross-Border Civil Litigation in the EU: What Can We Learn from COVID-19 Emergency National e-Justice Experiences?," *SSRN Electronic Journal*, 2020, https://doi.org/10.2139/ssrn.3737648.

28 Rozhnov Oleh, "Towards Timely Justice in Civil Matters Amid the COVID-19 Pandemic," *Access to Justice in Eastern Europe* 7, no. 2/3 (2020), https://doi.org/10.33327/ajee-18-3.2-3-a000028.

The European Commission has issued numerous guidelines on the use of electronic evidence in court hearings.[29] The Guidelines offer significant direction to national courts in ensuring the accuracy and reliability of the evidence submitted to virtual courts. More guidelines and procedures are expected to be issued by the European Committee on Legal Co-operation (CDCJ) on the development of digital dispute settlement processes to guarantee fair trials and appropriate remedies under Articles 6 and 13 of the European Convention on Human Rights, thereby ensuring that the Convention is enforced properly even in virtual court proceedings.[30]

Although the courts around the world are operating virtually and trying to reduce case backlogs, there are, of course, some obstacles that a virtual hearing may face.[31] The safety and security of online litigations may certainly create significant problems as the videoconferencing platforms (Zoom, Google Meet, Teams, etc.) have cybersecurity vulnerabilities. Since videoconferencing may frequently include documents, evidence, and screen sharing, the issues relating to cybersecurity and data protection must get priority. In an online dispute resolution mechanism, data privacy in legal services must be protected in the electronic facilities. Hence, the selection of an appropriate videoconferencing platform is significant in virtual court proceedings.

Some litigants have also addressed a variety of valid practical concerns that might emerge from electronic court trials. In the first place, taking testimony remotely could give rise to a question as to whether the judge should genuinely examine the actions of the accused persons and witnesses to assess the validity of the testimony and the integrity of the individual giving evidence, adding that witnesses testifying in the standard court should usually feel more compelled to speak the truth than to testify in the comfort of their homes. Second, there could be a possibility of inappropriate coaching or assistance to witnesses during a digital trial where attorneys may be present in the same room as the defendant give answers and testify evidence. Third, it is more challenging to perform a witness interview where witnesses require translators or sign language interpreters. In a recent English case of *Re P (A Child: Remote Hearing)*,[32] the court refused to take testimony remotely as there was a concern about its validity and integrity. The court observed:

29 "Electronic Evidence Guide: A Basic Guide for Police Officers, Prosecutors and Judges Version 1.0" (Council of Europe Data Protection and Cybercrime Division 2013). *See* also "Electronic Evidence – A Basic Guide for First Responders Good Practice Material for CERT First Responders" (European Union Agency for Network and Information Security 2014).

30 Remigijus Jokubauskas and Marek Świerczyński, "Is Revision of the Council of Europe Guidelines on Electronic Evidence Already Needed?," *Utrecht Law Review* 16, no. 1 (2020): 13–20, https://doi.org/10.36633/ulr.525.

31 Jan Petrov, "The COVID-19 Emergency in the Age of Executive Aggrandizement: What Role for Legislative and Judicial Checks?," *Theory and Practice of Legislation* 8, no. 1–2 (2020): 71–92, https://doi.org/10.1080/20508840.2020.1788232.

32 [2020] EWFC 32.

> . . . it is a crucial element in the judge's analysis for the judge to be able to experience the behaviour of the parent who is the focus of the allegations throughout the oral court process; not only when they are in the witness box being examined in chief and cross-examined, but equally when they are sitting in the well of the court and reacting, as they may or may not do, to the factual and expert evidence as it unfolds during the course of the hearing.[33]

There are also several cases where courts emphasized on the physical testimony and denied the virtual one.[34] Rule 43 of the Federal Rules of Civil Procedure of the United States provides that "[a]t trial, the witness's testimony must be taken in open court unless a federal statute, the Federal Rules of Evidence, or any other rules adopted by the US Supreme Court provide otherwise. For good cause in compelling circumstances and with appropriate safeguards, the court may permit testimony in open court by contemporaneous transmission from a different location."[35] The Advisory Committee Note on the 1996 Amendment comments that:

> [c]ontemporaneous transmission of testimony from a different location is permitted only on showing good cause in compelling circumstances. The importance of presenting live testimony in court cannot be forgotten. The very ceremony of trial and the presence of the factfinder may exert a powerful force for truth telling. The opportunity to judge the demeanor of a witness face-to-face is accorded great value in our tradition. Transmission cannot be justified merely by showing that it is inconvenient for the witness to attend the trial.[36]

Consequently, it is commendable that the legal assessment of witness testimony via digital platforms is experiential and, as such, essentially unwarranted. Subsequently, the legal scholars and the judges are on the same page, annotating that a sensitive case's virtual testimony should always be denied and, instead, taken in ordinary court proceedings.

Besides, one significant issue with virtual trials is that not all the parties involved in the proceedings have fair or sufficient access to the technical facilities at their disposal. Virtual hearings may not be possible for criminal trials where prisoners are not equipped with the requisite facilities, such as access to a secure Internet link and a suitable location for the accused to testify remotely before the court.

Except that the above difficulties are resolved, the virtual court is less likely to be the perfect place for considerably serious and complex hearings, particularly those involving witness testimony and extensive cross-examination. Although temporary, digital advancement can lead to some improvements in the future. For example, suitable trials can be heard easily and cost-effectively. Virtual hearings may

33 [2020] EWFC 32.

34 *Gould Elecs. Inc. v. Livingston Cty. Rd. Comm'n*, No. 17-11130, 2020 WL 3717792

35 Federal Rules of Civil Procedure, rule no. 43.

36 Notes of Advisory Committee on Rules – 1996 Amendment.

be more reasonable in some cases, and thus, digital trials may take into account a more customized structure in the post-COVID period. Perhaps COVID-19 has been the impetus required for courts to make changes. However, it is not yet clear whether any of the positive results of a transitory virtual legal framework can be stretched out in a post-COVID-19 era.

Importance of Legal Service in Ensuring Access to Justice in the Context of COVID-19

The COVID-19 pandemic and responses to it have affected the administration of justice and legal services. Closure, reducing working hours or changing the court's procedures affected the arrangement of trials and hearings. They added to the backlog of litigation and increased the duration of legal, judicial, and regulatory procedures. Many individuals, such as asylum seekers, illegal migrants, and refugees, have been profoundly and adversely affected by these reforms.[37] Children and women were also seen at risk of violence; however, they were less likely to seek legal protection from governments due to social distancing measures.[38] Reduced court hours also resulted in prolonged custody of pre-trial inmates or prisoners eligible for early release.[39] Without proper legal services, neither civil nor criminal trials could ensure adequate access to justice during the pandemic.

37 Ferdinand C. Mukumbang, Anthony N. Ambe, and Babatope O. Adebiyi, "Unspoken Inequality: How COVID-19 Has Exacerbated Existing Vulnerabilities of Asylum-Seekers, Refugees, and Undocumented Migrants in South Africa," *International Journal for Equity in Health* 19 (2020), https://doi.org/10.1186/s12939-020-01259-4.

38 Kim Usher et al., "Family Violence and COVID-19: Increased Vulnerability and Reduced Options for Support," *International Journal of Mental Health Nursing* 29, no. 4 (2020), https://doi.org/10.1111/inm.12735.

39 Many countries, including the USA and UK, have reduced jail populations in response to the pandemic, but this is not universal. In several US states, sheriffs and judges began to release high-risk and medically vulnerable prisoners. Nevertheless, the number of releases dropped even as COVID-19 began spreading through the jails in Dallas, Houston, San Antonio, and other states. On the other hand, there are few examples in Asia where the judiciary decided to release vulnerable prisoners. *See* also Jennifer Eno Louden et al., "Flattening the Curve in Jails and Prisons: Factors Underlying Support for COVID-19 Mitigation Policies," *Psychology, Public Policy, and Law*, 2020, https://doi.org/10.1037/law0000284.

"Access to justice" has been defined by several legal provisions,[40] constitutional articles,[41] and case precedents[42] as comprising the following elements:

i. the state must provide an effective adjudicatory mechanism;
ii. the mechanism provided must be reasonably accessible in terms of distance;
iii. the process of adjudication must be speedy; and
iv. the litigant's access to the adjudicatory process must be affordable.

Access to justice holds the same importance in the pandemic as access to healthcare.[43] Law practitioners around the world have cooperated to ensure that the legal system continues to function. Access to justice during the pandemic is probably the thought of providing the right to adjudication through any means, mainly in virtual forms. Such access to adjudication is undoubtedly better than no access at all. As Benjamin Cardozo once observed: "Existing rules and principles can give us our present location, our bearings, our latitude and longitude. The inn that shelters for the night is not the journey's end. The law, like the traveller, must be ready for the morrow. It must have a principle of growth."[44] The conditions induced by the pandemic have shown that the judicial system can be detrimental to maintaining access to justice if not ready to adopt changes for the future. Law, being a social mechanism, must adopt the required changes to ensure access to justice. Justice will only prevail if the application of law grows through changing processes according to the demand. In this changing notion of society and economy due to pandemic, the need for legal help has not ceased; instead, it has increased in the manifold.

Legal services and their professionals can ensure fair trials and equality before the tribunals and courts, as set out in the International Covenant on Civil and Political Rights. Only adequate legal services can safeguard the justice system by ensuring the rights to legal advice and access to court in case of deprivation of liberty. These rights must always be accessible even at the time of a pandemic; and hence, law enforcement and courts must maintain easy access to an attorney and mediator

---

40 *See*, for example, European Convention on Human Rights and Fundamental Freedoms, art 6; Legal Services Corporation Act, 42 U.S.C.A. 2996 (1995); Access to Justice Act 1999 (UK) and Malaysian Legal Profession Act 1976, s 112.

41 *See*, for example, Constitution of India, arts 14 and 21 and Federal Constitution of Malaysia, arts 5 and 8.

42 *See Gideon v. Wainwright* 372 U.S. 335 (1963), Robert W. Sweet, Civil "Gideon" and justice in the Trial Court (The Rabbi's Beard), 42 THE RECORD 915, 924 (Dec. 1997); *Anita Kushwaha v Pushap Sudan* (2016) 8 SCC 509, *Kerajaan Negeri Selangor & Ors v Sagong bin Tasi & Ors* [2005] 6 MLJ 289.

43 The Siracusa Principles on the Limitation and Derogation Provisions in the International Covenant on Civil and Political Rights, art 64 and the Universal Declaration of Human Rights, art 29(2) of set out the importance of the access to justice in a state of emergency. *See* also Human Rights Watch, "Human Rights Dimensions of COVID-19 Response," 2020, https://www.hrw.org/news/2020/03/19/human-rights-dimensions-covid-19-response.

44 Benjamin Nathan Cardozo, *The Growth of the Law* (Yale University Press, 1924).

to protect the rights of a fair trial of accused and convicted persons. Not only to the citizens, but similar rights also ought to be guaranteed to detained immigrants. They have the right to access lawful advice and the right to know the reasons for their confinement and challenge the detention under the regulatory oversight. Besides ensuring the rights mentioned above, legal services can help ensure justice by providing access to legal information. Legal education in a pandemic may equip the citizens to understand the emergency laws, attend to them to maintain the social distancing policy, and apply for legal action in case of rights violations.

So long as there are sufficient protection and security concerning COVID-19, court proceedings of criminal cases or cases relating to serious matters should be held in-person to preserve the interests of all involved and ensure the proceeding's fairness.[45] So far, in this pandemic, legal practitioners worldwide offered their expertise to clients at all levels of the court proceedings and provided essential legal assistance in digital platforms.[46] Nevertheless, access to justice in this pandemic partially depends on the technology. Legal advisors and their clients should be empowered to utilize innovation and technology to operate remotely and embrace social distancing measures. However, the protection of confidential data and information is another issue that legal practitioners must understand in utilizing technology for their clients.[47] Collaborative efforts and awareness of the legal practitioners can help to overcome this challenge and ensure uninterrupted legal services to uphold justice during the pandemic. Specific measures must also be taken to ensure that remote legal services do not conflict with customary court proceedings and fair trials, and the data protection is given due consideration.[48]

When states enacted crisis protocols to combat the spread of COVID-19, legal and judiciary oversight in the application of emergency measures was essential in order to prevent the disproportionate use of emergency powers. Nevertheless, in reality, very few jurisdictions and their administration have considered the legal and judiciary oversight before applying the emergency measures.[49] Hence, any emergency

45 Derrick Wyatt, "In the UK the Covid-19 Lockdown Has Accelerated the Use of Virtual Court Hearings, But Will It Bring Permanent Changes to the Judicial Process?," 2020, https://www.fidefundacion.es/In-the-UK-the-Covid-19-lockdown-has-accelerated-the-use-of-virtual-court-hearings-but-will-it-bring-permanent-changes_a1359.html.

46 Jan L. Jacobowitz, "Chaos or Continuity? The Evolution of the Role of the Lawyer and the Impact of Technology on the Legal Profession from Its Nascent Use to the Digital Age, in Response to the COVID-19 Pandemic, and Beyond," *Vanderbilt Journal of Entertainment & Technology Law* 23 (2020), https://doi.org/10.2139/ssrn.3647471.

47 Marcello Ienca and Effy Vayena, "On the Responsible Use of Digital Data to Tackle the COVID-19 Pandemic," *Nature Medicine* 26, no. 4 (2020), https://doi.org/10.1038/s41591-020-0832-5.

48 Audrey Lebret, "COVID-19 Pandemic and Derogation to Human Rights," *Journal of Law and the Biosciences* 7, no. 1 (2020), https://doi.org/10.1093/jlb/lsaa015.

49 Stephen Thomson and Eric C Ip, "COVID-19 Emergency Measures and the Impending Authoritarian Pandemic," *Journal of Law and the Biosciences*, 2020, https://doi.org/10.1093/jlb/lsaa064.

measures taken during the crisis should be subject to independent review. Legal service providers should support individuals' claims against fundamental rights violations during the crisis and ensure that they are processed in the appropriate courts. Legal services are also required to ensure that the restriction of fundamental rights and freedoms are lifted after countries recover from the emergency.

The socio-economic impact of the responses to the COVID-19 situation will be a primary concern for many people when the immediate threat of the pandemic passes. Across several nations, well before the pandemic, social movements were underway demanding that governments tackle systemic problems of corruption, injustice, and exclusion. The pandemic tests the social contract and people's trust in state institutions, as many governments are struggling to respond effectively to the crisis.[50] The crisis has presented severe socio-economic inequalities in a constructive forum. It is not just the poor, the day labourers, and the minorities who suffer, the detrimental impacts of insufficient policy responses are also faced by small business owners, freelancers, and lower-middle-class members. In post-COVID-19, pressure for wide-ranging social reform is expected to become even higher globally.[51] That can result in social unrest and instability. Increased social instability requires enhanced participation of legal service providers to cater for social-confidence. There is no certainty as to how long the crisis will last or whether repeated waves will follow. In any event, after the public health emergency recedes, COVID-19 effects will be felt for an extended period.[52]

Legal advice and support system will be required to resolve crisis-related issues like unemployment and social security benefits, labour disputes with increased job losses and unemployment, housing disputes resulting from expulsions and incapacity to pay rent, bankruptcies and insolvency, and health and safety threats faced by workers. Partnerships should also be strengthened between the legal service professionals and local civil society groups working on these issues to promote successful recovery strategies. A successful recovery strategy will improve stakeholders' capacity in the justice sector and renew confidence in social institutions.[53] The policies and plans should also consider the historical and systemic disparities in access to

---

50 Jay J.Van Bavel et al., "Using Social and Behavioural Science to Support COVID-19 Pandemic Response," *Nature Human Behaviour* 4, no. 5 (2020): 460–71, https://doi.org/10.1038/s41562-020-0884-z.

51 Edward B. Barbier and Joanne C. Burgess, "Sustainability and Development After COVID-19," *World Development* 135 (2020), https://doi.org/10.1016/j.worlddev.2020.105082.

52 C. Bryce et al., "Resilience in the Face of Uncertainty: Early Lessons from the COVID-19 Pandemic," *Journal of Risk Research* 23, no. 7–8 (2020): 880–87, https://doi.org/10.1080/13669877.2020.1756379.

53 In May 2020, the Task Force conducted a survey to help identify current and future legal needs arising from the Coronavirus Pandemic. The report recommended to adopt a recovery plan for improving the capacity of stakeholders in the justice sector. *See* also "Task Force on Legal Needs Arising Out of the 2020 Pandemic," American Bar Association, 2020, https://www.americanbar.org/

justice faced by various groups and minorities. Several ethnic, minor communities and groups are encountering more profound challenges in accessing justice in this pandemic.[54] Legal professionals also require support from community-based organizations and NGOs to support vulnerable and marginalized groups to realize their rights. Efforts to promote and endorse inclusive legal services for such groups are necessary to ensure a constructive approach to justice in an emergency.

Strategies and policies to prevent crime must invest in inclusive and responsive governance structures at the national and international levels to deliver more people-centred legal services. Identifying priority sectors for help is crucial to ensuring the effective responses of immediate demands of the communities. Besides, evidence-based policy implementation should be introduced as a recovery strategy to meet the requirements for equal access to justice under the SDG 16.3.3.[55] Safeguarding the right to access justice is also a basic component of endeavours towards accomplishing the SDG 16 objective.

The recourse to justice, the right to representation, and the right to a fair trial will never be fulfilled without the effective legal services in this crisis. Legal aid in this pandemic is important, particularly for people who do not have adequate financial means. Legal services can lessen the socio-economic impact of COVID-19. Legal professionals must have welfare attributes to ensure that social and economic benefits are maintained and distributed equitably to balance the community needs.

Law enforcement authorities are an integral part of the justice system and have a significant position in the resolution to COVID-19. Security and police officials must be educated with the required procedures and instruction to ensure human rights reasonably, even in emergency and quarantine periods. Separate instructions must so be provided to cherish particular care for vulnerable populations who could be limited with their ability to comply with quarantine laws (such as labourers, sex workers, migrant workers, or homeless people). The legal services are essential for guaranteeing the implementation of instructions and procedures to account the law enforcement agencies for their work.

Bar associations and other relevant bodies must actively participate to ensure justice by encouraging lawyers to respond to their clients' needs. Where law enforcement agents, judges, and prosecutors are exempted from travel limitations for participating in trials or other cases, the same exemption would be granted to attorneys so that

news/abanews/aba-news-archives/2020/04/aba-task-force-on-legal-needs-arising-out-of-the-2020-pandemic-1/.

54 Ruqaiijah Yearby and Seema Mohapatra, "Law, Structural Racism, and the COVID-19 Pandemic," *Journal of Law and the Biosciences* 7, no. 1 (2020), https://doi.org/10.1093/jlb/lsaa036.

55 SDG 16 (specifically Target 16.3) aims to promote the rule of law at the national and international levels and ensure equal access to justice for all. *See* also Janet Fleetwood, "Social Justice, Food Loss, and the Sustainable Development Goals in the Era of COVID-19," *Sustainability (Switzerland)* 12, no. 12 (2020): 5027, https://doi.org/10.3390/su12125027.

they can defend their clients. Efforts must also be made to strengthen the pro-bono and legal assistance programmes offered by private attorneys and legal aid agencies, both via the telephone and Internet. National human rights agencies and civil society should also track abuses of human rights, including inequality in the provision of COVID-19 assistance. This is also important to expand funding for legal assistance organizations to use preventive action to counter repressive state of emergency laws, as well as to enhance advocacy networks that work together to track and promote transparency of misuse of power.

Legal Assistance as an Essential Service

The concept of emergency services typically varies from one country to another. During the COVID-19 pandemic, several states shut down their non-essential services to contain the spread of the virus. The scope of emergency services extends to services crucial to people's overall welfare and are thus necessary to sustain even in a crisis. The definition of "essential services" can be found in the legislations of many countries, including India, Malaysia, Singapore, and the UK.[56] They normally include hospitals and support services, services relating to law enforcement, and services relating to essential goods, such as electricity, water, sanitation, and bank. However, none of the laws in these countries classify legal service as an "essential service".

Similarly, the operation of the courts or the judicial services is also not classified as an essential service. Nevertheless, the courts have continued their virtual functions in the pandemic. They had also returned to the normal proceedings when the governments lifted the emergency regulations. Many legal scholars believe that even in an emergency, the courts can function as per the needs.[57] The judiciary has the right to decide by themselves on their operations because they have a quintessential[58] role in upholding the law and order, and the judiciary is constitutionally independent from the other two government agencies, that is, the legislature and

---

56 *See* India's Essential Commodities Act 1955 and Essential Services Maintenance Act 1980; Malaysia's Industrial Relations Act 1967 (The First Schedule) and the Emergency (Essential Powers) Act 1964; Singapore's Emergency (Essential Powers) Act 1992 and the UK's Essential Services Act (Revised Edition 2013).

57 Julie Marie Baldwin, John M. Eassey, and Erika J. Brooke, "Court Operations during the COVID-19 Pandemic," *American Journal of Criminal Justice* 45 (2020): 743–58, https://doi.org/10.1007/s12103-020-09553-1.

58 While quintessential means "representing the most perfect or typical example of a quality or class", it defines essential as "absolutely necessary; extremely important".

the executive.[59] Because of the judiciary's autonomy, the government cannot temporarily or indefinitely suspend the judicial services under the constitution. The courts have an obligation to defend citizen's liberties and equality. At the same time, the state has a prime responsibility to safeguard the quality of living and public health in compliance with constitutional provisions.

In *Ratlam v Vardichan*,[60] the Supreme Court of India ruled that the courts following the English common law have the right to implement a wider concept of access to justice to ensure that civil rights are adequately enjoyed. In another case of *Imran Mohd. Salar Shaikh v State of Maharashtra*,[61] the High Court stated that the government must take into account the community's key concern when deciding what constitutes essential services. The court additionally opined that the State law of essential services must include the legal services provided by lawyers in the list.

Although courts can independently operate (especially in the common law countries) and believes that the legal services provided by lawyers should be considered as essential service, however, it has been witnessed that the law firms in many countries have to be closed down due to government's imposition of strict rules on physical distancing. The shift to remote hearings has transformed the work of litigators. Although it is appreciable that the lawyers have quickly adapted to using technology to work effectively during the pandemic, however, there remain specific practical challenges with many law firms being forced to be closed.

The situation induced by pandemic is rapidly demanding legal attention from commercial firms whose clients are seriously impacted. The difficulty felt by firms as they make the switch to remote work during COVID-19 depended upon two factors: court appearances and age of clients. Confidentiality remains as another key challenge, with lawyers adopting a new virtual environment to ensure that discussions with clients and colleagues can remain confidential as in regular practices. With the courts reluctant to adjourn hearings, various law firms are struggling with witness statements and other evidence being gathered on a virtual basis. Meetings with clients have also been a challenge, as many clients are not habituated in using virtual conferencing.

Although the law firms are reassessing and re-strategizing during COVID-19, the adjustments and transitions ultimately impact the employment of the legal professionals. It seems unlikely that there will be easily available employment in the law for all solicitors in a recession. It is also likely that trainees and apprentices will be amongst those who will find their contracts terminated. Many experts believe that the government must support the temporary changes to the legal services' operations,

59 Petrov, "The COVID-19 Emergency in the Age of Executive Aggrandizement: What Role for Legislative and Judicial Checks?"
60 AIR 1980 SC 1622.
61 Cri.WP-AS-DB-LD-VC-118-2020.

including allocating budget/fund for unexpected or exceptional expenses and incorporating a detailed national policy/strategy to tackle the COVID-19 crisis.[62]

Policies and response plans relating to COVID-19 must include all the inputs and consultations from essential legal services and its stakeholders, including judges, lawyers, law enforcement authorities, bar associations, civil society organizations, clients, and other related social support providers. Legal professionals in numerous countries are helping the judiciary to create a response plan in the context of COVID-19. Among them, prioritizing sensitive cases while protecting the rights of defendants is significant assistance that legal professionals are serving.[63] It cannot be denied that the law professionals are ethically obliged to render adequate assistance to victims of human rights violations even in the context of states of emergencies.[64]

Acknowledging legal assistance as an essential service is the first step that policymakers should concede to encounter the adverse effects of COVID-19 associated with justice and equity. Legal assistance is an essential service in the sense that it safeguards the right to justice promptly as a basic human right. Legal services help individuals to comprehend and utilize the law to understand their rights and privileges. Documentation and preparation of wills, affidavits, and contracts' execution require adequate services from the law professionals even in the pandemic.

Conclusion

The pandemic greatly impacts the progression of the Sustainable Development Agenda 2030.[65] States are struggling to maintain the progress that has been made for achieving the sustainable development goals (SDGs).[66] The present situation has created an impetus for rethinking and engaging in innovative approaches to make legal services more open and available to all. The challenge calls, in turn, for a collective commitment to creating more equitable and sustainable policies

62 Kumar Vaibhav, "Access to Justice during the Covid-19 Pandemic: An Indian Perspective," International Bar Association (IBA), 2020, https://www.ibanet.org/Article/NewDetail.aspx?ArticleUid=f1a1e3a6-675f-455b-b190-038306399cbb.

63 Zackary D. Berger et al., "Covid-19: Control Measures Must Be Equitable and Inclusive," *The BMJ*, 2020, https://doi.org/10.1136/bmj.m1141.

64 In the USA, the Civil Rights Act of 1964 and the Age Discrimination Act have explicitly provided provisions on the right to justice even in the emergency situation.

65 Walter Leal Filho et al., "COVID-19 and the UN Sustainable Development Goals: Threat to Solidarity or an Opportunity?," *Sustainability (Switzerland)* 12, no. 13 (2020): 5343, https://doi.org/10.3390/su12135343.

66 Fleetwood, "Social Justice, Food Loss, and the Sustainable Development Goals in the Era of COVID-19."

and strategies on SDG 16. The actors in the legal services – from courts, police to legal assistance agencies (such as pro-bono attorneys, community paralegals, and legal help-providing civil society organizations) and rehabilitation programmes – ought to cooperate in pursuing a comprehensive and people-centred approach to addressing justice issues. A particular focus on legal services is also crucial to improving technological resources. In this pandemic, adequate legal services can increase access to equal and reliable dispute resolution processes and achieve fairer access to justice for everyone.

Nevertheless, to ensure adequate legal services, standard policies must be established to guide the implementation of new procedures and practices related to the successful operation of the judiciary. This can include the use of technologies, such as the use of automated protocols to prosecute lawsuits, legal identification of electronic information and evidence, and legal information management programmes. This can also include the exchange of lessons between stakeholders in the legal services on the issues, such as access to information about their rights and how to seek redress in the context of emergency regulations, promoting direct participation of claimants and whistle-blowers in court cases, and ensuring oversight and transparency in the context of emergency regulations. Training and education on Information and Communication Technologies (ICTs) should be given to judges, lawyers, and court personnel to ensure effective electronic trials.

Adnan Trakic

10 COVID-19 and Business Law: Findings and Recommendations

Introduction

This chapter recapitulates the main findings discussed by the authors in their respective chapters. The chapter also provides concise recommendations for governments and other relevant authorities to consider when dealing with legal challenges caused by the COVID-19 pandemic. It needs to be noted, however, that both the findings and recommendations are based on the editor's reading and understanding of the substantive book chapters. While, for the most part, the chapter relates the findings and recommendations as correctly and concisely as possible, it also adds the editor's personal views on the matters in question where it was felt appropriate. This chapter, after all, represents a brief summary and review of the points raised and discussed by the respective authors. To get an unaltered version and full account of the authors' arguments, the readers are encouraged to read the authors' actual chapters in the book.

Relief for Contractual Breaches

COVID-19 has had a profound impact on parties' performance of contractual obligations. The performance might have been impeded by either COVID-19 (the disease) or by mandatory lockdowns imposed by the governments worldwide to contain the spread of the COVID-19. In either case, one would assume that the non-performance of the contract cannot be blamed on the non-performing party. If one party is to be excused from the performance of the contract on the grounds of COVID-19, then the other too should be given a concession. Suppose a landlord is unable to perform his contractual obligation to provide vacant possession of the premises to the shop holder due to the nationwide imposed lockdown. In that case, the lessee, too, should not be expected to perform his contractual obligation to pay for the premises for the duration of the lockdown. However, there have been numerous cases where this balance was either not achieved or was at least questioned. To understand the legal aspects of the issue at hand, in Chapter 2, Vazeer Alam Mydin Meera, Abdul Majid, and MeiYee Lee discussed the impact of COVID-19 on the performance of contractual obligations.

The authors considered the issue primarily in the context of the Malaysian law. However, occasional references to other jurisdictions were also made. They examined the matter mainly with reference to the common law doctrine of frustration

https://doi.org/10.1515/9783110723694-010

and the contract law concept of force majeure. While Malaysia's Contracts Act 1950 and the Civil Law Act 1956 provide a robust framework for the application of frustration in Malaysia, the doctrine, according to the authors, is not suitable for the contracts affected by the COVID-19. The authors pointed out two main reasons for that. First, the frustration doctrine was only intended to provide relief to individuals and not the who segments of society. Second, perhaps more importantly, the remedy for the frustrated contract, that is, the avoidance, would not be desired by most of the parties whose contracts have been affected by the COVID-19. Therefore, while conceptually, COVID-19 related events, including the lockdown, could be considered the frustrating event warranting the contract's frustration, the outcome of such a frustrated contract, that is, the avoidance, is not suitable for COVID-19 related breaches.

This brings us to the second legal concept discussed by the authors – force majeure. Force majeure is not the common law doctrine. Instead, it is a creation of contract law and can only be enforced if it is incorporated into a contract. The authors cited several judicial decisions where clearly written force majeure clauses were enforced and, as such, they absolved the liability of the parties for the breaches of the contract captured by the clauses. In the context of COVID-19, it is important that the force majeure clause contains a specific reference to a "pandemic". A general reference to the "Act of God", which typically includes a breach caused by natural sources that could not have been foreseen and avoided, may not be sufficient to cover the breach caused by COVID-19. The authors illustrated this by reference to a Malaysian case of *Khoo Tham Sui v Chan Chiau Hee*,[1] and concluded that "whether the COVID-19 pandemic is 'an act of God' is very much an open question".

The authors opined that the non-performance of the contractual obligations due to COVID-19 should be remedied through an act of Parliament, which would provide temporary relief measures to the affected parties. The authors pointed that, in 2020, the Malaysian Government introduced the Temporary Measures for Reducing the Impact of Coronavirus Disease (COVID-19) Act 2020. As the name suggests, the COVID-19 Act was passed to reduce the impact of COVID-19 by way of temporary measures. The authors discussed in detail the measures introduced in relation to contractual obligations and identified several weaknesses. They argued that the COVID-19 Act was narrow in scope in limiting itself to mainly business contracts and not providing for employment contracts, residential tenancies, vehicle parking facilities, and small businessmen and sole traders. Also, in comparison with Singapore's COVID-19 (Temporary Measures) Act, which provides relief for contractual breaches caused by the COVID-19 (the disease), Malaysia's COVID-19 Act only covers contractual breaches caused by measures adopted (i.e. the lockdown) to prevent the spread of the disease. Thus, an individual who might have breached his contractual obligation due to his COVID-19 hospitalization (the disease) is not covered by

1 [1976] 1 MLJ 25.

the COVID-19 Act in Malaysia as the Act is limited to the breaches of contract caused by the lockdown. This limitation is unnecessary and not helpful.

Recommendations

Non-performance of the contractual obligation due to COVID-19 should be remedied through an Act of Parliament. The Act should provide the affected parties temporary relief for the contractual breaches caused by both the COVID-19 (the disease) and consequent measures adopted to contain the spread of the disease (e.g. lockdown). Besides providing the appropriate relief to the affected business contracts, such legislation should also be extended to employment contracts, residential tenancies, vehicle parking facilities, and small businesses and sole traders. The parties who may wish to invoke frustration of the contract should know that it is not suitable due to its non-intended use in the circumstances of the pandemic and inaptness of its remedy of avoidance. Force majeure clause, on the other hand, may absolve liability for contractual breaches caused by the pandemic if the clause contains a clear reference to "pandemic" rather than just a general reference to "Act of God".

Work-Related Challenges

In Chapter 3, Ashgar Ali Ali Mohamed and Chithra Latha Ramalingam discussed several employment law issues that have been reinvigorated by the COVID-19 pandemic. The second-biggest loss caused by the pandemic, after the loss of lives, has been the loss of jobs and the ability to earn a livelihood. The disruption to labour marker around the world in 2020 was on a historically unprecedented scale.[2] International Labour Organization warned that nearly half of the global workforce could see their livelihoods destroyed due to the pandemic and resulting lockdowns.[3] Many companies have been forced to retrench their workers, while some had to shut down. While employment law relationship is often looked at through the lens of "us" and "them", that is, us being the works and them referring to the employers, the pandemic has taught us that the only way to survive this terrible disease is to work together. This has been the central theme of the authors' arguments in this chapter. They considered a variety of employment law issues that need to be urgently addressed, but they insisted that all the issues and the proposed solutions should satisfy both legal as well as social justice tests.

For example, the authors explained that the workers are entitled to annual, medical, and other leave types, which is their legal right. However, they should also

2 "ILO Monitor: COVID-19 and the World of Work. Seventh Edition," International Labour Organization, January 25, 2021, https://www.ilo.org/wcmsp5/groups/public/@dgreports/@dcomm/documents/briefingnote/wcms_767028.pdf.

3 "Nearly Half of Global Workforce at Risk as Job Losses Increase due to COVID-19: UN Labour Agency," UN News, April 28, 2020, https://news.un.org/en/story/2020/04/1062792.

be considerate to the employers' needs and try to accommodate them, especially in the time of the pandemic, which has impeded the employers' ability to generate revenue. Likewise, while the employer's unilateral reduction of the worker's salary would amount to a fundamental breach of employment contract, the worker should show understanding and be willing to take the pay cut if that is necessary due to the pandemic. The worker's willingness to sacrifice his legal right for the company's long-term good is consistent with social justice. If, on the other hand, the worker were to insist on his legal right entrenched in the employment contract or implied by the common law, then the employer, in the end, might be forced to retrench the worker. The blind insistence on only legal justice would serve neither the worker nor the employer in the time of the pandemic.

The same level of understanding is expected of the employers. The authors explained that employers should not easily retrench their workers. They should make sure that they have exhausted all the efforts to retain the workers, especially during the pandemic when many of them are vulnerable and when finding an alternative job is not easy. The employers should understand the difference between "redundancy", "retrenchment", and "lay-off" and when each is allowed under the employment law. They also must not use a "voluntary separation scheme", the authors argued, as a means of getting rid of underperforming or undesired workers. The authors also pointed out that employers should not use force majeure clauses to absolve their liability for the breach of the employment contract. The clause should not be used as a blanket defence to retrench workers on the basis that the pandemic has been identified as a force majeure event. The courts adjudicating employment law contracts, especially industrial courts, must show readiness to go beyond the contract law principles and pure legal justice and consider the matter with reference to social justice, equity, and good conscience.

The authors also discussed the difficulties surrounding work from home. Even though the flexible working arrangements remain unregulated in the employment law framework of many countries, including Malaysia, employers and governments should encourage it where the nature of the work allows for it. The workers' common law duty of fidelity and to act in the employer's best interest would ensure that flexible working arrangements, which are typically not monitored by the employer, are viable options. The authors also highlighted the employers' duty to provide a safe working environment for the workers. This is particularly important in the pandemic. The employer must make sure that the standard operating procedures mandated by the government authorities to contain the spread of the COVID-19 are fully implemented. They must also not ask the employees to do anything that may expose them or their family to the risk of contracting COVID-19.

Recommendations

When faced with employment law issues caused by the COVID-19 pandemic, particularly those relating to flexible work, deduction of wages, redundancy, retrenchment, lay-off, and occupational stress, employers and workers should try to resolve them amicably. There should not be "us" versus "them". They both should be prepared to go beyond the contract law principles and pure legal justice and consider the challenges with reference to social justice, equity, and good conscience. Employers and governments should encourage flexible work where the nature of the work allows for it. Governments should also amend the employment legislation to include flexible work arrangement provisions.

Tourism-Related Challenges

In Chapter 4, Joo Ee Gan discussed the implications of the COVID-19 pandemic for the tourism industry. It comes as no surprise that this particular segment of the economy was affected the most by closures of counties' borders, mandatory quarantines, and restrictions on movement imposed by governments worldwide. All these factors have caused a dramatic decrease in demand for tourism travel. It is estimated that global international tourist arrivals dropped 74% in 2020, making it the worst year on record.[4] United Nations World Tourism Organization World Tourism Barometer estimated the losses in 2020 to be around USD 1.3 trillion in export revenues.[5] The worst-hit regions have been Asia and the Pacific, with a drop of 84% in tourists' arrivals in 2020 (300 million fewer).[6] These countries have also imposed the highest level of travel restrictions. In absolute terms, the most affected region is Europe, with 500 million fewer international tourists in 2020, a 70% decrease in arrivals.[7]

In line with these figures, there have also been massive and unprecedented cancellations of travel bookings and tour packages due to the pandemic and the resultant restrictions. While some of the affected countries, like those in the European

4 "2020: Worst Year in Tourism History with 1 Billion Fewer International Arrivals", *United Nation World Tourism Organization (UNWTO)*, January 28, 2021, https://www.unwto.org/news/2020-worst-year-in-tourism-history-with-1-billion-fewer-international-arrivals.

5 "2020: Worst Year in Tourism History with 1 Billion Fewer International Arrivals", *United Nation World Tourism Organization (UNWTO)*, January 28, 2021, https://www.unwto.org/news/2020-worst-year-in-tourism-history-with-1-billion-fewer-international-arrivals.

6 "2020: Worst Year in Tourism History with 1 Billion Fewer International Arrivals", *United Nation World Tourism Organization (UNWTO)*, January 28, 2021, https://www.unwto.org/news/2020-worst-year-in-tourism-history-with-1-billion-fewer-international-arrivals.

7 "2020: Worst Year in Tourism History with 1 Billion Fewer International Arrivals", *United Nation World Tourism Organization (UNWTO)*, January 28, 2021, https://www.unwto.org/news/2020-worst-year-in-tourism-history-with-1-billion-fewer-international-arrivals.

Union (EU), have a robust regulatory framework to deal with these issues and offer the affected consumers adequate protections, other countries, most notably those in Asia and the Pacific, have struggled to do so. Joo Ee explored the situation in Malaysia, a country whose tourism industry has been hit very hard, and discovered that the current regulatory framework provided under the Tourism Industry Act (Malaysia) 1992 (TIA) and Tourism Industry (Tour Operating Business and Travel Agency Business) Regulations 1992 is inadequate to deal effectively with the ongoing crisis. She pointed out that neither the consumers nor the tour operators are satisfied with the existing legal framework.

Under the TIA and the Regulations 1992, only the outbound travellers are entitled to receive a full refund from tour operators for the cancellations caused by the pandemic and related events. These laws discriminate between outbound and inbound travellers, and this, according to the author, should not be the case. The other cause of action for a refund could be a more traditional contract law route as the COVID-19 pandemic is considered a force majeure event that renders the contract void. In that case, the refund would be deemed a compensation remedy provided under the Malaysian Contracts Act 1950. However, massive cancellations and demands for refunds have put an enormous financial burden on tour companies that are not adequately prepared to deal with this situation. Many of them have already paid third-party providers like airline companies, hotels, and transportation companies for the services which have been cancelled. This is why the Malaysian Association of Tours and Travel Agents had called the Malaysian Government to reconsider this, arguing that consumers should be bound by the airlines' and hotels' policies on cancellations and, as such, be entitled only to partial refunds.

The problem becomes more prominent when many of these travel companies become insolvent. The consumers are then treated as unsecured creditors and do not have insolvency protection like the consumers in EU countries have. This is precisely why, according to Joo Ee, a statutory priority through safeguards like bonding, guarantee fund, insurance, or trust is important. Joo Ee called on Malaysian authorities to consider the insolvency protection measures adopted in the EU Package Travel Directive 2015 and see if similar provisions could be introduced into the Malaysian regulatory framework. She argued that the UK's 2015 Directive and the Package Travel Regulations 2018, which implemented the EU Directive 2015, could be a useful guide on how to develop laws and insolvency protection system in which both the consumers and tour operators would be adequately protected and prepared for an unprecedented situation like the one we are currently in. The suggested legislative changes are meant to protect the consumers, prevent exploitation of the small service providers, and promote healthy competition.

Recommendations

The legislation governing the tourism industry, like Malaysia's TIA (Malaysia) 1992 and Tourism Industry (Tour Operating Business and Travel Agency Business) Regulations 1992, should not discriminate between inbound and outbound travellers. The insolvency protection measures adopted in the EU Package Travel Directive 2015, which address both consumers' and tour operators' concerns relating to the pandemic, seem reasonable and adequate. The Malaysian Government, and the governments of other countries for that matter, should introduce similar provisions into their regulatory frameworks. The UK's 2015 Directive and the Package Travel Regulations 2018 is a useful guide on how to do that.

Relief for Companies

In Chapter 5, Loganathan Krishnan explored the implications of the COVID-19 pandemic for the companies in Malaysia. After legislating the much anticipated Malaysian Companies Act 2016 (CA), the euphoria and hope quickly disappeared with the emergency of the pandemic. As Loganathan pointed out, it was quickly realized that many of the CA's provisions were not drafted with the worldwide pandemic in mind. The strict compliance with the provisions of the Act, which is typically expected of companies in normal circumstances, was an uphill task for most companies. But, companies that were affected the most perhaps were those that are generally most vulnerable – small and medium-sized enterprises. The pandemic restricted the movement of individuals, goods, and services. This, in turn, affected the companies' revenues. Many faced serious difficulties in paying their monthly rentals for company premises and wages to the employees. Perhaps the most serious threat arose from the debts owed to the creditors who could initiate insolvency proceedings against defaulting companies under the existing CA. The existing law did not take into consideration the pandemic and its impact on companies.

Loganathan explained that some countries like Singapore had offered various temporary reliefs to their companies through their COVID-19 legislation. According to him, this was an efficient and quick way to address some of the most pressing challenges the companies faced to keep them afloat. But, surprisingly, as Loganathan correctly observed, the Malaysian COVID-19 Act 2020 did not make any reference to the CA. In other words, all the strict legal requirements of the CA continued to be applied even during the pandemic. However, Malaysia did make some changes through Companies (Exemption) Order (No. 2) 2020 and the Direction of the Minister of Domestic Trade and Consumer Affairs in which the minimum debt threshold before the creditor could serve a statutory demand was increased from RM10,000 to RM50,000. According to Loganathan, this increase was insufficient, and he cited the example of the neighbouring Singapore, which increased the debt threshold from SGD$10,000 to SGD$100,000. The increase in the debt threshold is meant to help avoid insolvency proceedings due to the pandemic which creditors would otherwise be entitled to initiate. Loganathan also noted that the Minister's Directive, which extended the time period for the company to comply with the statutory demand issued by creditors from 21 days to 6 months, while welcomed in terms of substance, was ultra-virus as the minister did not have the power to do so. According to him, the CA allows such a change only through an Act of Parliament and not through subsidiary legislation. This is a major concern for companies, Loganathan notes, as creditors would be able to challenge this extension in court.

In any case, insolvency should not be the first option for every financially distressed company in the pandemic. There are other options, Loganathan explains, worth considering. For example, companies should consider "corporate voluntary arrangement" (CVA), a restructuring arrangement with creditors with minimal involvement from the court to see if the company could be saved from insolvency. However, CVA is only available to private companies with no secured debt. This is, as Loganathan noted, a serious limitation as most of the companies have loans with charges over their property. Another option to consider is "judicial management" (JM), a mechanism supervised by the court. The Judicial Manager appointed by the court is responsible for preparing a restructuring scheme for the company. The serious limitation for JM, however, is that it is not applicable to public listed companies. Loganathan also pointed out that strict wrongful trading provisions with regard to company directors under the CA must be relaxed during the pandemic. Otherwise, the company directors would be tempted to enter the insolvency process too quickly in the pandemic to avoid incurring personal liability. There should be relief offered to the directors for debts incurred in the ordinary course of company business. The pandemic has also brought about some corporate governance challenges for the companies pertaining to annual general meetings, written resolutions, board meetings, and lodgement of statutory documents. For the most part, the regulators and companies have managed these challenges well through the use of the internet and related technologies.

Recommendations

Company legislation, like Malaysia's CA 2016, should include provisions that would provide relief to companies during public health emergencies like the COVID-19 pandemic. In the absence of such provisions, the COVID-19 legislation, like Malaysia's COVID-19 Act 2020, should provide temporary relief to companies affected by the pandemic. Financially distressed companies should consider appropriate restructuring arrangements, such as CVA and JM before they file for insolvency proceedings. Wrongful trading provisions regarding company directors should be relaxed during the pandemic to offer directors relief for debts incurred in the ordinary course of company business.

Businesses – Cooperation and Dominance

In Chapter 6, Sunitha S Sivakumaran discussed the extent of competition law's application during the COVID-19 pandemic. While strict compliance with the competition law might not have been the priority for many businesses struggling to keep afloat during the pandemic, the law still exists, and businesses must adhere to it. Perhaps its relevance is even more important during the pandemic as businesses may be tempted to engage in anti-competitive conduct to remain viable. That said, like all other laws, competition law is not devoid of reality, and its application must take into consideration the interest of both the public and businesses.

The Malaysian Competition Act 2010 (CA 2010), as explained by Sunitha, is wide enough to allow for flexibility in the application of the law. The fact that the Act prohibits anti-competitive agreements, both horizontal and vertical, does not mean that businesses cannot cooperate. What is prohibited are the collusive agreements that significantly prevent, restrict, or distort the competition in the market, and not agreements that are in the public's interest and which help the businesses stay afloat and save jobs. In fact, as Sunitha clarified, the competition law and regulators worldwide have allowed businesses to cooperate and share information and resources, which otherwise would not have been allowed but for the COVID-19 pandemic. In this way, they helped businesses reduce their cost and risk exposure and, at the same time, ensured a steady supply of essential items that are in high demand to the public.

Another major problem that has been addressed by Sunitha is the abuse of the dominant position by some unscrupulous businesses during the pandemic. The excessive price increase for an essential item like facemasks during the pandemic could be indicative of the abuse of the dominant position that the business enjoys in a particular market. Malaysia's CA 2010, like the competition laws of many other countries, prohibits the abuse of the dominant position. Sunitha emphasized that regulators like the Malaysian Competition Commission should ensure that businesses do not abuse their dominance. One possible defence provided for in the CA 2010 for the accusation of dominant position is that that conduct has reasonable commercial justification or represents a reasonable commercial response to the market entry or market conduct of a competitor (the so-called meeting the competition defence). However, that does not mean, as Sunitha suggested, that businesses can simply rely on COVID-19 or the resulting events to justify their anti-competitive behaviour.

Despite the flexible nature of competition law and the pandemic challenges, Sunitha cautioned that businesses need to be reminded that competition law still applies during the pandemic and that temporary relief measures provided by regulators in some jurisdictions should not be seen as a condonation of the anti-competitive behaviour. Rather, the measures and exceptions under the competition laws are meant to help businesses navigate difficulties during the pandemic and ensure no shortage in the supply of the essential items to the public at reasonable pricing.

Recommendations

Businesses should be mindful of competition laws and the relief they provide to businesses during the COVID-19 pandemic. While anti-competitive, collusive agreements that significantly prevent, restrict, or distort the competition in the mark are prohibited by competition laws in most countries, cooperation and sharing of information and resources between businesses during the public health emergency like the COVID-19 pandemic and which is in the public interest, is not only allowed but somewhat encouraged. The regulators should also look for signs of possible abuse of dominance by businesses like sudden price hikes of essential items and take stern actions against such abuse.

Human Rights and the Rule of Law

In Chapter 7, Shanthy Thuraisingham and Danusha Rachagan have discussed the impact of the COVID-19 pandemic on human rights and the rule of law. Countries worldwide have been taking extraordinary measures to contain the spread of the disease. Many of these measures have been extreme such as countrywide lockdowns, intensified policing and checkpoints, and strict quarantines. The governments argue that extreme circumstances like the pandemic require extreme measures. There is no doubt, the authors contended, that the COVID-19 pandemic is a genuine emergency that requires immediate and robust measures to be introduced by the governments to contain the spread of the virus. The authors explained that even under international law, human rights such as freedom of movement, freedom of assembly, and freedom of association could be derogated if there is sufficient justification for that. In other words, individual human rights may be temporarily suspended if that is in the interest of the collective or the nation. However, the authors emphasized that derogation of human rights should be the last resort, and it should not be taken lightly.

When introducing measures to contain the spread of the coronavirus, the governments must ensure, the authors empathized, that those measures are in line with the international law principles of proportionality, legality, necessity, and timelines. The authors have mentioned examples of countries that might have been too quick to impose some of the measures that completely suspended some of the basic human rights when they could have achieved the same or similar results by limiting those rights. Therefore, the limitation should be preferred over derogation if possible.

The authors have also discussed the proclamation of emergency by some countries to deal with the pandemic. They cautioned that countries should be careful when proclaiming the state of emergency as it suspends checks and balances, which are necessary for an accountable and transparent democratic society. The emergency proclamation suspends the operation of parliament, which is supposed to oversee the work of the executive branch of government, and it gives an officer within the executive branch of government, normally prime minister or president, very broad regulatory making powers to do anything that he deems necessary in response to an emergency. The authors have suggested that some emergency powers may indeed be necessary in times of emergency like the pandemic, but those powers should be given by parliament for a specific period of time, and parliament should scrutinize the exercise of those powers by the executive. They mentioned examples of the UK Parliament, which introduced legislation allowing additional emergency powers to the Cabinet, but those powers must be renewed after six months and will automatically expire after two years. Likewise, in Spain, the proclaimed state of emergency expired after 30 days but was renewable for another 30 days.

The authors have also discussed the impact of the pandemic on individual privacy rights. This area deserves a special mention as people worldwide have expressed concerns relating to the private information that they are required to reveal to their governments because of COVID-19 tracing and containing measures. There have been many types of COVID-19 tracing apps like Australia's COVIDSafe app and Singapore's TraceTogeher app, temperature sensing drones, and phone apps to monitor the location and social distancing, which have been collecting vast amounts of private data and invading peoples' privacy. The authors have referenced studies that observed that people of some countries have expressed that they do not mind sharing their private information and location if that is in the interest of everyone's health. This goes back to the earlier point that collective rights override individual rights. The question is, as the authors argued, the extent of the information that governments need to contain the spread of the disease and the purpose for which such gathered information is going to be used. They cited an example of a minister in Singapore who reportedly said in parliament that information collected through Singapore's TraceTogeher app could be used by police for criminal investigations. The extent of gathering private information and its use by the governments will likely remain one of the widely debated issues even after the pandemic.

Recommendations

Derogation of human rights by governments due to genuine health emergencies, like the COVID-19 pandemic, must not be taken lightly and should be the last resort. Measures introduced by governments to contain the spread of the coronavirus must be consistent with the international law principles of proportionality, legality, necessity, and timelines. The executive's emergency powers, if necessary, should be given by parliament for a specific period of time, and parliament should oversee the exercise of those powers. The private data of individuals collected by governments through COVID-19 tracing apps and containing measures should only be used for the purpose of preventing the spread of the virus.

Human Trafficking of Migrant Workers for Forced Labour

In Chapter 8, Priya Sharma discussed the exacerbated problem of trafficking in migrant workers for the exploitative purpose of forced labour during the COVID-19 pandemic. Trafficking in persons, also known as human trafficking, is one of the most detested violations of basic human rights where individual fellow beings are being trafficked for exploitative purposes, such as forced labour, sexual exploitation, forced begging, forced marriage, removal of organs, child soldiers, and selling children.[8] Priya limited her discussion in the chapter to the trafficking in migrant workers for forced labour, which has been a major issue worldwide even before the pandemic. The situation, however, has deteriorated during the pandemic as the elusive traffickers, which normally operate in disguise and under the radar of the enforcement officers, became even more difficult to detect and prosecute during the pandemic. One of the reasons for that is that police, and other enforcement agencies have been quite understandably more preoccupied with the public health emergency to contain the spread of the deadly virus.[9] However, the traffickers also have made use of this situation and the lack of police oversight over their activities to exert even more oppression on already oppressed victims by threatening and forcing them to work without adequate pay even in the conditions where their health could be compromised.

The trafficking in persons, as explained by Priya, has been sanctioned under the Palermo Protocol.[10] The protocol is based on the so-called 3P paradigm framework (prosecution, protection, and prevention) to deal with the trafficking in persons offence, and countries are expected to adopt the framework into their own national legislations. Priya examined the extent to which protocol has been adopted in Malaysia's Anti-Trafficking in Persons and Ani-Smuggling of Migrants Act 2007 (ATIPASMA). Initially, trafficking and smuggling of persons offences used to be treated under separate legislations. But, in 2010, Anti-Trafficking in Persons Act 2007 was amended to add smuggling of migrants offences to it. Priya questioned the need to have the smuggling of migrants offences treated together with trafficking in persons offences. This amendment, according to Priya, is not helpful as it may cause

8 "Impact of the Covid-19 Pandemic on Trafficking in Persons," United Nations Office on Drugs and Crime (UNODC), accessed February 21, 2021, https://www.un.org/ruleoflaw/wp-content/uploads/2020/05/Thematic-Brief-on-COVID-19-EN-ver.21.pdf.

9 Christopher Johnson, "How Are Human Traffickers Taking Advantage of the Pandemic?," Reuters, October 18, 2020, https://www.reuters.com/article/us-global-trafficking-expertview-idUSKBN27300T.

10 A United Nations (UN) Protocol to Prevent, Suppress, and Punish Trafficking in Persons Especially Women and Children, Supplementing the United Nations Convention Against Transnational Organized Crime, accessed February 21, 2021, https://www.ohchr.org/EN/ProfessionalInterest/Pages/ProtocolTraffickingInPersons.aspx.

the two crimes to be conflated, especially by the police and enforcement agencies which may have difficulties understanding the difference between the victims of trafficking and smuggled persons. The difference between the two is important. The former do not consent to be trafficked while the latter consent to be smuggled and, as such, would be prosecuted under the country's immigration laws. If the victims of human trafficking are mistaken for smuggled persons, they too would be prosecuted by the state, which, instead of prosecuting, should treat them as victims and offer them the needed protection.

Another problem, highlighted by Priya, lies in the definition of "coercion" element under the trafficking in persons offence. Priya disagreed with the narrow approach to coercing adopted by the court in some cases where they took the position that the coercion is limited to the physical use of threat or force, thereby excluding mental, emotional, and psychological coercion. She argued that this narrow approach to coercion was inconsistent with the broader approach adopted in the Palermo Protocol, which serves as a core reference to ATIPASMA and informs its objectives. The forced labour problem faced by many migrant workers has been compounded by the lack of proper legal protection under other domestic labour laws. The contract for labour, in particular, has presented workers with many challenges in the past. Priya noted that the Malaysian Government made some progress, but the situation is still far from perfect. The domestic laws still, according to Priya, fail to indicate clearly the "employer obligations of the supplier" and the "employer obligations of the actual employer". Likewise, the "supplied employees" still tend to be discriminated against in comparison with the "employees of the workplace". Therefore, the only solution to this, Priya argued, is the abolition of the contract for labour system. All employees must be treated as employees of the workplace.

Recommendations

"Trafficking in persons" and "smuggling of migrants" offences should not be treated in the same legislation, as is currently done in Malaysia's ATIPASMA, for the fear of conflating the victims of trafficking with smuggled persons. The ATIPASMA should be amended to include mental, emotional, and psychological coercion under the trafficking in persons offences in addition to the physical use of threat or force. Governments should make the necessary legislative amendments to abolish the contract for labour system. As such, "supplied employees" should be considered "employees of the workplace".

Access to Legal and Judicial Services

In Chapter 9, Ridoan Karim talked about the importance of legal services during the COVID-19 pandemic. Legal services are not considered essential in many countries and, thus, have not been allowed to operate during the lockdowns. Ridoan pointed to the relevant legislative provisions in India, Malaysia, Singapore, and the UK and found that they all excluded legal services from the list of essential services. Should legal services be included in the list of essential services, Ridoan tried to answer by considering several factors.

In essence, if law firms are not allowed to operate, there will be serious economic repercussions for those firms and their employees. Lawyers cannot proceed with their client's instructions, which will affect their ability to generate revenue. If they cannot generate income, they would not be able to pay the rent or employees' salaries. As a result, many law firms would be forced to retrench their employees or, in some cases, to shut down. In this respect, it could be said that the law firms are not different from other business entities that faced similar cash flow problems due to the pandemic. But, there is another consequence of shutting the legal practice – the inability of an ordinary business transaction by individuals, businesses, and even governments to be conducted without legal help from relevant legal professionals. Furthermore, what would happen with the rule of law and judicial system if the lawyers cannot represent their clients in courts both in commercial and criminal cases.

Ridoan reiterated that the rule of law must not be suspended even in emergencies and mandatory lockdowns like those countries have experienced during the COVID-19 pandemic. Access to justice must never be halted. This is why Ridoan argues that the courts in many counties have embraced the digitalization of court proceedings, allowing the court proceedings to be conducted remotely via various video conferencing platforms like Zoom, Microsoft Teams, and the like. He mentioned the examples of the courts in the UK and Malaysia making history in March and April 2020, respectively, when they conducted for the first time entirely virtual court proceedings that were open to the public to watch. Online court proceedings are seen as more effective and less time-consuming. They also tend to be less costly as lawyers do not need to fly from other parts of the country to present their arguments in person before a judge for a few minutes. In some countries, Ridoan explains, the courts have worked with bar associations to introduce the guidelines detailing the conduct of online court proceedings.

It is not a surprise that the law profession has begun to embrace online technology more holistically. This is necessary, especially during a pandemic. The argument that lawyers should not be allowed to operate in person as essential service providers is also understandable given the contagious and deadly nature of the COVID-19. This, however, must not mean the suspension of the legal and judicial services. They must proceed to operate through an online environment. That said, they also must be aware of the dangers associated with the online environment. Ridoan raised concerns regarding cybersecurity and data protection. He also pointed that in-person witness testimony tends to be more compelling and authentic than the one given online and cited several court decisions to this effect. Indeed, these are genuine concerns that must be borne in mind by the parties involved in the online legal process.

Recommendations

Access to legal and judicial services should not be denied even during the pandemic. Both the courts and lawyers should embrace online technology. The courts particularly should allow the court proceedings to be conducted remotely via various video conferencing platforms like Zoom, Microsoft Teams, and the like. The practice of online court proceedings should remain even after the pandemic in cases where it is deemed effective and appropriate by the court and the parties.

Conclusion

It is highly unlikely that anyone would dispute the seriousness of the COVID-19 pandemic and its colossal impacts on individuals and businesses. The COVID-19 pandemic is a genuine global health emergency, and as such, it requires an understanding and cooperation from all the stakeholders to overcome its challenges. The affected parties, in particular, must realize that if they manage the effects of the pandemic in a collegial and collaborative manner, they will collectively be able to make it through and become even more resilient. This is best demonstrated in employment relationships. Employers and workers should be sensitive to each other's problems. They should not only insist on their strict contractual rights at all costs. Doing so may bring them short-term benefits, but the approach may not be sustainable for a long time. For example, the employee who refuses to accept a pay cut, which may be necessary to save the employer whose source of revenue is affected by the pandemic and whose reserves are not sufficient to cushion its effects, may end up being retrenched. Likewise, the retrenchment of the workers by the employers should only be considered as the last resort. Therefore, both workers and employers must work together to save jobs and livelihoods for their mutual long-term benefits. Governments also have a major role to play in mitigating the impacts of the pandemic. Most of the governments have introduced various temporary relief measures for the affected parties. Some of these measures may need to be more robust and encompassing. This book has pointed to a number of areas that COVID-19 legislation needs to address. We sincerely hope that the recommendations made by the authors in this book would be found helpful.

Notes on Contributors

Dato' Sri Ashgar Ali Ali Mohamed is a professor at Ahmad Ibrahim Kulliyyah of Laws, International Islamic University Malaysia (IIUM). He graduated with a Bachelor of Law (LLB (Hons)) and Master of Comparative Laws (MCL) from the IIUM, Master of Laws (LLM (Hons)) from the University of Auckland, New Zealand, and Doctor of Philosophy in Business Law (PhD) from the Graduate School of Management, University Putra Malaysia. His area of interest includes employment law, civil litigation, and alternative dispute resolution.

Joo-Ee Gan is the director of undergraduate studies at the School of Business, Monash University Malaysia. Her research is socio-legal in nature. Focusing on employment in the hotel sector and sustainable practices in the hotel and tourism industry, her studies evaluate the impact of legal measures. Her research on governance examines tourism as a vehicle for protecting the environment and advancing the socio-economic well-being of local communities, particularly the indigenous people. Prior to joining academia, Joo-Ee was a solicitor specializing in corporate matters. She was also a legal editor of the *Hong Kong Law Report & Digests*. She is an accredited mediator of the Malaysian Bar Council and is on the panel of the Malaysian Mediation Centre.

Ridoan Karim is a lecturer at the Department of Business Law and Taxation, School of Business, Monash University Malaysia. He has taught and researched in the fields of business and international trade law. Being a passionate researcher and academic, Ridoan has widely published in peer-reviewed journals and presented papers in several national and international conferences in his areas of interest, that is "legal and regulatory aspects of energy", "science, technology and law", "business law", "Asian and comparative law" and so on. Ridoan had acted as a consultant and fellow in projects funded by the University of Malaya, Malaysia.

Loganathan Krishnan pursued an LLB (Hons) at the University of London, LLM and PhD at the University of Malaya, postgraduate certificate in higher education at Curtin University of Technology. He was in practice at Thampa Solicitors, London. He was at SEGi University, Curtin University, and University of Tunku Abdul Rahman, and now at Monash University Malaysia. His research is on corporate law. His publication includes a book titled *Principles of Business and Corporate Law*, Malaysia (third edition), Wolters Kluwer, and book chapters with publishers, namely De Gruyter and Routledge. He has published in *Current Law Journal, INSAF Journal of the Malaysian Bar, International Company and Commercial Law Review, IIUM Law Journal, Journal of Governance and Development, Journal of Malaysian and Comparative Law, Journal of Legal Studies, Malayan Law Journal, Malaysian Journal of Law and Society, Malaysian Journal of Syariah and Law, Quarterly Law Review, Rekayasa Journal of Law, Ethics and Governance, Company Lawyer and Tax Guardian*.

Mei Yee Lee is a lecturer at the School of Business, Monash University Malaysia. She holds a PhD from Monash University. Lee has published in reputable journals and presented papers at international conferences. She is also a professional member of the Malaysian Institute of Accountants and the Malaysian Institute of Certified Public Accountants. Prior to her academic career, Lee had, for more than 18 years, held senior management positions in multinational corporations.

Abdul Majid is a senior lecturer at the Monash University Malaysia. He was at one time a professor of English at the University of Malaya and then a legal practitioner before taking up an appointment at the Chinese University of Hong Kong, where he was an associate professor in Law. He also held

https://doi.org/10.1515/9783110723694-011

an appointment as a visiting fellow in Commercial and Business Laws at the Hong Kong Polytechnic University. He has published extensively in business law areas with occasional forays into other academic disciplines.

Justice Datuk Vazeer Alam Mydin Meera is a judge of the Court of Appeal, Malaysia, and an adjunct professor at the School of Business, Monash University, Malaysia. He was in private law practice for about 20 years before his appointment as a judicial commissioner of the High Court of Malaya in May 2010. Justice Vazeer graduated with a LLB (Hons) from the University of Wales Aberystwyth, United Kingdom, and subsequently obtained an MCL degree from the International Islamic University, Malaysia. Aside from this, he also holds a Bachelor of Arts degree in Economics, Political Science, and Philosophy from the National University of Singapore.

Danusha Rachagan is a solicitor with the Office of Public Prosecutions Victoria. He completed his LLB at the University of Queensland and his Practical Legal Training, College of Law Victoria. He has been admitted as a solicitor in the State of Victoria. Before embarking on a career with the Office of Public Prosecutions, Danusha worked in law firms both in Australia and Malaysia.

Chithra Latha Ramalingam is a PhD graduate from the University of Malaya in the field of Socio-Legal. She had graduated with a LLB (Hons) from the University of Wolverhampton and has a Master of International Business Laws (LLM Merit) from Staffordshire University. Her research interest is in Human Governance that encompasses Sustainable Governance, Law and Ethics. She has undertaken research in the area of corporate governance and corporate law, employment law, sports law, and cyber media law. She has authored books on company law, elements of law and co-authored *Law and Technology Management* with Open University Malaysia, and is the subject moderator for Malaysian Business Law with a publishing house. Her experience in research is well compounded by the fact that she had trained a pool of MACC officers to understand the intricacies of the legal issues related to company and governance. She has also authored and co-authored book chapter publications and produced many peer-reviewed journal publications, and presented conference papers both locally and internationally in the above areas. Prior to her current portfolio as a senior lecturer, she has served as a lecturer locally at various private universities and abroad in the UK.

Priya Sharma is a lecturer in the Department of Business Law and Taxation and the School of Business's Principles of Responsible Management (PRME) ambassador at Monash University Malaysia. She is a recipient of the Dean's Award for PRME Education Excellence and the Purple Letter for Teaching Excellence. Priya is currently pursuing her PhD in the area of trafficking of migrant workers for forced labour. She is a recipient of the Monash Business School Prize for Research Strategies and Methods in Business Law. Priya has also published in the *Malayan Law Journal* entitled "The Exploitation of Children for Labour: The Malaysian Predicament" and has presented papers at various law conferences. Her area of research interest is in humanity and the law.

Sunitha S. Sivakumaran is an early researcher in the area of competition law. Her PhD thesis was on Pricing Abuses under Section 10 of the Competition Act 2010. She has published articles in legal journals, the most recent of which entitled "Competition law in the new normal" is published in *the European Competition Law Review.* Prior to joining academia, she was in legal practice for 7 years in both Messrs Shearn Delamore & Co and Messrs Azman Davidson & Co specialising in intellectual property law. In addition to being a researcher, she also works with children with special needs.

Shanthy Thuraisingham is the Academic Director at Kaplan Business School. She is also an adjunct associate professor with Monash University. Shanthy co-authored law books and is also instrumental in conducting the annual CEO Survey Malaysia, a collaboration between Monash University Malaysia, CPA Australia, Butler University, Indiana, and the Minority Shareholder Watchdog Group. Shanthy was a member of the OECD Taskforce on Corporate Governance and a member of the Listing Committee of Bursa Malaysia. She was also a member of the Adjudication Committee for the Malaysian ASEAN CG Awards. Shanthy works closely with professional bodies like the Institute of Accountants and CPA Australia. Shanthy is an Advocate and Solicitor and was engaged in both litigation and corporate conveyancing work in legal practice before moving to an academic career.

Adnan Trakic is an associate professor and head of Business Law and Taxation Department at the School of Business, Monash University Malaysia. He graduated with a LLB (Hons), MCL, PhD from the IIUM, and graduate certificate in higher education from Monash University. He has taught and researched in the fields of conventional and Islamic finance law, business law, and dispute resolution. He has published several books and numerous articles and book chapters.